How to Win

Order this book online at www.trafford.com
or email orders@trafford.com

The teaching methods, views, and opinions in this book are those of the authors alone. They are in no
way associated with or reflect the opinions or teachings of any other board review text, lecture, seminar,
preparation course, or teaching methods.

Most Trafford titles are also available at major online book retailers.

Note for Librarians: A cataloguing record for this book is available from Library
and Archives Canada at www.collectionscanada.ca/amicus/index-e.html

Printed in Victoria, BC, Canada.

ISBN: 978-1-4269-1582-6 (Soft)

*Our mission is to efficiently provide the world's finest, most comprehensive
book publishing service, enabling every author to experience success.
To find out how to publish your book, your way, and have it available
worldwide, visit us online at www.trafford.com*

Trafford rev. 07/13/2010

 www.trafford.com

North America & international
toll-free: 1 888 232 4444 (USA & Canada)
phone: 250 383 6864 ♦ fax: 812 355 4082

How to Win

On the
𝕬merican 𝕭oard of 𝕾urgery
Certifying Exam

Written by
Brad Snyder, M.D.

From the Notes of
Alex Nguyen, M.D.

Acknowledgments

I would like to thank the contributing author, Alex Nguyen, for painfully collecting and handwriting the notes that I used to study for my oral exams and in due course became the foundation for the content of "How to Win." Our mutual desire to create a well written and comprehensive study guide and his contribution to the development and writing of this review is the only reason it is in your hands today. Without him, it simply would not have happened. He continues to be a great friend and partner who is always there when I need him.

With loving devotion and gratitude to my courageous wife, my beautiful children, and all my amorous friends and family who have supported me throughout a very dim, but prolific, time of my life. Because of them, I pick myself up, brush off my knees, and have faith to try again! Somehow, it always works out the way it should.

Introduction

Morbid Humiliation

General Surgery 2007-2008 Certifying Examination, Dallas, TX, Jan. 28 Status: Completed Examination

Result: We regret to inform you that you were not successful in this examination.

These results are accurate and final. Please do not call the Board office to verify your results.

I have told myself, "I am a good surgeon," a million times since my "unsuccessful" attempt to pass the American Board of Surgery's certifying examination. It took everything I had to continue working at full steam after this letter, and I began to question my ability. In our profession, mistakes can result in significant morbidity and mortality. At this time, my friends all told me that I was a safe surgeon. I know they were right, but no matter what the truth was, I lived for nine months with self doubt and morbid humiliation all because of an exam.

Logical Thinking

On the up side, there is a silver lining. My failure on the oral exams made me realize that many of our residents and fellows have no idea what to expect from this exam never mind how to take it. Books and factoids are thrown at them, and they are asked to regurgitate it. How does this teach the essential problem solving ability, fundamental critical thinking, or systematic approach that makes general surgery very commonsensical? As a result, young surgeons are failing the certification exam (at least 20% every year). I want to change that.

I studied for three months in preparation for this exam. I read many of the most popular study guides available at the time and supplemented it with Cameron's "Current Surgical Therapy." I practiced scenarios out loud with a concurrent minimally invasive fellow, Alex Nguyen, and I assumed I knew the matter cold. I was right. I did know the answers; nonetheless, I didn't know how to articulate them!

You see, it's not about knowledge or facts; it is *all* about your ability to logically discuss a predicament that may or may not be surgical in nature. Most of these tribulations are straight forward, and the examiners are not out to get you (unless you have already annoyed them and they want to see you squirm. This is rare, and if it is happening then you probably deserve it). However, in order to pass this exam, you have to practice your presentation until it spills out of your mouth without thought. It is not about right or wrong but how good does it sound, and how well can you back up your answer. This test is a lot more than just sitting down and demonstrating to the person across from you that you have all the knowledge you are supposed to have. In fact, you can be fantastically brilliant and still fail this exam with one modest misapprehension. This is scary but true. Essentially, they are not testing your knowledge or your ability to care for patients. In fact, they are testing your logical thinking communicated out loud. For many people, this style of testing is not natural and requires a great deal of practice.

To quote Frank R. Lewis, Executive Director of the American Board of Surgery, in the closing paragraph of his response to my request for a critique, "Permit me to offer you two pieces of advice which I sincerely hope you will take. First, do not dwell on the results of this examination; what's past is past. Second, and in that connection, I would encourage you to 'practice' taking oral examinations in preparation for your next attempt. This means that you should ask a colleague, preferably a Board Certified general surgeon, to question you for two to three hours every week for the next several months. Your questioner should probe deeply enough into your answers to make certain that you have adequate evidence of problem-solving ability. If you can follow this course, your next oral examination should be less stressful and hopefully will have a different outcome."

There are many ways to say the same thing. You want to prepare for this exam by being familiar with all the possible scenarios that may be presented to you and be prepared to give the answer that you have practiced. Practicing how you will answer a very particular situation will make you very effective and efficient at the answering process and allow you substantial maneuverability and adaptability during the exam. It will help you sound like a smooth operator under enormous stress. That is what they want to see. That gets you a pass!

Using this Review Book

In the following pages, you are given a lot of facts and information that will be a satisfactory review for you. I highly recommend that you read through each section, not memorizing the information, but thinking about how you would communicate this out loud to your examiner. Then, literally speak out loud to yourself or a study partner, and do it over and over again. Unless you are fully prepared by way of practice, the brain and mouth will become disconnected when sitting down in that hotel room chair across from two surgeons attempting to test all of your surgical knowledge and training over the last nine years in just 90 minutes. You must be primed but relaxed.

To be most effective, be honest and think about things the way you would really do it. If you handle the situation like you would in real life, then you are less likely to say something stupid. Be candid with them. Let them see your sincerity. You are a human being, most of them know that. Try to relax. The exam goes by incredibly swift. The examiners want to cover a certain number of topics on their agenda, and there is not much time to do it. Answer the questions the way you were trained, not the way you read about in a book (including this one). You have to talk to the examiner just as you would talk to another doctor in your hospital. Use the proper language you have learned and imagine the presented problem. If you can do these things, you will handle the stress better.

Reading this book through once, then going back and re-reading the most common subjects is recommended. Doing this and taking an adequate review course will give you the organization, presentation, and understanding needed to pass the oral examination. I strongly encourage anyone reading this book to forget everything you have been told about the oral exams and how to take them. Furthermore, the examples given in this text should act as a guide and not as a "safe" answer.

Knowing what is important and what is not is crucial when studying. These authors have learned how the challenges are overcome; as a result, this book was created to have it all. It will give you pertinent pearls of wisdom quoted from others who have successfully taken the exam, 145 subjects of content, 26 bulleted descriptions of the most commonly probed surgical procedures, and 70 of the most commonly asked subjects stressed by invaluable example scenarios that show how content and technique should be employed synergistically. Intended to be more than just another book full of facts, this review includes examples of *how* the questions should be approached to be most effective in the delivery of the content. In addition, it categorizes the subjects by their frequency of appearance on the board exams over the last ten years so the reader knows where to focus the most effort. It is the opinion of these authors that this book acts as an indispensable corner stone of the foundation for high-quality, well-organized and objectively stressed material that you must know in order *to win* on this exam.

Quotes from Successful Candidates

"As so many have said before, speaking the answers out loud to practice is very helpful. You must get into your answer groove and then things will seem more routine (ABC for trauma, H&P, and pre-op studies for elective staging). Don't let them rush you to an answer. Order the EKG, stage the tumor with imagining before doing anything rash- it is being pushed into something uncomfortable that can be one's undoing."

"Ninety minutes passed in what seemed to be seconds. Perhaps I am just suffering from post-traumatic shock syndrome."

"Don't bluff unless you can provide a reasonable answer."

"The biggest challenge was balancing the need for information with the examiner's indignation when you asked for it. So, don't ask, just tell them what you are thinking."

"It irks them when you ask them about the history and they say it is negative, so I just say what I would do rather than ask them again."

"When you finish a room, forget about the room and move on, don't think about the past."

"...stay focused on what the examiner is asking you (most of the time they ask exactly what they want and don't lead you down the wrong path)..."

"It does help to have the beta blocker (propanolol 10-20 mg), pepcid, lomotil, and Benadryl at your disposal prior to the exam…if you are pharmaceutically inclined."

"The time leading up to the test was the most anxiety provoking experience of my life, I can't emphasize that enough."

"Each question had one or more pitfall or hidden points/key words that once you found they moved on. They also asked in disbelief or shock at your answer if that's what you really wanted to do, which could really mess you up if you weren't sure of your answer."

"Take the question out of their hands and into yours (if this then that, if not I would do this). They will definitely cut you off and take you somewhere else in the scenario when they want, or they will ask you about something specific."

"I thought the examiners were fair, wanted focused answers, and would probably be annoyed by statements like, 'I would do a complete history and physical.'"

"As I approached my trauma/critical care room the candidate before me came out looking a bit grim; I bit my bottom lip and waited for them to open the door and invite me in."

"In general, the more senior examiners were easier to deal with because they asked more straight forward questions and were less likely to start changing the scenario mid-question."

"In spite of advice from past residents, I did not explicitly go through ABC's and instead just asked if the hemodynamics and respiratory status were stable (and even stopped this at the first sign of boredom)."

"See the sheets. Imagine an actual patient standing in front of you and manage the patient just as you would an actual patient in your office, in the ER, or in the operating room."

"There are many right answers. If you can defend your answer and it's not too controversial you'll do fine."

"[As I sit down]...I feel my adrenals tighten up, I begin to feel my heartbeat in my neck and my mouth becomes as dry as the Mojave Desert."

"...go slowly, think out loud with words and imagine a real patient in front of you with the problem they present."

"It's really clinical, not esoterical, so you will do fine."

Table of Contents

This table of contents is a little unusual in that you will find a number in the front of every subject. This table of contents is a little unusual in that you will find a number in the front of every subject. This is the relative frequency that this particular topic may appear on your oral examination. There is an abundance of old test material available. Some of it is very useful in preparing for the boards and some is not. What I believe is the most useful part of studying old exams is that you learn the type of questions that are asked and get a feel of how the scenarios may change. With that in mind, not only do I do I give you a commonly played out scenarios at the end of 70 different and most common subjects (noted by the *), but I have listed frequency so that you know what is common and what is not (anything >5 is significant). There is such an abundance of material that you need to know in order to really do well on this exam that you should really focus on the things you have the highest chance of being asked on the exam. So, for example, I would not suggest spending an equal partition of time studying vaginal bleeding as I would breast cancer. This table of content is focused, as is this entire book, on giving you the highest chances for a successful attempt on the certification examination

(6) Skin/Head and Neck
(1) Skin Cancer*

H&P

Smoking, drinking alcohol, sun exposure and previous history of skin cancers are risk factors for skin cancer and are the focus of the history.

On physical examination, do an exam of the head and neck region, all the pertinent lymph node basins, and look at all of the skin for other lesions. The lesion itself should be inspected for color, characteristics, and size.

Diagnosis

As with any cancer, first get tissue for diagnosis so that you know what you are treating. You will excise the area with minimal margins. In sensitive areas like the face, or if the lesion is very large, you may consider punch biopsy to obtain the diagnosis.

Treatment

Once you have the pathology, you can decide on the margins you will have to take (e.g. for melanoma you need 1-2 cm margins depending on the depth, for BCC >2 mm margins, and SCC >5 mm margins); therefore, be thinking of the possible diagnosis and what margins you want to take.

You may be asked about reconstruction of the defects. Consider flaps (rotational or free) or wedge resections. Unless you do plastic surgery or have a well founded knowledge of flaps, I would defer great details of reconstruction.

Additional Therapy

Generally lymph node dissections are not performed for skin cancers, but if you have bulky nodal disease in a draining basin, then you should offer an anatomic node dissection (e.g. MRND, see procedures).

Radiation therapy is used when you can not get > 1mm margins, lesion very close to the eye or nose that can not be completely excised with confident margins, lymphatic invasion, or very large tumors with capsular invasion.

Example Case

An elderly gentleman who is a farmer comes to your office as a referral from his family doctor because he found a 1 cm lesion on his right superior ear that seems suspicious for cancer. How would you proceed?

I suspect that this farmer has been exposed to a lot of sun in his many years and this would increase the chances that this sun exposed area could have a cancer. Assuming that his other risk factors, such as smoking an ETOH are negative...

Oh, he smokes a pipe everyday, but no alcohol.

Well smoking is another risk factor, so I am highly suspicious of this area. I will also assume that he has never had skin cancer before and not had any other lesions removed.

Yes

Then, I would examine the lesion on the ear; you say it is 1 cm in size. I would also note any ulceration, vascularity, raised edges, irregular boarders and pigmentation. This would lean me toward the type of cancer. Assuming there is no pigmentation to think that this is melanoma, and then it is SCC or BCC. Regardless of what I think this is, he will need a biopsy. On the ear, this is best done with a wedge resection with minimal margins at this time until I get a diagnosis. Before I do that though, I am getting ahead of myself, I would finished the rest of the head and neck examination, look and feel for cervical adenopathy, and examine the rest of the skin over the body (especially sun exposed areas). Assuming the rest of the exam is negative, I would proceed with excisional biopsy.

The rest of the exam is negative and your pathology comes back as BCC with positive margins.

I am not concerned about the margins because I knew I would have to come back and excise this if it was a cancer. Since there are no suspicious nodes, then I would re-excise this area with at least 2 mm margins, again as a wedge resection. This should be adequate treatment for this lesion.

Why not just resect with 2 mm margins the first time?

I could have, and this would have saved a trip; however, the first time, I just wanted to make a diagnosis. I would hate to remove all that tissue for a benign lesion.

Would you do a node dissection?

There is no indication for node dissection for this lesion unless there is palpable adenopathy.

(3) SCC of the Oropharynx*

H&P

This is similar to skin cancer history and physical examination.

In addition to the above physical exam, you want to include a bimanual palpation and visual inspection of the oropharynx and indirect laryngoscopy.

Diagnosis

If this is an oral lesion or you have a cervical node with SCC on FNA then you should do a pan-endoscopy and a CXR.

Stage I is < 2cm and node negative

Stage III is >4 cm or node positive

Stage II is 2-4 cm and node negative

Stage IV is distant mets

Treatment

For the treatment of SCC of the head and neck, you have to re-excise the lesion. If it is less than two cm, then a 5 mm margin is ok, but more than 2 cm lesions need a one cm margin.

Additional Therapy

Once excised, the staging determines further treatment. For stage I or II lesions (i.e. node negative lesions less than 4cm in size), no further treatment is required. If there are really close margins, however, (i.e. that is less than 1 mm) or there is a high suspicion of nodal disease, then you should offer 5000 rads of XRT.

If the lesion is not accessible to resection, then you give 6000 rads of radiation and re-biopsy for residual tumor. Salvage surgery may be an option after radiation therapy.

Stage III lesions need a wide margin of more than 1 cm and a MRND plus 5000 rads to the entire neck.

Stage IV lesions get neoadjuvant chemotherapy and radiation.

Example Case

An elderly gentleman who is a farmer comes to your office as a referral from his family doctor because he found a 1 cm lesion on his tongue that seems suspicious for cancer. How would you proceed?

I would ask about smoking and ETOH.

He smokes a pipe everyday, but no alcohol.

Well smoking is a risk factor, so I am highly suspicious of this area. I will also assume that he has never had skin cancer before and not had any other lesions removed.

No he has not.

He will need a biopsy. This is best done with a wedge resection with minimal margins at this time until I get a diagnosis. Before I do that (I am getting ahead of myself) I would finished the rest of the head and neck examination, look and feel for cervical adenopathy, and examine the rest of the skin over the body (especially sun exposed areas). Assuming the rest of the exam is negative, I would proceed with excisional biopsy.

The rest of the exam is negative except a hard nodule at the anterior boarder of the SCM in the middle of the neck and your pathology comes back as SCC with positive margins.

So even though this is a SCC of the tongue, this node is suspicious and I would certainly want to try and diagnosis the pathology there. It could be metastatic and that would make this a stage III tumor (T1N+). FNA could tell if there is positive SCC in that node.

There is.

Then this is stage III cancer. I would explain to the patient that this is a cancer that has spread to the lymph nodes and treatment with be multidisciplinary. My role would be surgery, including re-excising this area with 1 cm margins and a MRND to remove all the lymph nodes draining this area; then, the radiation oncologist would give him 5000 rads to the entire neck area. This would be the best way to prevent recurrence of the cancer, and therefore increase his chance for cure and disease free survival.

What if I told you that the medical student ordered a chest x-ray before surgery and it came back as having a RUL mass?

(Ouch!)

I would thank that student. I should have gotten a chest x-ray when I found that node to be positive for cancer. In this case, I would have to make sure that this lung lesion is not a primary or metastatic disease. If this represents metastatic disease, then his treatment would involve neoadjuvant chemotherapy and radiation.

(1) Neck Mass*

H&P

You have to consider the differential diagnosis here. It is really long, but you should know that it could be a lymph node, primary neck tumor, or congenital mass Your H&P is focused on that differential and you need to know the age of the patient, duration of the mass, location on the neck, how it feels on palpation, and what color it is. For example, a one month old firm nodule in the cervical node basin in a 60 year old smoker is probable neoplastic as oppose to the year old, rubbery, midline neck mass in the 8 year old that moves with swallowing.

Differential Diagnosis of Isolated Neck Mass

Type of mass	Diagnosis	Locality	Age (Years)	Attributes
Congenital	Vascular malformation	Any	0–2	Soft, blue/red
	Branchial apparatus	Lateral	2–40	Cystic, round, distinct
	Thyroglossal	Central	2–30	Cystic
	Epidermoid	Any	0–30	Cystic
Inflammatory	Viral, bacterial, fungal		Any	Soft or solid
	Granulomatous (atypical mycobacterium)	Lateral	1–20	Solid
	Salivary		>15	Firm, solid
Benign	Thyroid		>15	Firm solid
	Schwannoma	Lateral	>15	Hard solid
	Chemodectoma	Lateral	>30	Pulsatile, CN palsy
	Lipoma		>20	Soft
Malignant	Salivary	Any	>25	Firm solid
	Thyroid		>15	Firm solid
	Sarcoma		>25	
	Lymphoma	Lateral	>10	Firm solid
Metastatic	Squamous	Lateral	>35	Firm solid/cystic
	Adenocarcinoma	Supraclavicular	>35	Firm solid
	Salivary gland	Lateral	>25	Firm solid
	Thyroid	Any	>15	Firm solid
Traumatic	Hematoma	Any	Any	Compressible-firm
	Pseudoaneurysm			Pulsatile
	Neuroma	Lateral	Any	Trigger point pain

Diagnosis

The history and physical examination goes a long way to make the diagnosis and culminating your suspicion for benign or malignant lesion.

Ultrasound should be done to tell you if the mass is cystic or solid, and it may tell you if it looks benign or malignant. It can also assist in FNA and diagnose positive nodal disease.

Unless you suspect this to be a vascular lesion, then you should do a FNA (+/- U/S guidance if needed) to get some idea of the pathology. If you suspect a vascular lesion then get a MRA.

A positive FNA without a primary may lead to other diagnostic test such as pan-endoscopy (bronchoscopy, upper endoscopy, and colonoscopy), chest x-ray or CT, abdominal CT, PET scans, etc. FNA has a 90% accuracy, which means that 10% will not get a diagnosis. If the pathologist needs architecture (e.g. follicular carcinoma), FNA is not useful. Lymphoma may be difficult to diagnose on FNA, requiring a larger biopsy sample by core or excisional biopsy.

CT of the head and neck is useful, especially if you suspect a malignancy (older age, with positive risk factors, or positive FNA for cancer).

Treatment

Treatment based on FNA depends on the diagnosis. Carotid body tumors, intravagal ganglinomas, schwanomas, cystic hygromas, teratomas, and brachial cleft cyst are excised.

You can find adenocarcinoma, SCC, BCC, sarcoma, or melanoma. These cancers need resection of the primary if known, MRND, and radiation plus chemo as indicated.

Lymphoma requires excision for pathology, staging CT scan, and bone marrow biopsy; and treatment is dictated by stage (I and II → XRT, III and IV → CHOP or MOAP). See lymphoma section.

Thyroglossal cysts get a Sistruck procedure (see procedure).

Hemangiomas can be observed if they are capillary or cavernous. AVMs should be embolized before excision.

Salivary tumors and thyroid tumors have algorithms presented later in this text.

Additional Therapy

Thyroglossal cyst can become infected, especially if they are aspirated. They do not require excision unless it is infected, increasing in size or you are worried about cancer. Papillary cancer is very rare in these cysts. If papillary cancer is found, and it is less than 1 cm with negative margins, then resection alone is probably enough as long as it is well differentiated.

Example Case

You have a 32 year old female referred to you by her FP doctor for evaluation of a 2 cm neck mass. She has no past medical history and no previous surgeries. She takes no medications.

This mass in her neck could be a lymph node, a primary tumor, or a congenital tumor. Due to her age; unless she has had it her entire life, it is probably not a congenital mass. Assuming she has not had a recent URI or scalp infections to suggest that this could be an inflammatory node, I would start by doing a complete examination of her head and neck. I would look over her skin to make sure that I did not find any malignant skin lesions that would suggest metastatic SCC, BCC, or melenoma. I would examine the thyroid and salivary glands to make sure there were no primary lesions here as well (this would include a bimanual examination in the mouth), I would examine the oral cavity for any lesions, and I would feel the rest of the nodal basins (including the groin) to make sure there is no other prominent lymph nodes to suggest that she has lymphoma. Finally, I would examine the mass itself and note the characteristic. Is it firm or soft? Does it appear vascular or not, and where is it located?

This mass appears to be in the midline and it moves when she swallows.

This may be a thyroglossal cyst that has gone un-noticed or ignored for the last 32 years. OK, then I would get an ultrasound to make sure that this is a cystic lesion, and that the thyroid is normal as well.

It is a solid mass.

So, this may be in the thyroid I would assume, and before I take any aspirations, I would check her thyroid function to make sure they are normal so not to cause thyroid storm, and I would ask her about any hyperthyroid symptoms.

She has no symptoms of hyperthyroid, and TFT are normal.

I would do an FNA.

How do you do an FNA?

I would prep the area of the mass, use a local anesthetic, and then pass a 25 gauge needle into the mass while creating a vacuum with a 20 ml syringe and making several passes with the needle in and out of the mass. The contents are then sprayed out onto the slide, and the slide is fixed and stained to look at under light microscopy.

Follicular cells are found.

So, I have a 32 year old woman who has no medical history and is euthyroid, with a 2 cm mass in the middle of the thyroid, and a FNA that shows follicular cells. I would explain to the patient that I can not rule out a benign tumor versus malignant tumor, so I would recommend excision.

Well, she agrees, but wants to know how much of the gland you are going to take out?

I will have to determine that in the operating room. She is young and female, the mass is relatively small, and if it is intrathyroid and one side more than the other, we may consider doing a lobectomy and waiting for the pathology report to come back. She would need to understand that if the pathology is cancer, then we would have to go back and remove the rest of the gland, but if it is benign then it is done.

She wants to know why you don't test it for cancer while you are in the operating room.

There is no way to tell if these cells are malignant on frozen section because you have to see capsular or vascular invasion and this can only be done on the final slides that are specially prepared. That usually takes two days to come back.

Fine, you do a lobectomy and it comes back follicular cancer. When you tell her this and the plan to go back to the operating room her husband interjects. Her husband is a lawyer and researched the internet and wants to know if it is really necessary.

In my practice, I would do a completion in this case. The mass is just large enough that it makes it risky to leave that other side in because she could develop another cancer on that side. It also allows us to use radio-active iodine to ablate any possible metastatic disease if found. However, it is not necessary, and we could leave the other side in, following her very closely for the development of any masses on the other side. I would do this by doing an US of the thyroid lobe every 6 month.

(1) Enlarged Cervical Lymph Node*

H&P

Your focus here is on metastatic cancer, lymphoma, or infection. So you should be focused on this. Ask about recent URI/TB exposure/ HIV, B-symptoms, history of cancer, radiation to the neck, thyroid symptoms.

Feel the mass and note its characteristics and location in the neck. Be sure to do a good oral examination (bimanual palpation), and you should note the level of the cervical node (level I = submental, level II, III, IV = anterior border of the SCM from the mandible to the clavicle, level V = posterior triangle of the neck, level VI = central lymph nodes, level VII = under the manubrium) which may give you an idea of the primary source.

Diagnosis

Start with a simple CXR to exclude infection or malignant spread from the chest. Get a CT of the neck (and chest if CXR shows something); and, finally, get U/S guided FNA for the diagnosis most of the time.

PET is an emerging technology; however, the jury is still out. Its primary use is looking at metastatic activity and recurrence of disease, but not being routinely used for the work up of the primary.

Treatment/Additional Therapy

Treatment is based on the FNA.

Benign causes can be inflammation. This should be observed for a couple of weeks and if it persist, take it out for definitive diagnosis. The lesions can be non-caseating (e.g. sarcoid) or caseating (TB). Either way, these lesions should be excised to make the diagnosis and start definitive treatment.

Lymphoma can be diagnosed by FNA, but this will require a complete excisional biopsy for final pathology confirmation. This will prompt you to order a CT scan of the neck, chest, abdomen, and the pelvis; in addition a bone marrow biopsy is done. This will stage the lymphoma and medical treatment can ensue from there.

SCC will prompt further workup with CXR and pan-endoscopy. There is a 70% chance that the primary is in the head and neck region. A CT of the neck and chest can be useful. If your work up to this point is negative, put the patient to sleep, do direct laryngoscopy with random biopsies of any suspicious tissue. If you still can not find a primary after this (rare, except on the ABS oral certification examination), then you should assume this is metastatic cancer and perform a radical neck dissection (see procedure) and give 5000 rads to the entire neck.

Adenocarcinoma can come from the thyroid, lung, breast, salivary glands, prostate, and GI tract. Work up all these areas. If no primary is found (or if it is found and treated appropriately), then perform a MRND, give 5000 rads XRT, and follow closely.

For thyroid cancer, see that algorithm.

Example Case

45 year old male, who has no pertinent medical history but is a smoker, presents with a 1 cm swollen node in the left anterior border of the SCM.

This node may be reactive, lymphoma, metastatic cancer, or not a node at all. After taking a careful history about the timing and symptoms associated with the node, I should have a good idea of where I think this is going. The fact that he is a smoker makes me more concerned that this is malignant, but if he is getting over a cold, then it may just be reactive and a course of observation is warranted. I would do a diligent search for any lesions on the head and neck, and I would perform an indirect laryngoscopy and bimanual examination of the orophayrnx. 70% of metastatic nodes in the neck are from the head and neck, but if I don't find it there, I would do an ultrasound and rule out other suspicious nodes and then FNA the node to get a diagnosis.

It comes back non-diagnostic.

So I would ask myself is it non-diagnostic because we did not do it right, or because no matter how much of this stuff I get I won't get a diagnosis. If it is the former, I would repeat the FNA, if it were the later, I would just excise the node and send it fresh to pathology for frozen, permanent, and lymphoma protocol.

You send it off and it comes back adenocarcinoma. Where do you think it could be coming from?

It could be coming from the thyroid, salivary glands, esophagus, lung, gastrointestinal tract, breast, and prostate. Hopefully the pathologist will stain this lesion and tell me where he thinks it is coming from.

He doesn't know.

So with that in mind, repeat physical exam of the thyroid and the breast should reveal any lesions if this is the source, a good chest x-ray and CT if that is positive would rule out lung mass, EGD to rule out an upper GI source, and a colonoscopy to rule out a lower GI source. A good rectal exam can detect a large prostate cancer, and I would send of a PSA. Most of the time a primary will be found.

Well not this time. No primary is found. Now what?

Although it may be in vain, I would CT the head, neck, chest, abdomen, and pelvis looking for the primary. I would also order a PET scan. If no primary is found after this exhaustive search, then I would do a MRND and give him XRT. But without having the primary found, I am concerned that more problems will arise in the future.

We'll see. Thank you.

(0) Salivary Gland Tumors

H&P

Just like any mass in the neck, you want a good history of presentation, time it has been there and growth rate. Check the patient's risk factors for cancer (ETOH and tobacco).

On physical exam you should get an idea of the size and location, and how fixed it is to underlying structures and the skin. Also find out if there is underlying nerve involvement as noted by cranial nerve deficits.

Diagnosis

You really have to have a high index of suspicion to be thinking salivary gland tumor, but keep that in your mind when you have a neck mass. CT scans, MRI, are helpful, but like everything else in the neck, you need an FNA. While this will not tell you if the tumor is benign or malignant, at least you now know that you have a salivary tumor. Excision will be required to determine if it is benign or malignant. If it is superficial, then you need to do a superficial parotidectomy. If it is deep then you need to remove the entire gland, sparing the facial nerve. Frozen section will determine treatment after that.

Treatment

Benign tumors are treated with excision only. For submandibular glands, total excision is done, sparing the lingual and marginal mandibular nerves. If the tumor recurs, then it can be re-excised. Warthin's tumor is a cyst adenoma and is the second most common benign salivary gland tumor.

Malignant, low grade tumors include mucoepidermoid and acinic cell carcinoma. Superficial or total gland excision with nerve sparing is done. There is no need for radical node dissection or post operative XRT or chemotherapy.

For high grade malignant tumors like mixed tumors, adenoid cystic and high grade mucoepidermoid tumors (as well as adenocarcinoma and SCC), more radical approach is needed. For the parotid gland, you need to do a total parotidectomy, sparing the facial nerve if possible (reconstruct with sural nerve or greater auricular nerve if needed), MRND, and post operative XRT. For the submandibular gland, WLE of the gland, floor of the mouth, involved tongue and mandible is done. This is followed by MRND and post operative XRT.

Additional Therapy

XRT is provided after WLE for malignant tumors. Facial nerve palsy or paralysis has a poorer prognosis (50% 5 year survival) for a patient with a malignancy and will make preserving this nerve very difficult.

(27) Esophagus
(1) Esophageal Reflux

H&P

These patients have a classic history of heartburn and the history should be well known to any surgeon. Specifically ask about regurgitation of food or dysphagia. Any thought of Zenker's or esophageal lesion should prompt a swallow study. Find out about NSAID use, previous treatment and history of *H. Pylori*.

Not much will be found on PE.

Diagnosis

Start with a swallow study because it is safe and diagnostic. You will often see the reflux on the film and determine if there is a hiatal hernia as well. In addition it will rule out other pathology such as diverticulum or solid tumor of the esophagus.

Next do an EGD to document esophagitis and rule out Barrett's or cancer.

Manometry is useful to measure the LES tone. For those with true reflux it is abnormally low (< 6 mmHg). The LES length is < 2cm in reflux patients and < 1 cm is in the abdomen. This study will also tell you if there is any dysmotility of the esophagus.

24 hour pH probe tells you how much time the esophagus sees a pH < 4 (90 minutes or 6% of the time is too long), and it can tell you if their symptoms are related to the reflux. DeMester score > 15 is positive for reflux.

Treatment

Life style modification and medical treatment should be tried first. You should do this for a total of 6 months. Failure of medical treatment after this time will prompt the work up for a Nissen fundoplication.

Patients with typical symptoms, who respond to PPI's, and have an abnormal pH probe have > 90% response rate to surgical therapy. (2 of these 70%, one is 50%). Nissen fundoplication is straight forward and needs no explanation.

Additional Therapy

The complications that may be asked about include stricture (pneumatic dilation q 6 weeks x 3), dysphagia, and recurrence.

(1) Esophageal Abnormalities and Motility Disorders*

H&P

These patients will typically have a history of long standing dysphagia with regurgitation of undigested food. You should be thinking about the reason we address these issues as doctors. They cause problems like pneumonia. So ask about adult onset asthma or recurrent admissions for URI or pneumonia. Their problems may cause chest pain, despite normal cardiac work up. That may be pertinent history to obtain. Of course, dysphagia may be due to a cancer and you should ask about tobacco and alcohol use, weight loss, family history of cancer and history of caustic injury.

On physical examination, there is not much to look for; however, you want to get a good head and neck examination, looking for lymphadenopathy and check for abdominal masses.

Diagnosis

Specific diagnoses that may be found include Zenker's diverticulum, achalasia, diffuse esophageal spasm (DES), parabronchial diverticulum, and epiphrenic diverticulum. The test used to diagnose them include barium swallow, EGD, manometry and pH probe as described below.

The first study to get in this situation is a good gastrograffin/ barium swallow. This is safe and will give you a lot of information. You should see reflux, hiatal hernias, achalasia, cork-screwing (DES), masses, strictures, and diverticulum on this study. Any masses or strictures should be followed by upper endoscopy.

Upper endoscopy will allow you to biopsy any masses or stricture and rule out Barrett's esophagus and cancer. Endoscopy is not used for the diagnosis of diverticulum or DES. It is used for achalasia to rule out severe esophagitis or cancer.

Manometry can be used to determine if there is achalasia, reflux, or other dysmotility. For achalasia, you can see high resting pressure of the lower esophageal sphincter (> 30 mmHg) and incomplete relaxation with swallowing. There may also be aperistalsis if the esophagus is mega dilated from long standing, vigorous disease. Manometry is normal in DES, and you will often see tertiary peristalsis (non-propulsive contractions). Epiphrenic diverticulum should have manometric studies to rule out achalasia that could have caused the pulsion diverticulum.

If the patients are having significant chest pain that seems to be related to their esophagus, but they have not had an appropriate cardiac workup, then it makes sense to rule out any significant cardiac disease that could be confounding the situation. A simple EKG and stress test (if warranted) should suffice. Of course, if they have a lot of risk factors, cardiac clearance should be sought.

Treatment

Zenker's diverticulum is a dyscoordination of the cricopharyngeous muscle. It is treated surgically by performing a complete myotomy of this muscle. The incision is made along the left anterior border of the SCM and the carotid sheath is pulled laterally while the trachea is pulled medially to expose the posterior-lateral diverticulum. A myotomy is performed of all transverse muscle fibers for about 3 cm up and down until all the muscle of the cricopharyngeous is divided. For diverticulum less then 2 cm, a pexy can be performed, but if it is more than 2 cm then a diverticulectomy is performed using a TA stapler over a 60 Fr. Bougie. Test for any leaks (using air or methylene blue), place a closed suction drain and close the neck in layers. Get a swallow study the next day and if there is no leak then start clears, remove the drain, and advance the diet. If there is a leak, then open them up, wash it out and drain it. Be careful not to injure the thoracic duct.

Achalasia can be treated medically, endoscopically, and surgically. The bottom line is that all but surgery has a high failure rate. Medical therapy includes nitrates, calcium channel blocker and botox. Pneumatic dilation may need several treatments, there is a risk of perforation, it makes the future myotomy more difficult because of scarring, should not be used for children or vigorous achalasia (high rate of iatrogenic perforation), and 50% fail by 6-12 months. Botox injections may be effective up to 3 months, but then additional treatments are needed. Heller myotomy has the best cure rate of 80% at 2 years. It is done laparoscopically with ports as you would place for a Nissen fundoplication and the esophagus is mobilized. The left anterior vagus is found and preserved and the myotomy is carried from the GE junction up the esophagus for 6 cm and onto the stomach for 3 cm. Finally, test for any leak and perform a Dor fundoplication. Fundoplication is used mostly to buttress the myotomy and the hiatal repair, no so much to decrease reflux symptoms.

DES is treated medically by reducing stress and precipitating factors, nitrates and calcium channel blockers

Parabronchial and epiphrenic diverticulum are treated with diverticulectomy, myotomy, and correction of the underlying disorder.

Addition Therapy

Symptomatic follow up is all that is needed.

Example Case

A 68 year old man is referred to because of several months of dysphagia. He is a smoker in the past and he has had a 10 pound weight loss recently.

This is concerning for cancer or a stricture given his symptoms, the weight loss and history of smoking; however, there could be other things going on here. I would get a better idea of the time frame this has been going on, and ask him about a family history of cancer. I would also ask him about vomiting.

Assuming that there is not much revealing on the history, I would do a physical examination, focusing on the neck and supraclavicular area looking for lymph nodes, and examining the abdomen looking for masses or groin adenopathy.

He tells you that he vomits undigested food.

Well now, that is sounding more like a diverticulum of the esophagus. I would get a swallow study on this patient. Assuming that the barium swallow shows a cervical diverticulum that is around 2 cm, I would discuss the findings with the patient and his treatment options.

That is exactly what you find. What are his treatment options?

Since he is symptomatic and it is 2 cm in size he can have an endoscopic procedure using a linear cutting stapler, which I don't do, so I would refer him to another doctor who does; or, I could take him to the operating room and resect this. In my hands, the later would be the safest thing for me to do.

Well, he decides that he wants you to do it because he likes you. What is the next step?

Assuming that the rest of the barium swallow is unremarkable and that the patient is otherwise pretty healthy, not on any medications (particularly anti-platelet or anti-coagulation medications), and he has no cardiac symptoms, then we can proceed to the operating room for a diverticulectomy

So no other studies are needed at this time, like an EGD?

No, I think his symptoms are related to the Zenker's and if there were any problems after the operation I would address them. The problem with EGD is that, even if I am very careful, there is a higher risk of perforating the esophagus. I don't want to do that.

So, all he needs is a diverticulectomy?

That and a myotomy should be done. The cricopharyngeus muscle is abnormal and needs to be split. So I would do a myotomy to include all the transverse muscle fibers for about 3 cm, expose the diverticulum, place a 60 Fr bougie down the esophagus, then fire a TA stapler across the diverticulum to remove it. I would test for a leak, leave a closed suction drain, and close the neck in layers.

Surgery goes well, when will you feed him?

I would get a water soluble contrast study the next day. If that is normal, then I would pull the drain and start him on clear liquids. He can be advanced as tolerated after this.

What would you do if you saw a leak on the swallow study?

I would take him back to the operating room, open my wound and wash it out, try to find the hole and repair it, then leave a drain and get out. I would leave the patient NPO for the next 7 days. I would start TPN in this time too.

(3) Hiatal Hernia*

H&P

Patients with hiatal hernias may not have any symptoms at all. For those that present, they may complain of reflux symptoms, dysphagia, nausea, vomiting, epigastric pain, postprandial fullness (the board likes this one), dyspnea (IS measurements improve after hiatal hernia repair – no such thing as asymptomatic hiatal hernia?), postprandial chest discomfort and history of anemia (high incidence of ulceration in herniated stomach).

On physical exam, you should listen to the chest for bowel sounds and examine the abdomen. Most patients will have a benign physical examination.

Diagnosis

If the patient is having chest pain, get an EKG to make sure it is not myocardial ischemia. Once that is done, proceed with a simple chest x-ray. While a chest film alone can be diagnostic, you need to determine the type of hernia in order to provide the patient with appropriate treatment options (type II and III should be fixed because there is a 30% risk of perforation, hemorrhage, or strangulation).

Hernia Type	Location of Gastroesophageal Junction	Hernia Contents
I (Sliding)	Intrathoracic	Gastric cardia
II (True Paraesophageal)	Intraabdominal	Gastric fundus
III (combination I and II)	Intrathoracic	Gastric cardia & fundus
IV	Intrathoracic	Gastric fundus, body and other abdominal organs

The type of hernia is defined by the position of the GE junction and that can be seen nicely by an upper GI contrast study.

EGD should be performed as well so that you can check for ulceration and biopsy any suspicious areas.

Finally, manometry should be done to evaluate the LES pressure and position, and to check the esophageal function. Most of these hernia repairs will be followed by a wrap and you need this information to determine the type of wrap you should create.

Treatment

Symptomatic type I hernias should be repaired surgically; all other should have surgery, regardless of "symptoms" because of the risk of perforation, strangulation, and hemorrhage. If they are "asymptomatic" and are not good surgical risk then one must consider the pros and cons of surgical repair.

The surgery is generally performed laparoscopically through the abdomen by most surgeons today. Ports are placed like you would for a Nissen Fundoplication, the hernia sac and contents are reduced along the cardia of the stomach (to reduce the chances of recurrence), and the fundus of the stomach is mobilized. The esophagus is cleared off circumferentially, taking care not to injure the vagi. You should achieve an adequate length of esophagus in the abdomen (at least 2 cm) or else you should consider a collies' gastroplasty. The diaphragmatic crura are closed with non-absorbable suture (e.g. 0-ethibond), and the hernia is patched with an alloderm patch to decrease the recurrence rate. Depending on the manometry studies and the surgeon's preference a wrap should be performed at this time. A suture should secure the repair below the diaphragm. For toupet closure sutures to bilateral crura is used. For Nissen an anterior stitch to the right crura is used. There is no benefit to gastrostomy tube placement, but it is still done with the thought that it will prevent the *entire* stomach from slipping back into the chest.

Additional Therapy

Complications that may arise after this procedure include esophageal perforation, bleeding, vagal nerve injury, recurrence and reflux. Follow up is symptomatic.

Example Case

A 40 year old woman presents to your office complained of non-specific abdominal pain, wt loss and anemia.

Given her vague history I would try to elicit a cause such as eating food or lying supine, and I would want to get a nature of the pain and ask her about a history of ulcer problems, gallbladder problems, or pancreas problems. I would ask her about alcohol usage. I suspect that this will not be an easy diagnosis with history alone, so I would examine her abdomen, looking for scars from previous surgery. Assuming this is not helpful, I would get some lab work, including a CBC to find out how anemic she is, check the amylase and lipase to rule out pancreatitis, chemistries with LFTs to see if there are abnormal electrolytes and if the bilirubin is high to suggest gallbladder problems or stones.

All negative.

I don't really have an idea of what is going on with her at this time, so I would get a CT scan of the abdomen and pelvis.

Why not just some plain films (hands me a chest x-ray with the stomach in the chest)?

I have to admit, I was not thinking about a hiatal hernia, but she obviously has a paraesophageal hernia that is symptomatic. I would explain the problem to the patient and the need for repair. Assuming she is a reasonable candidate, then I would take her to the operating room for a laparoscopic paraesophageal hernia repair.

First, I would definitely want to scope her myself to rule out any ulcers or malignancy in the area that needs biopsy, I would get a swallow study to judge the location of the GE junction, and I would get manometry to make sure the esophagus functions normally.

Describe your technique.

Place my ports in the upper abdomen as I would for a Nissen, place the liver retractor, and start by going through the pars flaccid, expose the right crus, work posteriorly to find the left crus as well. I would then take down a few cm of short gastric in preparation of the wrap I will do, and bring this up to the left crus, cleaning this off, and working anteriorly to expose the hernia sac. I would take a great deal of time and patience to fully reduce the sac completely and not leave any phrenoesophagel ligaments attached that might cause recurrence. Once this is done, I would mobilize the esophagus until the GE junction was several cm in the abdomen.

What if you cannot get the GE junction in the abdomen?

That is rare. Some would argue that shortened esophagus are non-existent; nonetheless, a Collis gastroplasty could give you extra length. I try not to do this because I have a problem leaving stomach in the chest. It is just not physiologic.

Fine, go on.

I would repair the crura posteriorly with interrupted ethibond, and then place an alloderm patch in place to decrease the recurrence rate. Finally, I believe in doing a partial 270 degree wrap or a full wrap depending on their preoperative manometry.

You did manometry?

I believe I did. If I forgot to, then I would certainly get manometry on any patient with a hiatal hernia that I would be repairing because you do not want to do a full wrap on a person with esophageal dismotility.

Would you do anything else?

No. I would do my wrap over a 60 Fr bougie and perform endoscopy at the end to make sure everything looked good. Then I would deflate the abdomen, close the 12 mm fascial defect and that is it.

How do you manage the patient post-operatively?

I begin clear liquids the next day. If they are tolerating this, and their lab work looks good the next morning, I generally let them go home. I instruct them to continue clear liquids for about 4 or 5 days, particularly to let the swelling go down, and then I have them start on full liquids for a week, purred food for two weeks, and then soft and slippery food after that, slowly working toward normal food again. I see them back in the office in about 2 weeks and make sure they are tolerating their diet well.

What if they are really having a hard time keeping anything down?

If it is immediately post-operatively, I give it time because it is probably edema. If it is several days or weeks later, then I just scope then to see what is going on, they may be too tight. If they are too tight, I would try dilation with a balloon a couple time before I consider going back to revise them.

(1) Barrett's Esophagus

H&P

Patients with Barrett's generally have a long standing history of reflux symptoms and possible dysphagia, and this will be the most common symptom on presentation. They may have weight loss.

Physical examination will not be very revealing.

Diagnosis

This diagnosis will be found on endoscopy and is not generally a diagnosis you expect to find. The work up is the same as for reflux disease and includes an UGI contrast study, manometry and a pH probe, but the upper endoscopy will be diagnostic. You will be able to see the metaplasia and biopsy it to rule out dysplasia.

Treatment

We treat Barrett's because it is a premalignant lesion and carries a thirty times increase in the risk of esophageal adenocarcinoma. When we discuss the treatment of Barrett's esophagus, we must know if there is the presence of dysplasia; and, if so, then what is the grade of dysplasia. 10% of patients will develop low grade dysplasia (LGD) and 2% will develop into high grade dysplasia (HGD).

Barrett's with no dysplasia should only be treated if the symptoms are not controlled with medications or the patient is relatively young (and the cost of lifelong PPI will be larger than the cost of a definitive operation). Of course, these patients should have surveillance scopes every two years to make sure that there is not progression of the disease (as there is rarely regression, even on medical therapy) or the development of dysplasia. If they develop dysplasia, then see below.

Dysplasia comes in two flavors: low grade and high grade. LGD can be treated with surgery or medical therapy. Surgery (Nissen or Toupet) controls symptoms, stabilizes nondysplasitc states and slows down progression of dysplasia, but does not prevent the development of cancer. If the patient is having reflux symptoms, then they should have surgery. If they are not having reflux symptoms, then they can undergo medical therapy. Young patients and those that can not tolerate the medical therapy should consider surgery sooner than later. Even after surgery, these patients should have a surveillance endoscopy every 6 months for 2 years, and if the disease remains stable then go to every three years. If they develop HGD, then see below.

HGD should be thought of as esophageal cancer, assuming that you just have a sampling error in your biopsy. A large percentage of these patients will go on to have frank cancer if left in place. They are considered candidates for transhiatal esophagectomy (THE). The diagnosis should be confirmed by two pathologists in high volume centers, and then you move on to the staging as if this is a cancer. This includes CT of the chest and abdomen, EUS, and +/- PET scan. Stage IIa or less can proceed with THE. If it is more than a stage IIa, then they should have neoadjuvant therapy and XRT and restaged in three months for resection (see esophageal cancer section).

Additional Therapy

Barrett's is followed with biopsies every three years.

Low grade dysplasia should be biopsied every year, whether they have had an anti-reflux procedure or not, until there is no evidence of dysplasia. Once there is no dysplasia, it can be followed every three years.

For those patients with HGD who are not ideal candidates for THE, you may consider the following therapies: photodynamic ablation, endoscopic mucosal ablation, or endoscopic laser ablation. These technologies are getting better and may become the standard of care for HGD; however, I would not answer them on the boards unless you use them and are familiar with the literature supporting their usage.

(6) Esophageal Perforation*

H&P

There is a significant amount of pain when the esophagus perforates, no matter where it occurs (neck, thorax, or abdomen). Before rushing into a diagnosis, consider all the aliments that can present with similar symptoms. You need to ask for a history pertinent to MI, pancreatitis, ruptured AAA, gastric volvulus, PUD perforation, and malignancy of esophagus.

On physical examination, you should make sure the patient's ABC's are ok, check the heart rate and temperature (rule out sepsis). Feel for crepitance in the neck and mediastinum. Listen to the breath sounds bilaterally (thoracic perforations can cause a left pleural effusion), and examine the abdomen for peritonitis.

Diagnosis

Send off a CBC to check the WBC, amylase to rule out pancreatitis, cardiac enzymes and troponin to rule out MI. Get an EKG and place the patient on a monitor. Get an upright CXR to check for pleural effusion, pneumomediastinum, and/or free air under the diaphragm. Finally get a gastrograffin swallow to rule out gastric volvulus, esophageal perforation or perforated PUD.

The swallow study will show the esophageal perforation and the level. It is not uncommon for the examiner to tell you that the gastrograffin swallow is negative, and then you have to do a thin barium swallow which will show the leak.

Treatment

Once you have diagnosed the esophageal leak, immediately stabilize the patient with IVFs, oxygen, Foley catheter, and antibiotics if the patient has signs of sepsis. Make them NPO and start them on IV PPI's.

Management can be conservative or surgical. Lean toward surgical; however there are circumstances that you may consider a conservative approach. Incidents where non-operative management may occur include instrumental perforation, secondary to esophageal variceal sclerotherapy or achalasia dilation, or perforation found several days after injury without symptoms. 25% of patients can be treated in this fashion. If the patient develops sepsis, pneumothorax, mediastinal emphysema, or respiratory failure then you should go straight to the operating room. Conservative management has failed and it is time to get control.

If the perforation is found within 24 hours, or if they fail to meet criteria for conservative management, then you are going to have to operate on these patients (you will need to operate on the general *surgery* oral boards).

Now, this could be an intimidating subject for most surgeons, but you have to think about this in a logical and systematic fashion so that you can discuss this in a slow, calm and deliberate manner. Think about the places there could be a perforation: cervical, chest, or abdomen. You should know the location based on the swallow. No matter where the leak is, keep these general rules in your mind: find the perforation, debride it, close it over a tube, test it and drain it.

Postoperatively, all patients will have an NGT, be NPO, and on TPN. You need to observe the wound for infection, monitor the drainage, and perform a gastrograffin leak test in 7-10 days post operatively. If this is ok, start clear liquids, advance as tolerated. If the drain output does not increase, then pull the drains. If there is still a leak, then continue to observe unless the patient gets septic (then you don't have sepsis control and you have to go back in to drain the area better).

If the perforation is in the neck, make an incision along the anterior border of SCM. Locate the perforation, using air or methylene blue if needed. Debride the tissue around the esophageal perforation so that you have healthy tissue to close, performing a myotomy as needed. Pass an NGT to stent the esophagus, and close the perforation in two layers (4-0 PDS on the mucosa and 3-0 silk on the muscular layer). Irrigate and wash out the area and perform a leak test to make sure you got it closed well. Buttress the area with the strap muscles and drain the neck with a Penrose drain. Close the wound in layers.

Thoracic perforations should be divided into the upper two-thirds and lower one-third. The upper chest should be accessed through the right posteriolateral thoracotomy and the lower esophagus is accessed through the left chest. Other than this, the treatment is the same. Move the lung medially after taking down the inferior pulmonary ligament. Open the pleura over the healthy distal esophagus, find the perforation using methylene blue, and perform a myotomy as needed. Debride the edge of the perforation, stent the esophagus with an NGT, and close the defect in two layers. Irrigate the chest thoroughly and buttress the repair with pleura, pericardium, or intercostal muscle. Test your repair with air or methylene blue, close the pleura, and place two chest tubes for drainage.

In the abdomen, the perforation will be at the GE junction. Approach this through a midline incision, mobilize the esophagus from the mediastinum to the crura, and identify the leak with methylene blue. Debride the tissue, make a myotomy as needed, pass an NGT, and close the perforation in two layers. Irrigate the abdomen well, and buttress your repair with a Dor or Thal fundoplication, and place two closed suction drains: one around the perforation and one in the left subphrenic space.

Additional Therapy

There are situation in which you will not be able to do a repair and drainage. This may be the case where the tissue is so torn up or infected (>24 hours after perforation) or the patient is very ill and septic and you don't have much time. In these cases you have two options: esophageal exclusion or T-tube diversion.

Esophageal exclusion is done by making a cervical esophagostomy, open gastrostomy, feeding J-tube, and wide drainage. You are trying to stabilize the patient. You can reconstruct the esophagus in 6 to 8 weeks.

T-tube diversion is when you place the tube directly in the perforation and secure it to the diaphragm, place a G-tube and feeding J-tube, and widely drain the area. In this situation you are simply trying to create a controlled fistula that can be dealt with later on when the patient is stable.

In the case of the patient with a peptic stricture, malignancy, or megaesophagus secondary to achalasia; you may need to resect the esophagus. If the discovery of the perforation is early, then a THE can be done. If there is a chronic perforation refractory to other treatments, then perform a three incision esophagectomy, gastrostomy, feeding J-tube, and reconstruct the esophagus in 6 to 8 weeks.

Example Case

A patient with achalasia has an esophageal perforation from a pneumatic dilation.

That is not good, and I am assuming that I am being given this diagnosis from the GI doctor or the emergency doctor who has stabilized the patient, given him IV fluids and antibiotics, and has a contrast study that shows the distal esophageal leak into the left chest. I am also assuming that the diagnosis has been made within a couple of hours of the perforation

Yes. What do you want to do?

I would take this patient to the operating room and make a left sided thoracotomy, (I am assuming the leak from the distal esophagus is in the left chest on the contrast study), through the 5th or 6th intercostals space, and exposes the esophageal perforation, debride the edges and close this with two layers, place a pleural or intercostals flap over it, leave two chest tubes and wash out the chest. The other thing to consider is that he is having dilations because he has severe achalasia, and before going to the operating room, I would want to know how functional the esophagus is. If the esophagus is not burned out, then I would flip the esophagus over after mobilizing it well and do a myotomy on the opposite side of the perforation.

Would you wrap him?

It is not a bad idea in this situation because I could cover my repair and myotomy with stomach and prevent reflux after the operation. Some do not believe in doing a wrap after Heller myotomy, but I do. The problem I have here is that I have never done a wrap in the chest, so unless there is someone there that can show me how to do it, I would not do it in this situation.

What if the patient did not present until he was 36 hours out from the dilation?

That is more concerning because now there is the potential for him to be a lot sicker. Also, in the operating room, the tissue will likely not hold a stitch because it will be badly infected and friable. So there are a couple of options. I feel the best option would be placing a T-tube in the esophagus to control the drainage, washing out the chest, closing the chest, then going in the abdomen laparosocpically to place a decompressing gastric tube and feeding J-tube. The other option I would consider if the tissue is really bad and I didn't think a T-tube is enough is to defunctionalize the esophagus by stapling it off proximally and distally, removing the perforated segment, place the G and J tubes, and performing an esophagostomy (spit fistula). I would have to bring him back another time to reconstruct the esophagus.

You have done this before? How do you do a spit fistula?

I have never done this before, but my understanding is that you make an incision along the anterior border of the SCM and dissect down to the esophagus, place a Penrose around it and deliver it up to the skin after mobilization. A loop ostomy is created with interrupted sutures

(0) Caustic Injury to the Esophagus

H&P

You will usually be given the history of a child accidently drinking a household cleaner or detergent or the adult that is trying to commit suicide by drinking "Drain-O." Your immediate focus is on treating this patient like a trauma. Consider the airway patency first. There can be significant swelling of the orophyranx. If you even suspect airway compromise (especially in a child) then intubate them. If the airway is intact, ask them about painful swallowing, hematemesis, retrosternal chest pain, and abdominal pain (these are questions that are trying to determine the location of injury…think about it).

On physical exam, again focus on the ABC's of the patient. Stabilize them, and then do a focus head and neck exam. Look at the orophyranx, asses the degree of injury in there and then work your way down. Feel the neck. Is there crepitus? Listen to the chest. Is there an effusion from a thoracic perforation? Perform an abdominal examination and rule out peritonitis.

Diagnosis

The diagnosis is given to you. You need to be concerned with the type of injury that has been done to the orophyranx, esophagus, and the stomach. Send off labs to check the electrolytes and the white cell count. Get a chest x-ray to look for thoracic perforation. Finally a gastrograffin swallow will demonstrate any perforation of the esophagus or stomach.

The next step in this patient, unless a perforation is obvious and you are going to the OR, is to perform an endoscopy to get an idea of the degree of injury. The scope (rigid or flexible) is placed in the esophagus until you reach the point of the esophagus where there is circumferential burn, and then you should stop and go no further. There are three degrees of burn starting from edema and erythema to frank necrosis, deep ulceration, and circumferential red tissue.

Treatment

Stabilize the patient, give them fluids; make them NPO, of course, and given them broad spectrum antibiotics. If you have found a perforation, then you will have to go to the operating room for treatment. If, however, the patient has minimal symptoms then admit the patient for observation, keep them NPO, give them fluids and perform endoscopy within 24 hours.

Final treatment is based on the degree of burn. In first degree burns, keep them NPO until they have resolution of symptoms, and then you can start them on clear liquids and advance as tolerated. After 3 weeks, get a gastrograffin swallow to look for a stricture. If you find a stricture, then EGD with dilation should be done and repeat every three months as needed.

Second or third degree burns to the esophagus require IV antibiotics and PPI's, NPO and TPN, and a high suspicion and worry about perforation. If, after 5 to 6 days, the patient remains stable, then the patient can start clear liquids. After 3 weeks, a gastrograffin swallow is done to rule out stricture and dilation should be done every 3 months as needed if one is found. Persistent stricture after 12 months is an indication for esophagectomy.

Perforation of the esophagus will take you to the OR where the neck, chest and abdomen should be prepped out and a three incision approach employed. Open the abdomen and evaluate the distal esophagus, mobilize the esophagus and stomach, resect the stomach if needed, and place a feeding G/J-tube. In the thorax, a right thoracotomy is done, the tissue is debrided and the esophagus is mobilized. Finally the cervical incision is made and the cervical esophagostomy is performed. Wait for 8 weeks, maximize nutrition status, and then reconstruct with a gastric conduit.

Additional Therapy

Caustic injury to the esophagus is a risk factor for SCC of the esophagus at 40 years post injury.

In children with second and third degree burns to the esophagus, stricture is likely. Since you cannot pneumodilate a child, a gastrostomy should be placed in these children early on so that retrograde dilation with savory dilators can be done up to a 36 Fr.

(9) Esophageal Cancer*

H&P

These patients will typically present with dysphagia and weight loss. You should ask them about risk factors for esophageal cancer (e.g. tobacco, ETOH, and history of caustic injury). You should ask about hematemesis, hoarseness, history of Barrett's, and history of reflux.

Physical is focused on the head and neck looking for supraclavicular adenopathy. Abdominal exam may reveal adenopathy or masses.

Diagnosis

UGI swallow study will often reveal the mass in the esophagus. Take note of the location because this will come into further work up and treatment (see below). A swallow will also rule out other pathology (e.g. achalasia, diverticulum, etc). Once the mass is found in the esophagus, the next step is to get the tissue diagnosis. Upper endoscopy is performed and biopsy is obtained.

Once you have a diagnosis of cancer, you must stage the patient before determining the course of treatment. You need an EUS to determine the depth of the lesion, determine if there are involved nodes (US guided FNA can have a positive predictive value of 95%). CT scan is performed on the chest, abdomen, and pelvis to look for adenopathy. PET scan should be considered. Bronchoscopy should be performed on any lesion that is in the upper third of the esophagus because involvement of the trachea makes the patient unresectable and they should only be considered for palliation.

Treatment

You must know the staging of esophageal cancer in order to know how to treat this. Surgical therapy is offered immediately to patient with "resectable disease," and those are the ones with stage I and IIa tumors.

Stage I is a T1 (submucosa) N0M0 lesion

Stage IIa is a T2 (muscularis propria) N0M0, or T3 (adventitia) N0M0

These patients should then have preoperative pulmonary and cardiac evaluation. Furthermore, their nutritional status should be evaluated. Those who have lost more than 10% of the weight benefit from 2 weeks of TPN leading up to the surgery to boost their nutritional status. Finally, they undergo esophagectomy (THE, Ivor-Lewis, 3-incision depends on the location of the lesion and your comfort, see below).

Patients that are staged as IIb and III will require neoadjuvant chemotherapy because this has been proven to downstage the tumors, increase resectability, and minimize micrometastasis; however, there is no improvement in survival. (5 year survival for stage I is 95% and stage III 10%, overall 12-20%).

Stage IIb T1N1 (paraesophageal nodes) M0, or T2N1M0

Stage III T3N1M0 or T4 (adjacent organ involvement) N1M0, or T4NxM0

These patients should have a feeding J-tube placed for nutrition and begin neoadjuvant therapy. This included 5-FU, cisplatin, mitomycin and radiation therapy (4500 rads). They should be restaged in 3 months and if they are down staged to a stage I or IIa, then they are considered resectable and can undergo and esophagectomy.

Finally, those unfortunate patients with stage IV [TxNxM1 (distant mets, M1a is celiac nodes for lower third cancers or cervical nodes in the upper third cancers, M1b is other metastatic lesions)] are not resectable and will need to undergo palliative therapy. This includes any combination of systemic chemotherapy, laser ablation, photodynamic ablation, stent placement, and/or radiation therapy.

Additional Therapy

As an addition to this section, the Ivor-Lewis and three incision techniques are described below as abdominal, thoracic and cervical incisions.

Abdominal incision is a midline incision. The abdomen is explored for metastatic disease that would make the cancer stage IV and unresectable (e.g. liver met or celiac node). If no such disease is found, then the stomach is mobilized, preserving the right gastroepiploic artery to create the gastric conduit. A pyloromyotomy is performed (because you will cut the vagi when you resent the esophagus), the hiatus is opened, and a J-tube is placed for postoperative feeding.

The abdomen is closed and the patient is placed in the left lateral decubitus in preparation for the right thoracotomy portion of the procedure. The chest is opened through the 4th intercostals space. The pleura are divided and the lung is retracted medially. The esophagus should be isolated and the thoracic duct and azygous veins are ligated and divided. The esophagus is transected and removed and sent for frozen section to make sure that you have at least 2 cm margins clear of the cancer (gross margins can be deceiving).

Finally, a left cervical incision is created and the esophago-gastrostomy is created in a two layered hand-sewn fashion. An NGT should be placed before final closure, and a Penrose drain is placed.

The complications include recurrence (5%), leaks (5%), and mortality (1%).

Example Case

You are asked by the PCP to see a 52 year old man with a long standing history of smoking and heavy drinking. In fact, he tells you that he can't drink as quickly as he used to when he goes to the bar. The PCP performed and UGI which shows an ill defined circumferential lesion in the mid esophagus.

This man sounds like a poster boy for esophageal cancer. I would get a better idea of his symptoms, including duration and progression of symptoms, and a history of weight loss (more than 10% is significant), and ask him a little about a family history of cancer. I would examine him for the presence of lymph nodes in the neck, supraumbilical, periumbilical and groin nodes. Assuming that the rest of the history and physical is unrevealing, I would proceed with getting a tissue diagnosis of this mid-esophageal lesion. I would do this with upper endoscopy.

EGD shows a fungating mass, but you get the scope pass it and the stomach and duodenum are normal. Biopsy shows a moderately differentiates adenocarcinoma.

So now I know. There are three things to do now. One, I need to stage this cancer to determine if it is resectable at this time; two, I have to assess his nutritional status; and, three; I have to asses his cardiopulmonary status.

So I would order a CT scan of the chest, abdomen and pelvis to see the extent of local invasion, involved structures, presence of distant mets or lymph node disease. I would also get a PET scan to assess distant disease. An EUS will tell me the depth of invasion and if there are any suspicious nodes, they can be FNA'ed at that time. Finally, I would do a bronchoscopy to rule out tracheal involvement because this is a mid-esophageal lesion.

I would then get an EKG and echocardiogram. If these were concerning then I would get a stress test. I would get a baseline ABG and PFTs since I would be opening the chest. I assume these should be normal, maybe a little decreased since he is a smoker.

Finally, since he is a drinker and has a big tumor in the esophagus, I assume his albumin and pre-albumin are low, indicating he is mal-nourished.

CT shows scanty nodes adjacent to the esophagus. Abdomen and pelvis are negative. EUS stages this tumor as a T3N0. His cardiac and PFTs are normal. He is malnourished and reports about 20 pounds of weight loss over the last month.

So if the EUS staged this as a N0, then I am assuming that they got and FNA sample of these nodes and they were negative. This is a stage IIa, and this is resectable disease. So since he is malnourished, then I would admit him, get central access and give him at least 2 weeks of TPN. I would then perform an Ivor-Lewis esophagectomy.

Can you explain that procedure?

Yes, it involves and incision in the abdomen and the chest. The chest incision is necessary here because the lesion is in the mid esophagus, and I believe that in order to do a proper resection of the tumor with the nodes around it, you have to go through the chest. So I would put a laparoscope in the abdomen first to make sure that I don't see any metastatic disease. 30% of people will be found to be unresectable at this point. Then I would make an upper midline incision, explore the abdomen, mobilize the stomach and hiatus and distal esophagus, do a pyloroplasty, and place a feeding J-tube. Then I would close the abdomen, place the patient in the left lateral decubitus and open the right chest. I would retract the lung medially; open the pleura, dissect out the esophagus, perform a lympadenectomy and remove the tumor with 2 cm margins, and send the margins for frozen to make sure I got all the cancer. If I have gotten it all, then I will pull up my stomach and create a two layer gastroesophagostomy over an NGT and buttress it with pleura or intercostal muscles. Finally, I will leave two chest tubes and close the chest.

(27) Esophagus

Four months later he presents to your clinic with disseminated disease with mets to the bone. He wants your input because the pain medication is just not helping with his pain.

Palliative XRT is all I could offer him.

(29) Breast

You will inevitably get a breast question on the exam. So you have to know this stuff cold, and you have to be able to stop and change the scenario on a dime. One of the most important pieces of advice I can give you about this is continue to clarify the situation with the examiner as he changes the scenario. He or she will be talking about DCIS in a premenopausal woman and then go to a cancer in a postmenopausal woman; therefore, you should state out loud what kind of patient you have in your mind or you and the examiner will be on different pages and they will fail you on a question that you know.

Spend as much time as you need to on this subject, it is a give me if you know the basics. Stay away from controversy, do not quote the literature (it pisses them off) or the latest ASBP trial, and stay within the last three years of surgical treatment of breast disease. You DO have to know the staging, the adjuvant therapy (dose and intervals), and the surgical treatment.

(5) Breast Mass*

H&P

The patient will usually present to your office after she or her primary care doctor has found a mass in her breast. You want to know how long it has been there and if it has changed in size. Ask about pain, skin changes, bloody nipple discharge, and history of breast cancer. This kind of history should just reflexively come out your mouth when you hear "breast." You also need to ask about the risk factors for breast cancer. The GAIL model for breast cancer is used to determine a patient's life time risk of breast cancer. This breast cancer risk assessment tool is provided on the internet by the National Cancer Institute and assesses the following information that you should ask about:

(29) Breast

1. Does the woman have a medical history of any breast cancer or of DCIS or LCIS?

2. What is the woman's age? (must be > 35 years old)

3. What was the woman's age at the time of her first menstrual period?

4. What was the woman's age at the time of her first live birth of a child?

5. How many of the woman's first-degree relatives-mother, sister, daughter- have had a breast cancer?

6. Has the woman ever had a breast biopsy?

    a. How many breast biopsies (positive or negative) has the woman had?

    b. Has the woman had at least one breast biopsy with atypical hyperplasia?

7. What is the woman's ethnicity/race?

This online calculator (which is available to all of us in our clinic) will assess the risk and if the woman is at a 1.6% five year risk for developing cancer, then she is considered high risk. From this point on, I will refer to a woman's risk factors as her GAIL model risk (GMR).

High risk by GMR or if they have a biopsy positive for atypical hyperplasia, there is a role for hormonal chemoprevention (tamoxifen for premenopausal lesions and aromatse inhibitors for postmenopausal women) to get a 50% permanent reduction in life time risk.

On physical exam, you have to do a thorough breast exam. No matter how you do it, inspect the breast for skin changes and symmetry and palpate all the breast tissue, looking for dominant masses or other findings (like adenopathy), examine the axilla and supraclavicular nodes, and evaluate for nipple discharge. Note the characteristics of any mass found in the breast: is it hard, mobile or fixed, well circumscribed or ill defined, etc.

Diagnosis

Now that you have established that the patient has a mass in her breast (regardless of her risk factors), you have to do some imaging of the breast. As a general rule, I would not stick a needle in or biopsy on a breast until it has been imaged.

The mainstay imaging for the breast is US and mammography (standard or digital). Ultrasound is most useful if you suspect that the lesion could be a cyst or if the patient is very young and will have dense breast tissue which would make MMG a less accurate imaging modality. Otherwise, get a mammogram on the patient.

MRI is being used. It is very sensitive, and it may be too sensitive. You may find a lot of suspicious lesions with MRI and would lead to many unnecessary biopsies. At this time MRI is suggested only for patients who are at high risk for breast cancer, have a history of BRCA, patient with breast implants, those who have a history of radiation to the chest, or a woman who has > 20-25% lifetime risk of developing breast cancer in her lifetime as determined by the modified GAIL risk assessment. I wouldn't mention MRI on the certification exam unless you know a lot about it and use it in your practice.

You should be familiar with the BIRADs system of classification. To date, there are six levels:

0. Indeterminate (do they have old films to look at? Or do we need US?)

1. Normal (repeat in one year)

2. Benign (degenerating fibroadenoma, no biopsy)

3. Likely benign (follow up MMG in 6 months, follow out 2 years then down grade to BIRAD 2 if it remains stable)

4. Suspicious, needs a biopsy (30-40% are malignant on biopsy)

5. Malignant, needs a biopsy (about 5% will not be cancer, so you have to biopsy)

6. Has a malignancy (undergoing systemic therapy)

Treatment

The breast mass that is found on the US or MMG could be a cyst (complex or simple), fibroadenomas, phyllodes tumor, fat necrosis, sclerosing adenosis, plasma cell mastitis, duct ectasia, subarealoar chronic abscess, or fibrocystic disease.

Breast cysts are fairly common. Their management requires ultrasound guided aspiration. Treatment depends on the characteristics of the fluid. If it is clear, then you are ok if the cyst collapses completely. They should follow up in 6 months. If it recurs, you can repeat aspiration and send the fluid for cytology, but a third recurrence requires excision of the cyst. If the fluid is bloody or particulate, then you should excise it right away.

If the cyst appears complex, or the mass is solid, then the woman should undergo core needle biopsy. This will provide architecture and cytology. If this pathology returns indeterminate, LCIS, atypical hyperplasia, radial scar (seen in fibrocystic disease) or papilloma; then the patient will need an excision of this area to make sure there is no underlying DCIS or cancer (25-30% upgrade).

Fibroadenoma, fat necrosis, and sclerosis adenosis requires local excision and routine follow up. Fibroadenomas is prepubescent or adolescent females require watchful waiting if less than 3 cm. Larger than 3 cm will not likely go away and are asymptomatic. In addition, the larger ones may be a Phyllodes tumor. Giant fibroadenomas may present in a young female, can be alarming and should be removed

Phyllodes tumor is a benign tumor 90% of the time (so we no longer use the term "cystosarcoma"), however it can be invasive. Local recurrence is the main concern, so you want to get 1-2 cm margins around the tumor. If it is invading local structures, this could be an invasive tumor and is most likely to metastasize hematogenously to the lungs, so a CXR should be obtained. If the tumor recurs the patient may need a total mastectomy.

Plasma cell mastitis, duct ectasia, and subareolar chronic abscess require incision and drainage, antibiotics, and subareolar excision. Granulomatous mastitis is an unusual finding, in younger woman, partial breast involvement. This is treated with steroid, not resection.

Fibrocystic disease requires you to rule out a solid mass or cancer. Once diagnosed, the patient is advised to decrease caffeine intake and fat intake, get proper fitting underwear, and take NSAIDs for the pain. If the pain persists, then a trial of primrose oil (prolactin inhibitor), danazol (testosterone derivative), or bromocriptine should be used. They should follow up in 6 month, continue self breast examines (SBE), annual clinical breast exams (CBE), and annual MMG.

Additional Therapy

Patients at age 20 years should do SBE monthly and have CBE every three years. At age 40 years, they should have SBE monthly, CBE annually, and MMG annually or biannually until age 70.

If the woman is a BRCA gene carrier they should start MMG at age 25 years and should consider alternating each year with MRI. High risk patients should start MMG 10 years earlier than premenopausal diagnosis age of family member diagnosed but not before 25 years of age. If the patient has a history of cancer, atypical hyperplasia, LCIS, or DCIS then annual MMG is done, starting at the time of diagnosis.

Example Case

A 28 year old woman comes to your office complaining of a breast mass that she has just recently noticed during self breast examinations.

This is a young woman with a breast mass, and most of the time this will be a benign mass, but I have got to rule out a cancer. I would start by getting an idea of her risk factors with her history (e.g. family history, history of breast biopsies, history of cancer, etc). Assuming she has no pertinent history, I would systematic inspect and examine both breast and axilla, palpating the nodal basins as well. If all of this reveals only this one small, mobile mass in a single breast, then I will need to biopsy it. Before doing any biopsy, however, I will get an ultrasound of the mass to make sure that it is not cystic, but solid, and make sure there aren't any other lesions. In addition to this, I would order a baseline MMG.

Ultrasound shows a cyst

I would aspirate this.

You get out some green fluid and it disappears.

Good, then I would send the fluid for cytology, and see her back in 3 months unless the cytology is positive or she develops a new complaint. If the cyst comes back, then I would do the same routine with US and aspiration. If it is bloody, does not disappear completely, has particulate matter in it, has an abnormal cytology, or recurs more than twice, then I would take her to the operating room for excision.

Well you do take it out and it comes back as fibrocystic disease. Now what do you do?

I assure the patient that this is benign and tell her to continue SBE, stay away from caffeine, stop smoking, and use supportive underwear.

Now it is LCIS.

I am assuming that this is on the excisional biopsy that I did.

Yes and there are positive margins.

This is not a cancer, so margins don't bother me. I would explain to the patient that this is a risk factor for breast cancer. There is a 25% lifetime risk, to be specific. She has three options at this time. My choice would be to closely observe this with monthly SBE and yearly CBE and MMG. In addition, I would offer her hormonal therapies if the LCIS is receptor positive, which they usually are. This would decrease the risk of her developing cancer by 50% (so to about 12% lifetime). Alternatively, she can forego the hormonal therapy and just observe, especially if there is concern about the side effects (blood clots, hot flashes, uterine cancer). Her final option, only reasonable in high risk patients, is bilateral simple mastectomies.

What if it is DCIS?

Assuming I have gotten negative margins, it is well differentiate, less than 1cm, and is receptor positive, then hormonal therapy may be all she needs. Some may offer radiation therapy as well, but if she has a recurrence, then BCT is out because you have already radiated the chest. If the tumor is > 1cm, has poor differentiation, or the patient is at high risk, I would give more consideration to radiation. Finally, simple mastectomy could be offered, but this should only be for woman who are BRCA1 or 2 positive, at very high risk, and absolutely desire this operation. SLN biopsy should be done at the time of simple mastectomy because if the specimen comes back with a focus of invasive cancer, I will not be able to go back and do this (and I would have to do a formal ALND).

Now it is Phyllodes tumor.

(29) Breast

I would go back and get 2-3 cm margins.

Really? Is this malignant?

No, but these tumors are prone to recurrence and the better the negative margins the lower the risk of recurrence. They can rarely be malignant.

What if it comes back?

I would re-excise it again.

(3) Occult Breast Lesion*

H&P

This would be the case when a woman is sent to your office after having a routine MMG that shows a BIRAD 4-5 lesion, but there is no palpable mass.

You should calculate her GMR and perform a full breast examination. Since this is an occult breast lesion, you will not be able to feel the mass. *(Sometimes the examiner will give you a very detailed history and tell you that the physical exam is negative. My advice is to not piss them off by re-examining the breast. They told you it was negative. Don't be paranoid; they are not trying to trick you!)*

Diagnosis

Since they are coming to you with an occult lesion, then they have probably already had a MMG or US. You may want additional images, or depending on the MMG finding and the patient's risk factors, you could consider MRI. Lesions seen only on MRI can undergo MRI guided biopsy.

Treatment

This is the heart of this question and it should not take you very long to get here (maybe 60 seconds). This lesion could be a cyst (see the previous section) or solid mass. Solid masses can be characterized as benign appearing (BIRAD 3) or suspicious (BIRAD 4). This will determine your treatment algorithm. Suspicious mass seen on MMG should be sent for a stereotactic core biopsy where a 14 G or larger needle is placed in the breast using MMG guided techniques and 10-15 cores are taken of the area with vacuum assistance. If the lesion is completely removed by this, then a clip is left in place in the event a future procedure is needed. If you cannot do a core biopsy for whatever reason (patient can not lay prone, breast are too large, etc.) then you can do a wire localized breast biopsy (again, leave clips at the bottom of your resection in case you have to come back for re-excision).

Biopsy results may come back as atypical or malignant (see breast cancer section). For the atypical biopsy results (atypical ductal hyperplasia, atypical lobular hyperplasia, LCIS, radial scar, papilloma, or Phyllodes) there is a 25% upgrade to DCIS or invasive carcinoma with surgical biopsy. This is why you have to go and excise these lesions when they are found on core biopsy.

Pseudoangiomatous stromal hyperplasia (PASH) is nonmalignant. It may present as a discrete mass or thickening, or incidental finding on core biopsy. This should be excised because they can grow and become locally recurrent. If it continues to recur, this may require mastectomy (this is very rare), and immediate reconstruction should be done since this is not a malignancy.

Additional Therapy

LCIS

If you have gotten a core biopsy of LCIS, then you have got to go in and remove this area of the breast (using wire localization if need be) in order to be sure that there is not DCIS or cancer in the specimen. Once you confirm that there is only LCIS, you need to explain to the patient that this is a risk factor for developing breast cancer in the future (about a 25% risk of developing a cancer in the next 20-30 years).

The woman then has three options:

She may consider chemoprevention. This is probably the best choice for you to defend on the boards. It has been shown that tamoxifen will reduce her risk (by 50%) of developing breast cancer in the future. However, it is not without significant side effects, and these should be discussed with the patient. Side effects include hot flashes, decreased libido, cataract formation, DVT/PE (especially in patients with a history of thrombotic disease or in smokers), and uterine cancer (they could consider hysterectomy, but it is a rare incident and usually has a good prognosis when it develops).

Observation alone is an option in a patient that does not want hormonal therapy and is willing to continue to come in for follow up and is reliable. Many women will opt out of the hormonal therapy for many reasons. That is her choice. However, if she has multiple risk factors and has a high GMR, then she should consider other options.

Finally, bilateral simple mastectomies will remove all breast tissue (theoretically), thus reducing her chance for developing breast cancer. This is a good option in a patient with many risk factors and a high GMR. Immediate reconstruction should be offered to this patient at the time of mastectomy. Nipple sparing mastectomies are controversial, and I would avoid discussing this with the examiners unless you are a plastic surgeon/oncologist who does this all the time.

Example Case

A 45 year old woman is referred to you with these mammograms (right breast lesion). Her exam is normal.

I don't look at mammograms very much in my practice, but this look like a suspicious lesion, maybe a BIRADS 4. Assuming that you meant my physical exam is normal, and there are no masses in the breast, I will need mammographic assistance to get a tissue diagnosis. First I would get a feel of the patient's risk factors using the Gail Model risk assessment tool.

What's that?

The Gail model takes into account a woman's risk factor and predicts her 5 year and lifetime risk of developing cancer. It can be found on the NIH website and is readily available. It will look at factors such as age, age of menarche, age of first birth, if the patient ever had any atypical breast biopsies and how many, their race, and how many 1st degree relatives have been diagnosed with breast cancer.

I never heard of that, sounds interesting. So her mother and sister had breast cancer at an early age.

That makes me concerned that there is a genetic cause in this family, specifically BRCA1 and BRCA2 genes could be at play here. I would certainly recommend that she be tested because it may significantly alter the treatment plan depending on the results.

How?

Well, if she is a BRCA1 carrier, then she has a 30% lifetime risk of developing cancer. If this lesion in her breast now is a cancer, then she would have about an 80% chance of developing a recurrent breast cancer. So she may elect to have both breasts removed at one time (including oopherectomy for BRCA1+).

I see. Well she says that she will consider genetic testing, but wants to know what we are going to do right now for this lesion.

Since this lesion is seen on MMG, the rest of those films I assume are normal (the other breast), and I cannot feel this on physical exam, then she will need a stereotactic core needle biopsy.

There is a 1 cm focus of invasive lobular carcinoma.

Lobular carcinoma is rare, but it should be treated like any other breast cancer. I would offer her breast conservative therapy with sentinel node biopsy.

Well, she says she read on the internet that for lobular cancer, the lesion can mirror itself on the other side and biopsy there is needed.

That is for LCIS; I would explain the difference and reassure her that it would not be useful in this situation.

What if it was a 1 cm focus of DCIS?

Now we are dealing with a non-invasive (as of yet) cancer and this will need to be re-excised with negative margins to make sure that there is no invasive cancer associated with it. There are a couple of different approaches to DCIS. Some surgeons would offer all these patients radiation to the breast after removing the DCIS because it will reduce the risk of recurrence by 50%. Once you give them radiation, then a recurrence commits them to a MRM. However, there are some surgeons, including myself, who use the Van Nuys score to determine how much risk there is of developing a recurrence or cancer based on the size of the DCIS, the negative margins around it, the presence of comedo necrosis, and the grade or differentiation. Based on a score from these factors, a patient may be offered simple excision, excision and radiation, or simple mastectomy. Regardless, I would offer her hormonal therapy if her tumor is ER/PR positive.

How would you treat the patient with lobular carcinoma if her lymph nodes were positive?

Well if her sentinel node was positive, I would complete a formal ALND. If the ALND was positive, then she would need addition systemic therapy for her N disease, making this at least a stage IIb tumor. In addition, if there were more than 4 nodes that are positive, then I would have her receive radiation to the axilla. If the tumor was hormone receptor positive, then she should receive hormonal therapy for five years after her systemic and radiation therapy.

What if the receptors are negative?

Then I could not offer her therapy with hormonal antagonist.

What about the one with DCIS, should she get tamoxifen?

Yes, as I said, if she is receptor positive, then she should get it because this will reduce her risk of developing recurrent DCIS by 50% in both breasts. We know that when these tumors do recur, half the time they are invasive. So while there is no good data right now that say hormonal therapy increases survival, you can infer that it does and the long term data should eventually show this.

(6) Early Breast Cancer*

H&P

GMR and usual physical examination

Diagnosis

Patient is usually sent to you with a diagnosis of breast cancer on core biopsy. You want to look at her MMG yourself and make sure that she doesn't have any other synchronous lesions that need to be addressed.

Once you are satisfied that you are dealing with a true early breast cancer, then you have to stage the cancer. This is done with a CXR to rule out mets to the lung, LFTs (if elevated CT scan the abdomen and pelvis), and bone scan if the patient has any complaints of bone pain.

Atypical • • • • • •DCIS • • • • • • •Cancer

Breast cancer is a spectrum of diseases, not just a diagnosis. It can range from atypia on the left to advanced cancer on the right. When you make the diagnosis of cancer, find out where you are on this scale, it matters.

DCIS lies in the middle, and has a good prognosis. DCIS is a cancer that is not invasive yet, but has a 35% chance of becoming invasive over the next 20 years if left in place. 2% of DCIS will have local recurrence, and half the time they recur, they are invasive.

Treatment

DCIS and invasive cancers are included in this discussion of the treatment of early stage breast cancer.

The treatment of DCIS is essentially removal. Traditionally, this disease was rare and found incidentally when cancers were removed. Because of better screening techniques, we are seeing more of it. Traditionally simple mastectomies were used to control the disease, but several studies have shown that lumpectomy can be used for most patients.

The treatment depends on several factors: tumor size, multifocal/ unifocal, comedo necrosis, differentiation, and grade of tumor. All of these factors will determine how to treat this disease, and there are two camps on the management of this non-invasive cancer.

First, there is the camp that is well trusted in the NSABP trials that has a large number of people in a well designed prospective trial that states that DCIS should be excised with at least negative margins, then the remaining breast tissue irradiated to decrease recurrence (and with long term follow up studies, probably survival), and hormonal therapy if the tumor is estrogen receptor positive. These trials showed that radiation therapy reduced the risk of recurrence from 42% to 12%. Hormonal therapy further cut this in half.

Then there is the Van Nuys camp that states that there is a spectrum within the DCIS patients and that we need to look carefully at those factors mentioned above and assign a score (4-12) to determine the treatment. You can look up Van Nuys if you like, but the bottom line is that for low scores (small, well differentiate tumors in older women that you can get a negative margin on) you probably only need to provide a lumpectomy and not radiation because the risk of recurrence is very low; on the other hand, those with high scores (poorly differentiate or comedo necrosis, large tumors that are difficult or impossible to get clear margins, multi focal disease, young patients) should have a simple mastectomy to remove the higher risk of recurrence (remember 50% will be malignant when they recur. We fail our patients if DCIS recurs!). *(If you do a simple mastectomy for high risk DCIS, then do a sentinel node biopsy at that time, because you will not get a second chance at this, and you may find an invasive cancer in the final pathology).* Patients in the middle (moderate size tumors, low grade, decent margins, and middle age people) probably benefit from lumpectomy and radiation. Hormonal therapy is given to any patient that is receptor positive because it will reduce the risk of recurrence by 50% whether they have radiation therapy or not.

Invasive breast cancer, once diagnosed, must be staged. As stated above, this would include CXR, labs, and possibly CT scans and bone scans as needed. If it is a localized, early staged breast cancer, the patient has a good prognosis and an excellent chance at cure.

Breast conservation therapy (BCT) with sentinel node dissection (SLND) is the standard of care. This should be offered to every patient unless they have the following contraindications to BCT: large tumor to breast ratio, two lesions in separate quadrants of the breast, diffuse calcifications, persistent positive margins, pregnant (see below), collagen vascular disease (don't tolerate radiation well), central subareolar mass, and previous history of radiation. For these patients, a modified radical mastectomy is performed.

If the SLND is positive, then the patient should undergo a formal axillary node dissection (ALND). You should review the techniques of SLND and ALND. Skin sparing mastectomies can be offered for really small tumors and patients that are good candidates. Immediate reconstruction is also an option, but be aware of the complications that radiation can have on the reconstruction.

Contraindications for SLND include IBC, prior axillary surgery, and biopsy proven positive axillary node.

Additional Therapy

For any woman that is found to have a cancer larger than 1 cm, she should be offered chemotherapy (especially premenopausal women). If there are positive nodes, they should have chemotherapy. Adjuvant therapy includes AC (adriomycin and cytoxan) and is a 6 week course. 5-FU is added to some regiments. Taxol is added for advanced tumors or non-responding tumors.

Hormonal therapy is given to patients that are receptor positive. Her-2-nu receptors (an oncogene that is amplified in 20% of patients) should also be tested for and treated appropriately.

The radiation dose provided to the breast and chest is 5000 rads. This is given to the axilla as well if more than 4 nodes are found to have invasive cancer in them.

Example Case

A 35 year old woman comes to your office with a 1 cm breast mass on mammogram. The radiologist did a core biopsy which was non-diagnostic. There may be some abnormal cells. What do you want to do?

I am assuming that the biopsy was adequate and he sampled the abnormality and left clips.

Yes.

Then I would get an assessment of her risk factors, assuming she has none I would examine both breast and axilla to prove to myself that there is no palpable lesion.

There is not one.

Then I would get some baseline labs including LFT, which if they are elevated would prompt a CT of the abdomen and pelvis, and a CXR to rule out a lung lesion. If she had any symptoms of bone pain, then I would get a bone scan.

It is all negative, what do you want to do?

Needle localized biopsy.

What kind of margins?

I would get one cm margins since I done know what it will come back as.

It comes back as invasive ductal carcinoma with an area of DCIS which has a 2mm free margin.

I am ok with 2 mm free margin for the DCIS as long as I got good margins around....

What are good margins?

I mean if the margins are negative, then I am concerned more about the invasive cancer that is her life threatening problem at this time. So I would explain to her that she has an early cancer, the prognosis is good, but we have to sample her nodes and this can be done with a minimally invasive technique called sentinel node biopsy. (20 SLND are required before you are given privileges to perform this in most hospitals).

When you do the SLNB, your frozen section comes back positive. What do you do now?

I would complete the ALND.

What if your biopsy was negative, but the final pathology showed micro-metastasis?

Then she will need to go back for a completion node dissection.

Really, you would do that for micro-mets?

That is my understanding of the literature, but I am not a breast surgeon. I suppose that if there is a very low risk of finding more nodes positive, and she is going to get systemic therapy, it may be reasonable not to go back and that would be a conversation to have with the patient. I think that is controversial, I would just go back.

She wants to know what the chances of finding another node that is positive if you do the ALND.

There are nomograms that can be used to figure that out, but I do not know of the top of my head.

What about isolated tumor cells?

That is considered node negative, and I would not go back for that. They may have got there from biopsy manipulation rather than a metastasis.

Does it matter how many nodes you take out of the axilla when you go back?

In terms of prognosis, like for colon cancer we need 14 nodes, no. This has not been shown to be true for breast cancer, but you want to do an adequate node dissection.

Fine, the SLN is negative. So now what do you want to do with her?

I want to send her to an oncologist to receive chemotherapy (AC) for 4 cycles, and then radiation therapy to the breast. Once she has completed that, I would advise her to start hormonal therapy if her tumor was receptor positive. In addition, Her-2-nu receptor positive patients should be offered herceptin with their chemotherapy regiment.

How will you follow her?

I would like her to do SBE monthly, and come and see me every 3 months for PE in the first year, and every 6 months after that. Furthermore, she should have yearly bilateral MMG.

Is there anything else?

No.

(9) Advanced Breast Cancer*

Let's go over the TNM of breast cancer.

T0 - in situ
T1 - < 2cm
T2 – 2-5 cm
T3 - >5 cm
T4 – Extension into the skin/chest wall
N1 – Axillary nodes
N2 – Matted axillary nodes
N3 – Infra/Supraclavicular nodes or inframammary nodes
M0 – No mets
M1 – Mets

Stage I - T1N0
Stage IIA – T0-1N1, T2N0
Stage IIB – T2N1, T3N0
Stage IIIA – T0-2N2, T3N1-2
Stage IIIB – T4N1-2, TanyN3
Stage IV – M1

H&P

This scenario may start off as a patient that presents for initial evaluation of a breast mass and is found to have advanced cancer, or the patient comes back with distant metastatic disease. The woman may have a local recurrence, large mass adhered to the chest wall, or inflammatory breast cancer.

Get a pertinent history related to these scenarios, calculate the GMR, and perform the routine physical examination.

Diagnosis

Again, it is all about staging. In these cases, you are going to have positive finding in the nodes or distantly

Treatment

Stage IIB (T2N1 or T3N0) or stages IIIA (T3N1) have two options: Modified radical mastectomy or primary systemic therapy (neoadjuvant) and BCT with SLND if they respond.

If you perform the mastectomy, the patient will require adjuvant chemotherapy. If they are receptor positive, they will need hormonal therapy. Radiation therapy should be given if they have 4 or more nodes positive.

For those that receive primary systemic therapy, there will be responders and non-responders. Those that respond can undergo lumpectomy and ALND (SLN is contraindicated in the presence of documented node positive disease, so this is only offered to stage IIB, T3N0). These patients will need post operative radiation therapy. Tamoxifen and chemotherapy is given as indicated.

For those that do not respond, they will require a MRM. Chemo, XRT, and hormonal therapy as needed.

Stage IIIa (T0-3N2), stage IIIb (T4), or stages IIIc (N3) are offered primary systemic chemotherapy for 6 weeks or 4 cycles. If they become resectable then you can perform MRM. Postoperative chemotherapy is give for 8 more cycles and radiation. Hormonal therapy is given as indicated.

If the patient is unresectable after primary chemotherapy, they should be given radiation therapy, and add Taxol to the chemotherapy regiment (some may add this routinely in the beginning of the therapy for all advanced cancers). The patient is then reassessed for resectability. Hormonal therapy is given as indicated.

Treatment of stage IV (M1) is based on menopausal status. If they are premenopausal, then they will need oopherectomy or ovarian ablation with lupron shots, tamoxifen, and chemotherapy with Taxol if there is no response with the above. For postmenopausal women, aromatase inhibitors are given. Tamoxifen is given if they are not responding to that. Finally, chemotherapy is added for nonresponders.

Inflammatory breast cancer should be considered in any inflamed breast; and other diagnoses to consider include acute mastitis, breast abscess, and Mondor's disease. An incisional biopsy is made, including the skin, to make the diagnosis. The patient is diagnosed and started on paxlitaxel (taxol) every week for 12 weeks, followed by CAF for 4 cycles. If the patient has a partial or complete response, then she undergoes a resection and postoperative radiation therapy. She is given hormonal therapy as indicated. If there is no response to the taxol and chemotherapy, then she is given radiation therapy upfront, undergoes surgery if possible, and then given hormonal therapy as indicated.

Additional Therapy

Immediate breast reconstruction becomes an issue in some patients with stage IIb or III cancers that would benefit from post operative XRT. This includes patients with node positive disease and tumors more than 5 cm before neoadjuvant therapy. Tissue expanders may be a good choice in this situation, otherwise the patient will have their flap radiated. The reconstruction may be a little hard after this, and if the patient is alright with that then you can do that.

It is very useful for patients with early breast cancer. Patient may refuse lumpectomy with radiation because they refuse radiation and opt for MRM. Multicentric DCIS is another situation that immediate reconstruction is a good option.

Example Case

A 45 year old woman comes in to your office because she has noticed a mass in her right breast for the last six months but has delayed coming in because she was scared that it would be cancer. She is otherwise healthy and not on any medications.

That is concerning that she has waited so long, now we may be dealing with an advanced tumor. I would assess her risk factors using the Gail Model risk predictor tool and do a physical exam of both breasts. I am assuming that this is a large breast mass with palpable adenopathy.

Yes, it is, and she has small breast. The mass in her right breast measures 6 cm. Her other breast is normal. She has multiple palpable lymph nodes.

So, if I assume that this mass is not fixed, then this is a T3 lesion. The nodes are mobile, so this is N1 disease. This is an advanced tumor. I would image her breast with a MMG for a base line image, and then get a core biopsy of this lesion in the office so that I can make the diagnosis. In addition, I would FNA the nodes in the axilla in order to confirm that this is metastatic cancer. While waiting for the tissue diagnosis, I will send her for a CT scan of the abdomen and pelvis and get a chest x-ray, looking for metastatic disease. I would scan the brain or chest if I had any suspicion of mets to these areas. If she had any bone pain, I would get a bone scan. Hopefully, I find no evidence of metastatic disease.

Since this is an advanced tumor, I am going to give her primary systemic therapy before I offer her surgical resection. The chemotherapy offered is taxol for 12 weeks, then chemotherapy (cyclophosphamide, doxorubicin, and 5-FU). The doxorubicin is cardio toxic, so I would get an echo of the heart to make sure there is good function there.

The pathology is infiltrating ductal carcinoma in both the breast and the axilla. There is no distant metastatic disease that you find on further workup. What now?

I would give her the primary systemic therapy. She should receive 4 cycles, and then we can assess her response.

What if there is no response?

Then I would give her radiation therapy to the chest wall and add Taxol for another 4 cycles, followed by modified radical mastectomy.

What if she does respond, what operation would you offer her?

She is a T3N1. This is a stage IIIA, and even if she had a good response, I believe she would do best with a MRM. She has small breast and the risk of recurrence by leaving some breast tissue behind and the poor cosmetic result we would probably have is just not worth it. If her breast was large enough and the mass is very small, I could theoretically offer her lumpectomy. I would discuss the risk and benefits with her. She will definitely need an ALND (not SLN) because of her node positive status.

She really wants to keep her breast.

I would not feel comfortable doing breast conservative therapy for this patient. I would discuss the options of immediate breast reconstruction, but she needs to understand that she will need radiation therapy postoperatively and so I would even recommend waiting for that option as well.

So, she has the operation, and you do a MRM. Now what?

She should receive another course of systemic therapy and get radiation to the chest wall and axilla. After this, if her tumor was ER/PR positive then she should receive hormonal therapy for five years. In addition to this, the presence of Her-2-nu receptors is an indication to treat her with herceptin.

How does herceptin work?

I really do not know, but my understanding is the Her-2-nu is an oncogene and the drug blocks its receptors so that it is not effective.

Let's change this a little and say that this woman is 60 years old and comes in with a 7 cm mass in her breast and has a very strong family history, and she is complaining of back pain.

So she has a large tumor and the back pain makes me worry about bone mets. I would start with the metastatic work up and get the CT of the abdomen and pelvis, and I would get a bone scan.

She lights up all over. The back has bone mets, and the liver is full of metastatic disease. What would you do now?

I would start her on an aromatase inhibitor. If she did not respond to that then I would add tamoxifen, and finally chemotherapy if she did not respond to that. The breast cancer is going to kill her, and I would only do surgery on the breast to remove the tumor if it became painful or infectious.

How long do you think she has to live?

She has 6 months, maybe. I don't know.

(2) Breast Cancer Recurrence

H&P

Consider the possibilities here: Local recurrence (in the breast), regional recurrence (in the axilla), or systemic (distant metastasis).

Typical history here is irrelevant, she already has cancer. You need to know the original pathology, get the previous operative report to know what she had done and what they found, know about her adjuvant therapy (chemotherapy and radiation, did she get tamoxifen?), and ask about symptoms of bone pain or abdomen pain that may suggest bone or liver mets, respectfully.

Physical exam is focused on the size and location of the recurrence, presence of hepatomegaly, and lymphadenopathy.

Diagnosis

Perform a core biopsy on this mass to confirm that it is a cancer recurrence. Check typical labs (including LFT's and alk phos to rule out liver and bone mets). CT scan and bone scans may be needed depending on the lab results. CXR should be done routinely to rule out lung mets.

Treatment/Additional Therapy

In order to treat this problem, you need to consider the type of recurrence and the previous treatment that she has received.

For a woman that has a systemic recurrence, she should receive chemotherapy, hormonal therapy as needed. If they have a response to this therapy then a chest wall resection can be done.

If the patient has already had a mastectomy and has a local recurrence then she needs total field radiation to the chest wall, internal mammary, and supraclavicular area. If there are no distant mets, then she can undergo chest wall resection. If there are distant mets, she needs systemic chemotherapy; depending on the response, subsequent resection can be undertaken.

If there is a regional recurrence after mastectomy and she has had no previous ALND, then she needs an ALND as long as the nodes are not matted. If they are matted down or immobile or if she has had a previous ALND, then she should have chemotherapy and hormonal therapy.

For those women who have had BCT and now have a local recurrence, they should have a mastectomy. If the woman had previously undergone an ALND, then you should offer a simple mastectomy and chemotherapy. If the woman has not had an ALND (e.g. she had SLN), you should offer a MRM and chemotherapy.

For those women who have had BCT and now have a regional recurrence and never had an ALND or had undergone SLN and has mobile nodes, an ALND should be done. If the nodes are immobile, then just give chemotherapy and hormonal therapy. For those women who have had an ALND, they are offered chemotherapy and hormonal therapy.

(2) Bloody Nipple Discharge*

H&P

You want to ask if it the discharge is spontaneous, unilateral, and bloody or clear discharge (all would suggest that it is may be malignant, although even with these factors it is most likely benign papilloma). Calculate their GMR.

Perform a physical exam on the breast, paying close attention to any responsible quadrant of the breast that causes the nipple discharge.

Diagnosis

The diagnosis is mostly determined by the history and physical exam, but you definitely want to get a MMG or US to determine if there is any underlying pathology. All of these will need excision.

Treatment

If there is a benign presentation (non-bloody, bilateral, not spontaneous, no masses) then focus on the color of discharge. If it is colored then observe for 6 to 8 weeks, have the patient do SBE to localize the responsible quadrant, stop smoking and decrease caffeine intake, and reassess. If it is milky or clear, then check a prolactin level. If it is high, then get a CT or MRI of the brain. If it is normal, then do as if it is colored discharge.

If there is a responsible quadrant and the MMG and PE are negative (no dominant mass) then do a subareolar wedge resection. If the MMG or PE is positive, then follow the breast mass work up as already described above and perform a subareolar wedge resection. If you cannot find a responsible quadrant on reassessment and the MMG and PE are negative, then perform a complete subareolar ductal excision.

If you suspect a possible malignancy (spontaneous, unilateral, single duct, bloody, or associated mass) and the MMG, PE, and SBE is negative, and the fluid is heme positive then perform a complete subareolar ductal excision. If the MMG is negative and the PE and fluid are positive then perform a subareolar wedge resection. If the MMG, PE and fluid are negative, then send the fluid for cytology. Abnormal cytology is cause for a subareolar wedge resection. If the cytology is normal, then observe for 6 to 8 weeks and have the patient do SBE to localize, have them stop smoking and decrease caffeine intake, then reassess. If there is still a negative MMG, PE and SBE then perform a total subareolar ductal excision.

Example Case

A 35 year old woman presents with unilateral bloody nipple discharge.

Most nipple bleeding is benign, but the unilateral and bloody make it concerning and it needs to be worked up for a malignancy. I would question the spontaneity of the discharge and about her risk factors for breast cancer, and assuming she has none, I would proceed with examination of both breast for any dominant masses, and the axilla and supraclavicular nodal basins for any enlarged nodes. Of particular interest would be the nipple discharge, and if I could find a responsible quadrant or particular duct. I would make note of these findings and send her for a mammogram. If the MMG and physical exam are negative for any suspicious masses or lesions, then I would ask her to consider removing the responsible quadrant of ductules.

How would you do that?

In the operating room, I would find the responsible duct again and I would catheterize and inject it with a small amount (few drops) of methylene blue so that it will be visible during the dissection. I could also just leave a probe in the duct. I would make semicircular incision around the areola complex and dissect out the ducts in this area, including the blue duct, tying off the distal and proximal ends, taking 1 cm area of tissue around the duct, and orienting the specimen for pathology. 10% of the time there can be a malignancy, so you want to know if there were positive margins and where they are.

Why not just stick one of those little scopes in there and get some biopsies?

It is not useful in this case because even if your biopsy was benign papilloma, there is an increased risk of cancer being associated with this, and I would not want to take the chance of leaving caner behind.

What if you find an abnormality on MMG?

If the lesion is a BIRADS 4 lesion or higher that warrants biopsy, then I would order a stereotactic core biopsy and treat the pathology accordingly.

It comes back DCIS.

Then I would take her to the operating room, perform a wire localized excision of the DCIS to get negative margins (and I would leave a clip in the areas of resection in case I have to come back for more tissue), do the subarealoar wedge resection, and treat her accordingly.

Accordingly how?

So, if the wedge is benign and I got negative margins on the DCIS, then I would consider the size and differentiation of the DCIS to determine if she should get radiation therapy. If she is receptor positive, then she should get hormonal therapy for five years.

(0) Gynecomastia/Male Breast Cancer

H&P

The typical history and GMR does not apply to men. You should suspect that this is not cancer, but it can be. Ask about marijuana or steroid usage, get a medication list, ask about liver disease or cirrhosis, and change in libido or sexual function.

Physical exam should be similar to that for woman. Notice if it is symmetric or unilateral. Is there a mass, and if so, is it rubbery and oval shaped under the nipple or is it a hard mass eccentric to the areola? Check the lymph node basins, and find out if it is tender.

Diagnosis

MMG can be used to aid in the diagnosis. US can also be used in this situation. You want to test HCG and LFTs which may rule in steroid producing tumors or liver disease, respectfully.

Treatment/Additional Therapy

If there is a hard, eccentric mass, then assume that it is cancer. Core needle biopsy should be performed. If it is positive for cancer then perform a MRM. Male breast cancers are usually receptor positive and tamoxifen should be given if they are. Radiation and chemotherapy are given just as they would be for female breast cancer.

If there is diffuse enlargement of the breast, this is probably pseudogynecomastia. Plastic surgery is considered if the patient wants this removed.

Rubbery, round mass, found behind the areolar is probably gynecomastia. When in doubt, perform an FNA. Testicular tumors (high HCG), hyperthyroidism (high LH, and high testosterone), prolactin secreting tumor (low LH and low testosterone), adrenal tumor (high estradiol), leydigs tumor (high estradiol), and sertoli tumors (high estradiol) can cause this. Treatment is observation and NSAIDS. Tamoxifen or danazol can be used with some success. Plastic surgery can be done for removal.

(0) Enlarged Axillary Lymph Node

H&P

Ask the patient about a history of infection, hiradenitis, cat scratch fever, generalized adenopathy, tobacco use, GMR for breast cancer assessment, GI cancer risk factors, "B" symptoms, and melanoma risk factors.

25% of the time, adenoma in an axillary lymph node will be breast cancer.

On PE, examine all the possibilities. Do bilateral breast examinations, check the cervical lymph node basins and groin nodes, do a skin exam, do a rectal exam, and examine the abdomen to rule out abdominal masses.

Diagnosis

Assuming that the H&P will be unrevealing *(for the board exam, this is the design of this scenario. In the real world, it is uncommon not to be able to find the primary tumor. On the board it is a standard question. In addition, whatever you don't look for, that is what it will become)*, then perform a core needle biopsy or excisional biopsy to determine the diagnosis. Send the excised specimen fresh for flow cytology (rule out lymphoma), ER/PR (rule in breast cancer), and mucin (to rule out melanoma and lymphoma). MMG, CXR, CT scan of the abdomen and pelvis, upper and lower endoscopy, and CEA levels should be done in an attempt to find the primary tumor.

Treatment

So you have a metastatic tumor but you cannot find the primary. The most likely site of disease is the ipsilateral breast. This may be a situation where you want to get an MRI of the breast to rule out a mass that is missed on standard or digital MMG and ultrasound. You can discuss the options of MRM with the patient, but this is not a great choice. Perform an ALND and observe.

(0) Paget's disease of the Breast

H&P

This woman may present as a referral or show for routine exam and you find this scaly lesion on the nipple area. You will want to know the duration of symptoms, whether she has had any infection, if there is any drainage from the area, or trauma to the nipple. Assess her GMR.

Do a complete breast examination.

Diagnosis

MMG and/or U/S are used to examine the breast in the usual fashion. 95% of Paget's disease of the breast has an underlying cancer.

Treatment

Do not treat with steroid creams. This can cause regression of the Paget's disease and cause a delay in the diagnosis.

If the MMG and the PE is negative, then perform a wedge resection of the nipple areolar complex. If this is positive for Paget's disease, then the treatment is simple mastectomy or central lumpectomy with SLND and radiation therapy.

If the specimen contains invasive cancer deeper in the breast, they may not be good candidates for BCT and you should perform a MRM.

(2) Breast Cancer during Pregnancy*

H&P

GMR and typical examination is done.

Diagnosis

The diagnosis is given to you in this case. They just want to know what you are going to do if she is pregnant.

Treatment

Antimetabolites (e.g. methotrexate) and radiation is out. The rest is the normal algorithm.

Consider which trimester the woman is in. MRM is the only option for a woman who is diagnosed in the first trimester. No chemotherapy can be given during this time of fetal development; you have to wait until the second trimester.

In the second trimester, you can do a MRM and give chemotherapy. You can not give the radiation while she is pregnant, so this makes BCT hard to push. However, if she is in the late part of the second trimester, then consider the fact that she will be getting six weeks of chemotherapy before you give her radiation. So, can she deliver the baby six weeks from now, and what is the risk of postponing XRT for a week or two?

In the third trimester, you can do a MRM and give chemotherapy; also, you can do BCT with SLN (no blue dye, but tech-99 sulfa colloid is ok) and defer the radiation therapy until she is postpartum.

Example Case

A patient in her third trimester of pregnancy is sent to you for the treatment of a small breast mass that is biopsy positive for breast cancer.

(29) Breast

These patients are treated like any patient with breast cancer with the exception that they cannot be given antimetbolite chemotherapy (e.g. methotrexate) or receive XRT during pregnancy. Therefore, after I have reviewed her films, operative reports and pathology reports; and I have had a chance to interview the patient to get an idea of her risk (I will assume she has no significant family history) and perform my own physical exam, then I would offer her breast conservative therapy.

But you just told me that she cannot receive radiation, so how would you do breast conservative therapy?

She will need chemotherapy for 6 weeks after surgery, and if she is in the third trimester, then she will have delivered the baby already and will be able to receive the XRT.

What chemotherapy would you give her?

I would offer her doxorubicin and cyclophosphamide. I would consult with a medical oncologist, and I would not be the one administering these drugs. I have no experience in this.

You didn't do a metastatic work up on the patient. Would you not do this if the woman is pregnant?

No, I definitely would do this. I am sorry I skipped that step. I would order LFTs, and get a chest x-ray. If there is elevation in the liver functions I would get a CT of the abdomen. The CXR can be done with an abdominal shield, but if there is anything concerning on that I would CT the chest. If the alk phos is elevated then I would get a bone scan.

Is CT safe in pregnancy?

Yes. In the second and third trimester it is perfectly safe.

Would you do a sentinel node on this pregnant woman?

Yes, I would, but I would not use blue dye. The radioactive material, ironically, is fairly safe and this would let me perform a SLN biopsy; however, the blue dye can cause problems with the baby.

What kind of problems?

There is a risk of anaphylaxis from the blue dye, and this could be harmful to the fetus.

(18) Stomach/PUD
(3) Gastric Ulcer*

H&P

Epigastric pain, dyspepsia, vomiting, dark stools, anemia, weight loss and history of ETOH or NSAID usage are suggestive of gastric ulcer disease.

Physical examination is generally normal unless they are having a clinically significant bleed from the ulcer. You should check the stool for blood.

Diagnosis

The diagnosis is made with endoscopy and this should be set up on an outpatient basis if the patient is stable. Gastric ulcers may harbor a cancer, so they must be biopsied several times at the center and around the edges (getting 8-10 biopsies). Endoscopy allows you to define the ulcer type. Brush cytology will increase the sensitivity of the biopsies, and biopsies for *H. pylori* should be done.

Treatment

Medical treatment is the first line of therapy for benign gastric ulcers. If the patient *is H. pylori* positive, then they should be treated for two weeks with PPI and a triple antibiotic regiment like amoxicillin, clarithromycin and Pepto-Bismol. After treatment, check a breath urea test to confirm eradication (repeat treatment if this is positive). Smoking and ETOH cessation is required, and you may treat the patient with additional H2 blocker, sulcrulfate, and/or cytotec. Most ulcers should heal within 12 weeks of treatment. Repeat endoscopy should be done in 6-12 weeks to make sure that they are healing, and biopsies are done at each scope. If they fail to heal after 24 weeks, then there should be a high index of suspicion for malignancy or

ZES. ZES should be ruled out before considering surgery, and this is done by checking a gastrin level. If the gastrin is greater than 1000 and pH is < 2.5 then this is consistent with ZES and the gastrinoma should be localized (see that section). Resection should be considered for failure to heal after adequate medical therapy in the absence of ZES.

Indications for surgical resection of the ulcer include **IHOP**: **I**ntractability, **H**emorrhage, **O**bstruction, and **P**erforation.

Intractability (or giant ulcers >3cm that are suspicious for malignancy and unlikely to heal with medical therapy) is defined as failure to heal after 24 weeks of adequate medical therapy. If the biopsies to date have been benign, then the surgery is based on the location of the ulcer. Type I gets an antrectomy to include the ulcer but does not need a vagotomy as this is not associated with high acid secretion. Type II and III ulcers are believed to be the result of hyper acid secretion and should have an antrectomy and vagotomy. Type IV ulcers require a Csendes procedure to remove the ulcer.

Hemorrhage from a gastric ulcer has a 10% mortality rate and can be severe if it erodes into the gastroduodenal artery. Outcomes are improved if the patient is treated surgically before they receive more than 4 units of blood and have early intervention within 48 hours of endoscopic intervention. On presentation, the patient should be stabilized and transfused as needed to do so. Upper endoscopy can be used to inject and heater probe the ulcer to control bleeding. Ulcers with visible vessels (especially if there is active pulsatile bleeding) are at high risk for re-bleeding. If they re-bleeding or bleeding cannot be controlled then they are taken to the operating room. For type I ulcers, the ulcer is resected with an antrectomy, but no vagotomy is done. For type II and III ulcers, vagotomy and antrectomy is performed. For type IV and V ulcers, a gastrotomy is made; the ulcer is biopsied and over sewn. If the patient is too unstable for this procedure, the ulcer should be wedged out or over sewn and the antrum biopsied for *H. pylori*.

Obstruction from gastric ulcer is treated with antrectomy and BI or BII reconstruction.

Finally, **perforation** may present with early peritonitis (within 24 hours) or late peritonitis (>24 hours). For early presentations that are in good condition for the operation and have no history of PUD, then a wedge resection of the ulcer and gram patch is adequate. If they have a history of PUD then an antrectomy should be done. For those patients that are unstable or present with late peritonitis, a biopsy of the ulcer and graham patch is all that is done.

Additional Therapy

Always send a biopsy for *H. pylori*. Postoperatively, patients are treated with NPO, NGT, IVF's, antibiotics, Foley catheter, PPI drips, and *H. pylori* treatment. On POD #5, a gastrograffin swallow is done. If that is negative, then they can start clears and advance as tolerated. They should all undergo an upper endoscopy at 12 weeks to re-evaluate the therapy.

Example Case

You are referred a patient with a 3 cm lesser curve ulcer.

That is a giant ulcer and I am already thinking that this thing is not going to respond to medical therapy and could be harboring a cancer. I would get a history of the patient's past symptoms, risk factors for ulcers like smoking and NASIAD abuse, and previous medical treatments that he has undergone. Since he is coming to me with the diagnosis, I am assuming that he has already had an EGD, they told me the size and location which is great, but I would also like to know the *H. pylori* status and, hopefully, they took many biopsies of the gastric ulcer which are all benign. If the *H. pylori* test is positive I would treat it with triple antibiotic therapy, leave him on a PPI for 6 weeks, and then I would repeat his scope. Assuming it has not healed; I would re-biopsy this thing many times, and counsel the patient on surgical options. My concern is cancer or ZES. I would send off a gastrin level as well.

Gastrin is normal. What operation would you do?

Before any operation, I would stage the patient like he had a gastric cancer and get a CT of the chest, abdomen, and pelvis.

Not interested, what operation would you do?

Well this is not really an anti-acid operation because this is a type I ulcer, so the resection is just to rule out a cancer. Since it is on the lesser curve, I would put in a laparoscope, examine the abdomen to rule out enlarged nodes or evidence of peritoneal seeding from cancer, and I would biopsy any suspicious tissue. If that is negative, I would proceed with an upper midline incision, and rule out metastatic disease. Then I would do an antrectomy and send it for frozen. If the frozen comes back negative, then we are done, if it is cancer, then he will need a gastric resection with 6 cm margins confirmed with frozen sections.

What if the lesion was really high on the GE junction?

Then I would try to wedge this out leaving a gastric sleeve (Csendes procedure) trying to get negative margins. If that is not possible, then I will have to do a total gastrectomy with a roux-en-Y esophago-jejunostomy. I have only seen one of those, and hope I never see that again.

Fine, now let's say the guy comes to your office after 6 months of "observation" from the GI doctor and you diagnose cancer and the guy says, "let's level, did he screw up?" Would you turn him in?

I would tell the patient that we need to focus on the treatment now and not any neglect by the GI doctor. But I would sure call the GI doctor once he left my office and let him know that the guy has cancer, and he should be aware that he is asking questions. Let's face it, he was negligent.

(0) Recurrent PUD

H&P

Patient will present with a recurrence of his symptoms: epigastric pain, nausea, melena, chest pain, vomiting. He may have a history of *H. pylori* treatment, previous biopsies, and NSAID use.

Physical exam is not helpful

Diagnosis

You need to think of the causes of recurrent disease, and that list is long. The top three causes are incomplete vagotomy, retained antrum, and NSAID use. Other things to think about include gastric outlet obstruction (GOO), suture granuloma at the anastomosis, long afferent limb, ZES, *H. pylori,* hyperparathyroidism, bile gastritis, and antral G-cell hyperplasia.

So your initial approach will be to get the patient's old records, including operative reports and pathology reports. Rule out other confounding diagnosis like MI (with EKG) and pancreatitis (amylase and lipase). All of this is generally negative.

Next, you should start with an UGIS that will show you what kind of previous surgery they had done (because the examiners won't give you an operative report), if there is GOO, the length of the afferent limb, and the patency of the gastro-jejunosotmy.

EGD will let you visualize the ulcer and biopsy it. You can take biopsies for *H. pylori* and look for suture material or masses (like a gastrinoma).

All of these patients should have a gastrin level and serum calcium level sent off to rule out ZES and hyperparathyroidism, respectfully. If gastrin is > 1000 then it is ZES, if it is equivocal, then do a secretin stimulation test (it will increase > 200 if it is ZES).

Technetium scan will diagnose retained antrum.

DSIDA should be done if you suspect bile gastritis.

Steak meal test will diagnose G-cell hyperplasia if there is a 200-300% increase in gastrin when the patient eats high protein meal. Smaller increases may suggest retained antrum, and no change suggests ZES.

Treatment

First line treatment should be conservative therapy with PPI, avoid NSAIDs, cholestyramine and reglan for bile gastritis, and suture removal for suture granulomas.

Surgery is performed for incomplete vagotomy. Previous PCV gets an antrectomy and vagotomy and previous P&V gets an antrectomy.

Retained antrum patients need an additional resection from the duodenal stump and see Bruner's glands on frozen pathology.

GOO is fixed with an anastomotic revision, or gastro-J.

Long afferent limb syndrome is treated by revising the roux limb so that the limb is closer to the gastro-J.

Antral G-cell hyperplasia is treated with an antrectomy.

(0) Stress Ulcer/Erosive Gastritis

H&P

This is becoming a rare entity since the wide usage of PPI for inpatients (especially ICU patients). Three types of stress ulcers include erosive, Curling's, and Cushing's ulcers. Overt bleeding occurs in < 10% patients on prophylaxis.

Prevention of this is with H2 or PPI drips, carafate usage, and misoprostol drips through the NGT.

Diagnosis

Blood coming from the NGT or hematemesis is often the first sign and the diagnosis is made with upper endoscopy.

Treatment

These patients should be treated medically if possible. Cold normal saline lavages via the NGT, octreotide and vasopressin drips, and heater probe during endoscopy can be used. You must correct any coagulopathy and may have to transfuse up to 10 units of packed red cells.

Surgery is performed if the bleeding cannot be controlled. If they are reasonable candidates, then an anterior gastrotomy is made away from the lesser curve and over sewing of the major bleeders is attempted. If this fails, then gastric devascularization is done by ligating all vessels except the short gastrics and performing a truncal vagotomy. If this fails, the last option is a near total gastrectomy which carries up to a 30-100% mortality.

(10) Duodenal Ulcer*

H&P

Patients may present with GI bleed, obstruction or perforation. They may be seen in the clinic with complaints of epigastric pain, chest pain, nausea or vomiting, hematemesis, or history of PUD. 90% of duodenal ulcers are associated with *H. pylori.*

Diagnosis

Patients who present with acute upper GI bleed from a duodenal ulcer need immediate resuscitation and diagnosis with upper endoscopy. Perforations present with acute peritonitis, and the diagnosis is made based on the H&P and free air on upright CXR. Patients who present with obstruction are diagnosed with EGD or UGIS.

Treatment

For the bleeding ulcer, the first line of therapy is endoscopy. The ulcer should be injected with epinephrine and heater probe can be placed on the ulcer to try and get hemostaisis. The patients should receive a couple of liters of fluid to obtain a normal blood pressure, and a type and cross-match for 6 units of PRBC should be done. Conservative treatment will work in 80% of people. However, those that re-bleed will most likely need an operation.

The indications for surgery in the bleeding duodenal ulcer include failure of conservative therapy with 6 units of blood transfused over 24 hours, hemodynamic instability, re-bleeding, or high risk of re-bleeding. For old or high risk patients, a truncal vagotomy and pyloromyotomy with over sewing of the ulcer is performed at three points (the proximal GDA, distal GDA, and medial and transverse pancreatic artery). For the young patient that is stable and good risk, the size of the ulcer and history of PUD is important. If the ulcer is more than 2 cm or they have a history of PUD, then a vagotomy and antrectomy (V&A)

should be performed. If the ulcer is less than 2 cm or they have no history of PUD, then the ulcer is simply over sewn and a pyloromyotomy and vagotomy is performed (P&V).

Surgery	Recurrence	Mortality	Morbidity
V&A	1%	1-2%	15%
V&P	10%	1%	15%
PCV	15%	0.5%	5%

This data may stand a little outdated, especially in regards to the recurrence rate of the V&P of 10%. This data is based on studies that were done before PPIs, and the duodenal ulcer was still being bathed in acidic fluid even when the patient was on the strongest H2 blockers around. Now, while on PPIs, the stomach pH is neutral and allows the DU to heal with a much lower recurrence rate. P&V is safe and effective and seems to be the most logical operation for most cases.

Patients that present with peritonitis and free air under the diaphragm on an upright CXR buy an operation. They should be immediately resuscitated, started on a PPI drip and taken to the operating room for exploration. If they are elderly, more than 24 hours out, or are at high risk, then an omental patch should be placed over the perforation and the abdomen washed out. For the young patient, less than 24 hours after perforation, and good risk, an omental patch and lavage are done. In addition, if they have a history of PUD or *H. pylori* negative in the past, then they should have an antrectomy and vagotomy for definitive control of their disease or else the recurrence rate will be very high (as high as 80%).

Finally, obstruction from a duodenal ulcer requires admission, NGT decompression, PPI drips, antibiotics, and TPN. Their electrolytes should be corrected. The UGI or endoscopy should be repeated in about 7 days to see if they have opened up after this treatment. If they are still obstructed then repeat the treatment for another week (while they are on TPN). If, after 2 weeks, they have still not opened up, then they will need an operation. A V&A should be done in this case. If the duodenum is too scarred, they will need a gastro-jejunosotmy; and, since this is an ulcerogenic procedure, you need to do a vagotomy as well.

Additional Therapy

Patients should be empirically treated for H. pylori after surgery for DU bleed, obstruction, or perforation.

Example Case

You are asked to see a 56 year old male in the emergency room who presented with hematemesis. He is a healthy man who takes only a single agent antihypertensive. You perform an EGD and you see a duodenal ulcer. You take biopsies of the antrum and it is clo (-). What do you do?

So this middle age man has a duodenal ulcer that has bled, and I am scoping him in the ED and see no signs of active bleeding. I hope there is not visible vessel or clot on the ulcer that may suggest a high risk of re-bleeding. I will assume he is stable this whole time, not tachycardia, otherwise asymptomatic, and the history is pertinent to only what you have told me. I would admit this man at this time, check his hemoglobin to see how much he has bled or if he is chronically anemic, and monitor his hemoglobin's every 6 hours for 24 hours in the ICU or step down unit to make sure he does not start bleeding again. I would make him NPO, start him on a PPI drip to neutralize the stomach, and give him IV fluids.

He re-bleeds the next day.

Well, if he re-bleeds then he will need an operation. I would, start making the preparations, again make sure he is stable, transfuse to keep the hemoglobin above 8 mg/dl, and re-scope him to make sure I cannot stop any active bleeding while I am on the way to the operating room.

Once in the operating room, I have a few things to consider. Since he is stable, I can do a good operation to treat his ulcer disease. He is not a big NSAID user (I suppose I will assume that since he only take a single antihypertensive) and he was clo (-), and so these things lean me more towards a bigger operation. My job is to stop the bleeding and treat the disease. In this case, I would open the duodenum longitudinally across the pylorus, identify the bleeding ulcer and sutures ligate it in three places to get it to stop bleeding. I would then close the duodenum in two layers, transversely, and perform a truncal vagotomy.

Why are you doing a vagotomy?

I would do this to prevent the recurrence of the ulcer disease. The reported recurrence rate with V&P is about 10% (and that may be a little high these days). Without the vagotomy, the recurrence rate would be very high, even if he had *H. pylori* and I treated it appropriately post-operatively. He is a young, relatively healthy, stable man in the operating room and he needs me to stop this ulcer from bleeding, and fix the problem that started it.

What if the patient was unstable in the operating room?

Then my focus would be on stopping the bleeding and get out. I would at least try to re-biopsy the antrum while I have the duodenum open and test it again for *H. pylori*, but I would not go for the vagotomy. I would treat him postoperatively with PPIs and empirical *H.pylori* treatment.

After your V&P, how do you manage him?

I would keep him NPO, NGT decompression for the next 5-7 days, and then get an UGI swallow with water soluble contrast. If there is no obstruction or leak, then I would remove the NGT and start him on clear liquids, advancing his diet as tolerated. I would keep him on PPIs for 6 weeks to allow complete healing of the duodenal ulcer, and then re-scope him to make sure it all looks well.

Would you keep him on antibiotics?

Only for 24 hours post-operative, and then stop them unless I have a concern for infection.

You are now seeing a 25 year old man in the ER with acute onset of abdominal pain. He can tell you the exact time he started hurting.

I am concerned that he has perforated a peptic ulcer. However, there are other things that can cause this problem, including ruptured AAA, gastric ulcer, pancreatitis, or gallbladder disease to name a few. I would ask him about a history of ulcer disease. Being so young I think AAA is out, and I would ask him about gallbladder problems, recent weight loss, and alcohol usage. I would focus my exam on the vital signs and the abdominal exam.

He has been treated for ulcer disease 5 years ago and completed treatment for H. pylori at that time. His abdomen is rigid.

I am quite sure he has perforated an ulcer, so I would order a CBC to check the white count and chemistries to replace lytes and look at the renal function. I would get an upright chest x-ray to look for free air, and an abdominal series as well. Assuming all these point toward the perforation, I would fluid resuscitate him and give him broad spectrum antibiotic on the way to the operating room. I would make a midline abdominal incision and explore the abdomen.

What operation would you do?

This is a healthy young man and has a long time to live with possible re-occurring problems and has been treated once before for this problem, so I would wash out the abdomen, graham patch the hole in the duodenum, and perform a definitive anti-ulcer operation. For him, a vagotomy and antrectomy is probably the best option. It has the lowest risk of recurrence and the added morbidity and mortality for a young person is a reasonable risk. If he was at all unstable and I had to get out of the operating room, I would do a vagotomy and pyloroplasty. I have never done a HSV, but that is also an option, it has the highest recurrence rate.

(0) Mallory-Weiss Syndrome

H&P

These patients will present with the triad of vomiting, retching, and hematemesis. They may have a history of hiatal hernia, ETOH use, or portal HTN.

On physical exam, make sure that they are stable and put them on a monitor. Feel for crepitance in the neck and mediastinum. Abdominal exam is done to check for peritonitis.

Diagnosis

H&P and endoscopy is used to make the diagnosis.

Treatment

90% of the time this is self limiting. You need to stabilize them and monitor them like an UGI bleed. Starting a PPI drip and following serial H&H's is routine. T&C is done, and endoscopy should be performed not only for diagnosis but also so the areas of bleeding can be injected with epinephrine, hemo-clipped, or heater probed. This is successful in 75% of cases. If the patient has portal HTN, then start an octreotide drip to decease the portal pressure. Vassopressin drips can decrease bleeding. If none of these maneuvers help, then take them to the angio suit for embolization of the left gastric artery, splenic branches, and inferior phrenic arteries.

Surgical treatment is reserved if all fails, take the patient to the operating room, perform a gastrotomy high and anterior. All of the mucosal tears should be suture ligated with 3-0 PDS. If the esophagus tears then go in the left chest, perform a myotomy to reveal the full length of the tear, and perform a suture ligation.

Additional Therapy

Blakemore tubes have no role in this situation because this is arterial bleeding and is usually associated with a hiatal hernia.

(1) Complications of Surgery for PUD*

H&P

You have to have an idea of all the possible complications in order to take a focused history on this patient. Anemia, dumping syndrome, post vagotomy diarrhea, alkaline gastritis, bleeding from the anastomotic line, afferent loop syndrome, gastroparesis, and duodenal stump leak are the complications. Therefore, you should ask about weakness, postprandial symptoms of dizziness or flushing, diarrhea, pain, bloating, nausea or vomiting, and hematemesis.

Physical exam is not revealing for these diagnosis, except that if they are bleeding you want to make sure they are stable.

Diagnosis

For patients with anemia, you may find that there is an iron deficiency or B12 deficiency and a history of weakness should prompt this work-up.

Dumping syndrome is diagnosed by the history of postprandial symptoms.

Post vagotomy diarrhea is explosive and not associated with eating. This diagnosis is made based of history as well.

You need to be sure of the diagnosis of alkaline gastritis before you proceed with treatment for this problem. The diagnosis is secured by performing an EGD where you will see bile in the stomach, and a DISIDA scan will show bile reflux.

Most bleeding from the anastomotic line will stop spontaneously. If it does not, the patient may become unstable and require emergent diagnosis with endoscopy and resuscitation

Afferent loop syndrome patients present with intermittent abdominal pain and bilious vomiting. The diagnosis is made by UGIS.

Gastroparesis is diagnosed by UGIS where there is a delay in the passage of contrast through the stomach in the absence of obstruction or stenosis.

Duodenal stump leak is diagnosed by the findings of an acute abdomen, free fluid in the abdomen, and high suspicion.

Treatment

Replacement of iron and B12 is the treatment for these deficiencies that lead to anemia.

Dumping syndrome is initially treated with small meals, decreased carbohydrates and increased protein in the diet. If this fails to improve the problem, and the patient remains desperate for intervention, then converting the patient to a Roux-en-Y or creating a reversed jejunal segment between the gastric stump and the roux limb may be necessary.

The treatment of post vagotomy diarrhea is decreasing fluid intake with meals, lomotil, and cholestyramine. If this fails, then a reversed jejunal segment 100 cm from the ligament of Treitz or a gastro-jejunosotmy may be needed.

If a patient is having alkaline gastritis, medical therapy with cholestyramine and reglan is tried at first. If this fails then converting the patient to a roux-en-Y gastro-jejunosotmy is warranted. In this case, you should perform a truncal vagotomy because this procedure is ulcerogenic.

Bleeding at the anastomosis is treated with endoscopic heater probe or clip. If necessary, you may have to re-explore the abdomen and ligate the bleeder directly.

Afferent loop syndrome is corrected by a side-to-side jejuno-jejunostomy.

Gastroparesis is initially treated with reglan or erythromycin. If this does not work, then you will have to perform an antrectomy.

Duodenal stump leak is disastrous, and if it is caught early is treated by re-exploration, duodenostomy, drainage, NPO and TPN, antibiotics, and control of the fistula for at least 12 weeks. If this is a late complication, then CT drainage should be attempted, patient is made NPO and placed on TPN, antibiotics started, and the fistula controlled for at least 12 weeks.

Example Case

You are seeing a 60 year old man who is S/P choledochojejunostomy and gastojejunostomy for unresectable pancreatic carcinoma who develops an upper GI bleed. Go.

Well, I would establish if the patient is stable or if I have to start giving him boluses of fluid and getting some blood for him. I expect he is bleeding from his anastomosis. I would immediately give him 80 mg of protonix IV and start a protonix drip at 8mg/hour. I would get him as stabilized as I can and perform an EGD.

The staple line is bleeding.

I would inject epinephrine and heater probe anything that I think I can stop bleeding.

You do this yourself?

I am very comfortable with therapeutic endoscopy, but if my GI colleagues were immediately available, I would let them do this.

This fails to work. He continues to bleed and has now received 4 units of PRBC.

He is receiving blood, he is still bleeding, and I am assuming that his Hgb is not coming up (we should be checking this regularly) and that I have checked his coagulation and this is normal. Then I have no other choice but to take him to the operating room and revise my gastojejunostomy. I will hand sew the anastomosis this time.

The next day he bleeds again, and he requires another 2 units of blood.

I would repeat the scope, I would be surprised to see my anastomosis bleeding now that I hand sewed it.

No, he is bleeding everywhere, diffusely.

Diffuse gastritis and hemorrhage on a PPI drip would be very rare, but if he is bleeding like this I would start a vasopressin drip to cause vasoconstriction of the mesenteric vessels and hopefully this would slow down the bleeding. Again, I would check the coagulation studies and make sure he is normal. If this fails to work then I would be forced to return to the OR and ligate all vessels to the stomach except the left gastric.

The family wants to know if all this is really necessary given the fact that he has unresectable cancer.

If I do nothing, then he will die. If the patient and his family agree that we should not do anymore, then I would respect their wishes and continue to manage this non-operatively. Maybe, I would even discuss the case with IR to consider embolization. However, as a surgeon, I want to stop this and give him some time to live.

What if you devascularize the stomach and he still bleeds?

Then I would have to do a subtotal gastrectomy.

What do you think his mortality is for that?

Very high, 80-100% I would think.

(1) Post-Gastrectomy Problems

H&P

These problems can occur early or late, and the history is target to these specific problems just as they were for complications of surgery for PUD. The early problems include leak from the anastomosis or duodenum, bleeding, and obstruction. Generally the patients are still in the hospital for early problems and the history and physical is problem focused.

Late complications include dumping syndrome, diarrhea, marginal ulceration or recurrent PUD, gastroparesis, bile gastritis, roux syndrome, afferent limb syndrome, internal hernia, long afferent loop syndrome, gastro-colic fistula, adenocarcinoma of the gastric remnant, and nutritional or metabolic problems. H&P is focused on specific symptoms discussed in the diagnosis section.

Diagnosis

<u>Early Problems</u>

Leaks usually present themselves after the third or fifth postoperative day. Tachycardia is the most common sign of a leak, but abdominal pain and shortness of breath is concerning as well. CT and UGIS are the diagnostic test of choice and can demonstrate extravasation of contrast into the abdomen.

Bleeding can occur within two weeks of surgery and is usually from the staple line, re-bleed from the prior ulcer, or an extra-luminal vessel secondary to line dehiscence. Diagnosis is made by endoscopy.

Obstruction can be at the afferent or efferent limb, from an internal hernia, an O-loop, or gastroparesis. Afferent limb obstructions present with abdominal pain and patients will have elevated amylase and LFT's. CT scan shows the dilated duodenum. Efferent limb obstruction presents like any small bowel obstruction and is diagnosed with KUB/UGI series. Internal hernia will present with pain and vomiting and can be diagnosed with a CT scan. UGIS may show gastroparesis (look like an obstruction but EGD shows that the anastomosis is patent).

<u>Late Problems</u>

Dumping syndrome is diagnosed by history of postprandial abdominal cramping, diarrhea, diaphoresis, weakness, lightheadedness, and tachycardia.

Diarrhea is diagnosed from history.

Marginal ulceration and recurrent PUD disease is diagnosed by history or EGD.

Gastroparesis diagnosis is made with EGD and UGI.

Bile gastritis may present with nausea, vomiting, and epigastric pain and is diagnosed with endoscopy, UGIS, and CT scan to rule out afferent/efferent obstruction and gastric stasis.

Roux syndrome is difficulty of the roux limb to empty and leads to vomiting and epigastric pain. It is diagnosed by endoscopy (to rule out bezoar, gastric remnant dilation, or roux limb dilation), UGIS (to rule out delayed gastric emptying), and gastric emptying study.

Afferent loop obstruction is diagnosed by history of postprandial pain and bilious emesis with relief of pain. CT scan will rule out SBO and UGIS can rule out stricture. EGD can be employed as well.

Internal hernia is diagnosed by CT scan.

Long afferent loop is diagnosed by symptoms of diarrhea secondary to bacterial over growth, marginal ulceration, and bloating. UGIS and endoscopy are used to make the diagnosis.

Gastro-colic fistula is caused by Chron's disease, NSAID usage, cancer, PEG, or marginal ulceration. This problem is diagnosed by the history of feculent vomiting, malnutrition, and diarrhea secondary to bacterial stasis.

Adenocarcinoma of the gastric remnant is diagnosed by endoscopy and biopsy.

Nutritional and metabolic problems present in patients that are losing a lot of weight and are diagnosed by lab work. Bone pain, weakness, and numbness of the extremities are common complaints.

Treatment

Early Problems

Leaks are treated by conservative or surgical means. If the patient is stable and there are no signs of sepsis then small fluid collections can be drained percutaneously. The patient should be kept NPO, started on TPN, and given antibiotics as needed. Surgical treatment is for those that are septic or show signs of peritonitis and involves re-explorations, over sewing the leak, and placement of a drain to control the drainage. A feeding tube should be left for postoperative enteral feeding.

For duodenal stump leaks, you must determine if the tissue around the leak is healthy, friable, or frankly necrotic. If the tissue is healthy then you may over sew the hole and place a graham patch or you may choice to place a 16Fr catheter into the duodenum and purse string it in place. If the duodenum is ischemic, then it must be debrided until it is healthy, re-suture the area, buttress with omentum, place the catheter in the duodenum laterally for decompression, and widely drain the area. If the tissue is friable, then you should place a lateral duodenal tube, buttress with omentum, widely drain, and drain the stomach with a gastro-jejunostomy. A feeding jejunosotmy tube should be place for all these scenarios.

The treatment for bleeding is early diagnosis and control of the bleeding. Make sure that there is no coagulopathy and the patient is on PPI drip. If it is from prior ulcer disease, then heater probe, injection, and clips can be used to control the bleeding endoscopically. Bleeding from the staple line usually stops on its own, but if it does not may require re-exploration and suture ligation. Arteriogram is a possibility.

Treatment of obstruction is directed to the problem. For afferent limb obstruction you need to decompress them endoscopically and place an NGT into the limb. Efferent limb obstruction is treated with NGT trial unless you suspect an internal hernia. Internal hernias require re-exploration for correction of the mesocolic, mesenteric, or Peterson's defect. Gastroparesis should be treated with NGT, TPN, and pro-motility agents. Give it time (6 to 8 weeks) to improve.

Late Problems

Dumping syndrome is treated medically with octreotide, high fiber diet, and decreased liquids with meals. Generally this will improve, but if it does not, then you may need to do a roux reconstruction or a takedown of the loop gastro-J.

Diarrhea is treated with cholestyramine and lomotil.

Marginal ulcer/recurrent PUD treatment is the same as the work up for recurrent PUD already discussed above.

Gastroparesis is treated with pro-motility agents. Surgical options include subtotal gastrectomy with BII anastomosis or a roux-en-Y reconstruction.

Bile gastritis is treated with a roux-en-Y reconstruction (making the roux limb 45 to 60 cm in length) or a BII with Braun enteroenterostomy.

Roux symptoms are treated medically with reglan, domperidone, and erythromycin at first. If this fails, then surgical options include decreasing the gastric remnant size or reconstructing the roux limb.

Afferent limb obstruction is treated with LOA, reduction of internal hernia, or reduction of volvulus if found. If the afferent limb is too long, it can be shortened.

Internal hernia is treated by exploration and reduction of the hernia with repair of the defect.

Long afferent limb syndrome is treated by taking down the gastro-J and recreating it high on the afferent limb.

Gastro-colic fistula is treated by en-bloc resection of the fistula and interposition of omentum between the staple lines.

Adenocarcinoma of the gastric remnant is treated by total gastrectomy with roux-en-Y pouch.

Nutritional and metabolic problems are addressed and replaced as they are diagnosed. Weight loss, anemia, and bone loss are the most common problems encountered. These require supplementation with multivitamins and calcium.

(2) Gastric Malignancy

H&P

Patients with gastric malignancy will typically present with abdominal pain, weight loss, anemia, nausea, and early satiety. You want to question their diet, tobacco usage, and history of *H. pylori* infection.

On physical exam, the abdomen may not be revealing unless you find a sister Mary Joseph's node. Do a rectal to feel for Blumer's shelf node.

Diagnosis

EGD will discover the gastric mass and allow you to take biopsies to confirm the diagnosis. Once the diagnosis is confirmed, you have to stage the tumor. This involves obtaining a CT scan of the chest, abdomen, and pelvis. EUS can tell you the depth of invasion. Check their hemoglobin if they seem anemic. Send a pre-albumin to assess their nutritional status.

Treatment

Surgery is for cure. You should begin by putting in a laparoscope because 30% of the time, you are going to find metastatic disease that was not seen on CT, making the tumor unresectable.

A distal antrectomy is done in order to obtain 6 cm margins free from gross tumor. Histological margins should be free on frozen section. An omentectomy, lymph node dissection (regional dissection, D1 and 2), and en bloc resection of involved adjacent organs (except pancreatic head and CBD) is performed.

If the tumor is unresectable, there are cases where palliation may be necessary. This includes bleeding, perforation, or obstruction. In these situations, you should try being least aggressive as possible. Palliative chemotherapy, laser recanulization, dilation, and stenting are all possibilities. Surgical bypass has fallen out of favor and is only done if it can be done with little morbidity.

Additional Therapy

There is no adjuvant chemotherapy given after surgical resection for gastric cancer. Primary Systemic chemotherapy is offered if there is disease beyond the stomach (neoadjuvant, which includes etoposide, cisplatinum, and 5-FU or doxorubicin) because it provide an improved survival with resection in phase II trials. Radiation therapy can reduce local recurrences when used in combination with 5-FU.

Tumor:	Tx	Primary tumor cannot be assessed
	T0	No evidence of primary tumor
	Tis	Carcinoma in situ: intraepithelial tumor without invasion of lamina propria
	T1	Tumor invades lamina propria or submucosa
	T2	Tumor invades muscularis propria or subserosa
	T2a	Tumor invades muscularis propria
	T2b	Tumor invades subserosa
	T3	Tumor invades serosa (visceral peritoneum) without invasion of adjacent structures
	T4	Tumor invades adjacent structures
Nodes:	Nx	regional lymph nodes cannot be assessed
	N0	No regional lymph node metastases
	N1	Metastases in 1 to 6 regional lymph nodes
	N2	Metastases in 7 to 15 regional lymph nodes
	N3	Metastases in more than 15 regional lymph nodes
Metastases:	Mx	Distant metastases cannot be assessed
	M0	No distant metastases
	M1	Distant metastases

Stages:

	0	Tis	N0	M0
	IA	T1	N0	M0
	IB	T1	N1	M0
		T2a/b	N0	M0
	II	T1	N2	M0
		T2a/b	N1	M0
		T3	N0	M0
	IIIA	T2a/b	N2	M0
		T3	N1	M0
		T4	N0	M0
	IIIB	T3	N2	M0
	IV	T4	N1-3	M0
		T1-3	N3	M0
		any	Tany	NM1

Gastric lymphoma is surgically resected with lymph nodes if it is stage I or II. The liver should be biopsied and a splenectomy is done only if it is grossly involved. Post-operatively, they get chemotherapy. Low grade MALT tumors just need *H. pylori* treatment.

Gastric carcinoid may be sporadic, associated with pernicious anemia, and ones associated with ZES. The sporadic ones can be malignant, and the 2 cm rule applies. Atrophic gastritis and pernicious anemia is usually benign and are multiple very small tumors, and antrectomy to reduce the gastrin level will cause regression of the carcinoid usually. 24-urines are not sensitive. Chromogranin A level is more sensitive. Liver metastasis may be treated with chemotherapy embolization, RFA, or resection; however, there is not much to do when you have metastatic disease, but this is rare from gastric carcinoma.

(1) GIST Tumors*

H&P

There is a history of pain and discomfort, UGI bleeds, and obstructive symptoms with these tumors.

The physical exam may reveal and abdominal mass if the tumor is very large

Diagnosis

Diagnosis is made with an EGD to visualize the tumor and biopsies are taken to confirm the diagnosis and find out the grade of tumor. CT scan of the abdomen and pelvis may reveal a large, well vasularized, and well circumscribed mass. PET imaging will demonstrate increased FDG uptake in these tumors.

These tumors should not be biopsied percutaneously because these are highly vascular and may bleed; you could precipitate tumor rupture, hemorrhage, and tumor dissemination.

Treatment

If there is no evidence of metastasis, then the tumors should be resected with 1 cm margins. Although it is rare for the tumor to invade other organs, en bloc resection should be done if needed.

If the tumor is a proximal lesion at the GE junction, then a total gastrectomy and roux-en-Y reconstruction is needed. If the duodenum is involved, then this may need resection as well (Whipple).

If there is metastatic disease, the patient should receive Gleevac treatment for one year. A CT scan is done every 6 months to assess the response (PET scan can be used). If the patient responds well, then surgery can be done if all gross tumors can be removed. If there is progression of the tumor, then chemotherapy and hepatic artery embolization may be needed.

Additional Therapy

Post-operatively, patients are treated with Gleevac. CT scans are done every 6 months for the next three years, then annually after that. Tumors > 5cm or that have more than 5 mitosis/50 HPF are more likely to recur. If there is recurrent disease, then Gleevac is given for a year, re-evaluated every 6 months with CT scans, and operate if all gross disease can be removed.

Example Case

A middle age man who is having vague upper abdominal pain complaints has an EGD performed and a small polyp is found and biopsied. It comes back adenomatous. What do you do for this?

I haven't seen too many gastric polyps, but the concern of course is that this could be or turn into a malignancy. Assuming that the polyp is of a pretty decent size, a couple of cm, and sessile, so it could only be biopsied and not snared or completely removed with cold biopsy forceps, then there is still tissue in there that is premalignant. The other thing to be concerned with is that he could have FAP because this is associated with foregut polyps, so I would be interested in looking in his colon with a colonoscopy. So once I have looked in the colon and made sure there aren't any polyps there, this is not FAP, all I have to deal with is the polyp. If this thing is more than 3 cm, I would be more concerned with biopsy error and leaving a cancer in the stomach. If it is less than 3 cm then I would go back on multiple endoscopies and piece meal this thing out.

What if it was an inflammatory polyp?

Then I would leave it alone, treat him for *H .pylori* if he was positive and put him on PPI. I would re-scope him in 3months.

What if it is a GIST tumor?

GIST tumors need to be resected. First I would get CT scan of the abdomen to make sure that there is no other solid organ involvement that I may have to remove with the tumor. I would also be looking for any metastatic disease. If it is rather small and amendable to resection, then I would wedge this out with a 2 cm margin.

What if there were positive perigastric lymph nodes?

I would resect them with the specimen. I would try to get all gross disease. Post-operatively, I would treat the patient with one year of Gleevac. I would re-evaluate him every 6 months with a CT scan.

(8) Small Bowel
(7) Small Bowel Obstruction*

H&P

Nausea, vomiting, abdominal distension, history of previous surgery or cancer, and history of IBD are all presenting symptoms of bowel obstruction.

The physical exam will reveal a distended, maybe tender abdomen, with high pitched bowel sound.

Diagnosis

Labs should be sent off to rule out biliary obstruction, infection, and pancreatitis. Abdominal films will reveal any dilated bowel or air fluid levels. In stable patients, a CT scan should be done early because it is very sensitive to rule in complete small bowel obstructions (90%); in addition, this can reveal mass lesions or an unappreciated hernia and recognize edematous or incarcerated small or large bowel.

Treatment

The patient should be given IV fluids, NGT decompression, and correction of any electrolyte abnormalities.

If there are emergent surgical indications (fever, peritonitis, shock, and leukocytosis) or evidence of complete bowel obstruction then the patient should be given antibiotics, resuscitated and taken to the operating room.

If the patient has a partial bowel obstruction, then you should continue close observation, give them fluids, and continue NGT decompression. Abdominal films are taken every 12 hours. If there is slow improvement, continue conservative management up to 5 days. After five days, a gastrograffin UGIS is done. Failure of the contrast to reach the colon in 24 hours is an indication to go to the operating room. If the contrast reaches the colon in 24 hours, then 75% of the time the SBO will resolve with conservative management. If there is no improvement over the first 48 hours, get the contrast study right away and follow the same guidelines.

Bowel obstruction in the virgin belly may be due to a hernia (in which case therapy is directed to reduction of the hernia, assessment of the bowel, and repair of the hernia) or to a tumor or intussusceptions. Chron's disease can be another cause for SBO in the virgin abdomen, and conservative management should be attempted first (follow above algorithm for PSBO).

Post-operative bowel obstruction usually resolves within 14 days. The patient should be kept NPO, NGT, and started on TPN within the first 7 days of NPO status. If the patient worsens before 14 days, then take to the operating room. After 14 days, the adhesions are dense, poorly defined, and highly vascular. If there is a low grade partial obstruction, wait 3-4 weeks, then go back and do a complete LOA.

If the patient has a known history of abdominal cancer; then 30% will have adhesions only, 30% will have a resectable malignancy, and 30% will have carcinomatosis.

Example Case

A 45 year old woman comes to the ED complaining of nausea and vomiting and the absence of flatus or stool.

Sound like this lady has a bowel obstruction. I will need to find out what kind of bowel obstruction this is, where it is, and why she has it. So I would be thinking of the most common causes of obstruction and ask if she has had any previous surgeries that could have resulted in adhesions. If she has not had any surgeries...

She had a C-section through a low midline incision about 7 years ago.

So that makes me think she probably has adhesions, but hernias and malignancy are still possible. I would examine her to make sure she does not have any peritonitis, rule out any incarcerated hernias, and examine her scar.

Her abdomen is distended without pain and very tympanic with high pitched bowel sounds.

So, I am thinking that the high pitched bowel sounds and very tympanic abdomen may be a distal small bowel or large bowel obstruction. I would make sure that she has a good IV line and getting some fluids to replaces her losses from vomiting. I would check her electrolytes and replace any deficiencies and check her CBC to make sure there is no leukocytosis to suggest a more urgent surgical problem. I would get a flat and upright x-ray of the abdomen to get a better idea of the bowel gas pattern and try and determine what kind of obstruction I have here, and I would get a chest x-ray (upright) to make sure there is no free air.

Her WBC is 9,000 and she has some dilated loops of small bowel, but there is no free air.

This seems to be a small bowel obstruction, probably from adhesions from her previous surgery. I would place an NGT in her to decompress the bowel and make her more comfortable, hopefully. Of course, I would make her NPO, but I would not start any antibiotics since her WBC is normal. I would check her urinanalysis to make sure there is not a urinary infection causing an illeus, and check a pregnancy test just in case. I would admit her with the plan of conservative management, hoping that she will open up with just nasogastric decompression. Though some surgeons would not do it, I would get a CT scan of the abdomen because this is a very sensitive test for complete bowel obstruction. If the radiologist calls a transition point, they are usually right, and I can go in earlier, resulting in a better outcome and shorter hospital stay for the patient.

Your CT scan does not show anything like that, and the rest of her labs are normal. How will you continue to manage her in the hospital?

I would do serial abdominal exams and abdominal films every 12 hours to see if there is any change in the status. In addition, I would check labs in the morning to make sure the white count is not increasing and that the electrolytes are being appropriately treated.

Well, the next morning, she is still much distended, and the NGT output is 2 liters. Her WBC is 10,000 now.

So this is not much improvement despite the NGT. That worries me, but she is still afebrile, and that small change in the WBC is not too alarming. The other nice thing about the CT is that she gets oral contrast and I can follow that oral contrast through the abdomen serially. If the contrast has made it to the colon within 24 hours, then that makes me happy and I am more content to sit on this because more than 50% of these patients will likely open up with conservative management. If the contrast has not made it to the colon within 24 hours, on the other hand, then it is more likely she will need surgery to open her up.

Well it has not made it to the colon, so you take her to the operating room and find a dense adhesion in the lower midline around which a loop of small bowel is torsed. You un-torse it and it looks a little dusky and mottled.

I am surprised with this finding since she did not have any abdominal pain on exam; however, you have to be concerned about the viability of this short segment of small bowel. There are a few ways to assess this. I would use intra-operative Doppler on the antimesenteric border of the bowel to listen for flow. If there is good flow, I would place warm, moist laparotomy sponges on the bowel and give it some time to see if it pinks up. The other thing you can do is give IV flourascein and use a wood's lamp to see if there is good blood flow through the bowel. If there is any question about this, then I would just resect this portion of the bowel and do a primary anastomosis.

There are definitely areas of the bowel that do not "pink" up. In all, this is about 15 cm in length. Would you consider a second look laparotomy instead of a resection?

No. I think an open abdomen is more morbid than a 15 cm bowel resection.

What if you were worried about the ends of the small bowel?

I am there looking at it, and I would resect the small bowel until there were healthy ends before anastomosing it together.

Ok, the next day her temperature is 101F and her WBC is 15,000.

Immediately post-operatively like that, I would round up the usual suspects and get a chest x-ray to look for atelectasis or pneumonia, get blood cultures, and send urine to rule out UTI, look at her wounds and IV sites for cellulitis, and feel her calves to rule out thrombitis. I would continue her on the pre-operative antibiotics, usually that is some first or second generation cephalosporin.

You find nothing, and she does ok until POD #5, when you find succus coming from the wound.

Well, I would open the wound and make sure there is no un-drained fluid collections, make sure she is stable, clean the wound up and place a device on her skin to protect it and measure the output, make her NPO, and give her maintenance fluids, and get central access with a plan to start TPN.

OK, then what.

Well, as long as she is not septic and needing a return to the OR for source control, then I would get a CT scan of the abdomen to rule out any kind of distal obstruction or abscess in the abdomen. If this is negative, then I would continue this plan for 5 to seven days and let the fistula mature. I would then do a fistulogram to make sure there is no distal obstruction again and find out where in the bowel this fistula is. Most fistulas will heal on their own. I would measure the output and classify this as a high or low output fistula. I would give it about 6 weeks to heal. If it doesn't heal in this time, it probably won't heal, and I would take her to the operating room for an elective fistulectomy.

(0) Small Bowel Chron's Disease

H&P

Patients generally have the history of Chron's disease already when they are seeing you. They may have abdominal pain, diarrhea, fever, fatigue, anemia, anal pain, weight loss, etc. On physical examination, you should evaluate the patient for IHOP. Make sure there is no peritonitis and guiac his stool.

Diagnosis

Get abdominal films to rule out free air or obstruction, colonoscopy to get smears and cultures and rule out ulcerative colitis, barium UGIS with SBFT to make note of the severity and extent of disease and the presence of any strictures, and a CT scan of the abdomen (especially before any surgery) to identify the relationship between the disease segments and adjacent organs. If there are any abscesses seen on CT, they should be addressed.

Treatment

If the patient is having an acute flare up and there is no obvious indications to go to the OR right away (IHOP), and then the patient is treated medically using prednisone (20 mg po bid), ASACOL (800 mg pot id) and 6-MP (80 mg po qd). They should all be given PPIs as well. The prednisone is tapered over the next 4 weeks. Remicaide is used to help establish remission in refractory patients. Rowasa enemas and flagyl is used for colorectal and anal involvement, respectfully. Patients should be put on a low residual diet and multivitamins.

Surgeries are indicated for fistulas, abscesses, duodenal involvement, suspected appendicitis, obstructing or bleeding lesions, and strictures. Fistulas must be taken down, and the small bowel must be resected at that point.

Abscesses can usually be drained percutaneously. The patient is given antibiotics and time to heal. Elective surgery is done 4 weeks later to resect the involved limb. In the meantime, the patient should be kept NPO and on TPN.

If there is severe duodenal involvement, you may consider truncal vagotomy and gastro-jejunostomy.

Suspected appendicitis but you find Chron's is not an uncommon scenario on the oral boards. In this case, you do an appendectomy only if the appendiceal base is not involved. If the base is involved, then forego the appendectomy for fear of fistula formation.

Obstructing or bleeding lesions in the bowel require segmental resection.

Indications for stricturoplasty include non-phlegmonous fibrotic stricture, in short bowel segments, with history of major bowel resection in the past, and diffuse involvement of the small bowel with multiple strictures. If there is a short stricture (<10 cm) then a Heineke-Mikulicz stricturoplasty is done. For long stricture (10-20cm) a Finney type or a side-to-side antiperistaltic stricturoplasty is done.

Contraindications to stricturoplasty include perforation, multiple strictures in a short segment, colonic stricture, suspicious for cancer, and stricture close to proposed area to resect.

(0) Small Bowel Tumors

H&P

Patients may have symptoms of abdominal pain, obstruction, bleeding, weight loss, perforation, and jaundice. On physical exam, feel the abdomen for masses or hernias.

Diagnosis

You need to rule out other causes of obstruction (hernia) or bleeding (EGD, colonoscopy, capsule endoscopy). UGI with SBFT will identify most lesions or tumors and tell you the location. CT scan of the abdomen and pelvis is done to evaluate the extent of the tumor, the presence of lymph node involvement and if there is intra-abdominal spread.

These tumors may include adenomas (as seen in FAP), lipomas, hemangiomas (often bleed), hamartomas (risk for developing adenocarcinoma), adenocarcinoma (most common), carcinoid, and lymphoma.

Treatment

Obstructing lesions are dealt with as described for SBO. There needs to be a resection of the mass, lesion, or intussusceptions.

Bleeding requires that the patient be stabilized and EGD should be done to exclude stomach or esophageal causes. Angiogram and tagged cell scans are then employed and capsule endoscopy may tell you where it is in the small bowel.

Malignant tumors require proper staging with CT scans and resection with 6 cm margins on both sides with a wide en bloc lymphadenectomy. If the tumor is in the duodenum, then you need to do a Whipple. If the tumor is in the terminal ileum, then a formal right hemicoloectomy should be done. Post-operative chemotherapy will likely be needed.

(8) Small Bowel

Lymphoma of the small bowel is most commonly found in the ileum. The treatment of stage I or II is segmental resection with the mesentery. If this is stage III or IV disease, then chemo-radiation is given.

GIST tumors of the small bowel are treated with segmental resection with 1-2 cm margins. There is no need for mesenteric resection (these tumors rarely spread, and when they do it is by the hematogenous route). Post op gleevac is given.

(1) Carcinoid Tumors

H&P

Patients may have crampy abdominal pain, obstruction, diarrhea, flushing or palpitations. You should consider IBD, pheochromocytoma and hyperthyroidism in you differential and focus a history to exclude these diagnoses.

On physical exam, feel for abdominal masses.

Diagnosis

Urinary 5-HIAA levels are 100% sensitive/specific for carcinoid syndrome (not carcinoid tumors). These levels are only 75% sensitive in asymptomatic patients. Chromogranin A is a more sensitive tumor marker.

CT scan of the abdomen and pelvis is the most common initial test in which you may find mesenteric shortening and fibrosis. This may visualize metastatic disease to the liver.

Somatostatin receptor scintigraphy may be able to localize a primary and mets better than CT or MRI. This is useful for staging before surgery.

Treatment

The treatment of carcinoid is surgical resection, but it depends on the location and size of the tumor. There is something magical about 2 cm, and when a carcinoid grows beyond this it becomes malignant and metastatic.

In the duodenum, tumors less than 2 cm are locally resected. Those more than 2 cm require a Whipple. If there are hepatic mets, then local debulking and post-operative medical therapy is used.

For the ileum and jejunum, wide local resection with en bloc mesentery resection is done. Hepatic mets are debulked if safe.

Carcinoid of the appendix is a good board question. They will continue to change the scenario. Remember, if it is >2 cm, it is malignant and needs a right hemicolectomy. If it is at the base of the appendix, it may extend further than you think; therefore, you should assume that it is > 2cm, and do a hemicolectomy. If it is at the tip of the appendix and < 2cm, then an appendectomy is adequate.

Rectal carcinoid is treated with wide local resection for tumors less than 2 cm. For those tumors more than 2 cm, or those tumors that invade the muscularis propria, an APR should be offered to the patient for cure.

Metastatic disease to the liver only need wedge resection at the original surgery. Extensive resection should not be done, generally. The primary lesion is removed, the base line 5-HIAA is taken, and the patient's symptoms observed. Plan resection or ablation of these lesions after there is a clear assessment of the disease.

Additional Therapy

Carcinoid syndrome occurs in about 10% of patients and is characterized by flushing, diarrhea, palpitations, and edema. The treatment is medical with octreotide (150 mcg sq bid), lantreotide IM q 1 week, sandostatin LAR IM q 1 month, and interferon alpha. The side effects of treatment include glucose intolerance, steatorrhea, and gallstone formation.

Carcinoid crisis can occur in the perioperative period in which the patient develops cardiac arrhythmias and can become hemodynamically unstable and go into cardiac arrest. The treatment is ACLS, and octreotide (50 mcg sq tid).

Non-resectional tumors that are refractory to somatostatin and interferon are candidates for trans-catheter arterial chemo-embolization with doxorubicin, RFA, In^{111} pentreotide (radioactive agent that binds serotonin receptors), I^{131} MIBG (taken up by neuro-endocrine tumors), and chemotherapy with cytoxan and streptozocin (with little affect).

(0) Enterocutaneous Fistula

H&P

While I have a (0) in front of this subject, I must admit, it is common on the boards; however, it is usually not asked directly. There is generally a leading case that gets to the EC fistula. So you need to know this subject.

Ask the patient about a history of Chron's disease, previous surgeries, and notable weight loss.

Physical exam focuses on the patients overall appearance, stability, wound care, peritonitis, and signs of systemic infection. Just because you see fluid coming from the wound does not necessarily mean they have a fistula. The dehiscence scenario is out there. This is usually serosanguinous fluid, and you should check the fascia at the bedside or in the operating room.

Diagnosis

History and physical exam will reveal the diagnosis of fistula. Look for signs of malnutrition, electrolyte imbalance (send a chem 20), and sepsis (check WBC). You should try to clarify the output of the fistula as low (< 200 cc/day), moderate (200-500 cc/day) or high (> 500cc/day).

Treatment

There are five steps to the treatment of an Enterocutaneous fistula: resuscitation, investigation, decision, definitive therapy, and healing.

Resuscitation is the first step and involves aggressive IVFs, correction of electrolytes, NGT, Foley catheter and central venous access for TPN. The fistula output should be controlled and skin cared for. Placing an ostomy device will save the skin and help measure the output of the fistula. Keep the patient NPO and on GI prophylaxis to decrease fistula output. Ocreotide may decrease output, but will not increase the chances of closure. CT scan should be done early in the treatment to rule out any drainable fluid collections or abscess collection. Antibiotics are only used if there are signs of infection.

In the second phase, you have to get some information about the fistulas. Fistulas will not heal if there is a foreign body, radiation, infection, epithelialization, neoplasm, or distal obstruction. After 7-10 days, the fistula tract is matured enough to place a catheter in it and shoot a fistulogram with gastrograffin. This will tell you the length of the tract (longer than 2 cm more likely to heal), site of the bowel entry, nature of adjacent bowel, intestinal continuity, and distal obstruction.

Next you have to make a decision about the intervention you want. Depending on the site of the fistula (stomach, lateral duodenum, LOT, and ileum are less likely to heal then the orophyarnx, esophagus, duodenal stump, pancreatico-biliary, and jejunum), nature of the adjacent bowel, presence of an abscess, and the presence of distal obstruction you will decide if and when to operate. After 5-6 weeks, if the patient is nutritionally acceptable, it is unlikely that the fistula will heal and you should consider surgery. If the patient has uncontrolled sepsis, you may need to operate early, but make sure there is no abscess that needs drainage. If the patient's situation is in extremes, then divert the bowel and repair the fistula later.

Finally, definitive therapy is undertaken by opening the abdomen and taking down all the adhesions. The small bowel segment with the fistula is taken down and resected. You should place a feeding tube at this time.

Additional Therapy

TPN should be continued 5-10 days after surgery. Start tube feeds, and follow the nutritional status with pre-albumin.

(0) Small Bowel Diverticular Disease

H&P

The patient may have a history of diverticulitis, perforation, abscess formation, UGI bleed, obstruction or jaundice.

Physical exam is usually unremarkable.

Diagnosis

Traditional endoscopy can be used to diagnose foregut diverticulum. The midgut disease is diagnosed by UGI with SBFT or capsule endoscopy.

Treatment

Treatment depends on the location. For disease in the duodenum, asymptomatic lesions need no therapy. If there is inflammation or perforation, then the duodenum is kocherized, the hole is closed, and the area drained (+/- pyloric exclusion). Peri-vaterian lesions will require choledochojejunosotmy and cholecystectomy. Those that present with UGI bleed will require endoscopic interventions or angiogram with embolization.

You don't have to do anything to jejunoilleal lesions that are asymptomatic. If they are inflamed or perforate, then they will require resection with primary anastomosis. UGI bleed from these will require angiogram with embolization or resection.

Meckel's diverticulum in the adult will require resection when found unless they are asymptomatic. For children, however, they should always be resected when found.

(O) Short Bowel Syndrome

H&P

Patients with a history of Chron's, radiation enteritis, and multiple bowel resections may present with diarrhea, weight loss, dehydration, malnutrition, and steatorrhea. These are all signs of short bowel syndrome.

Physical exam is not revealing.

Diagnosis

History is the main way of diagnosis. Vitamin deficiencies can be found when tested for.

Treatment

Maintain adequate vascular volume, correct their electrolytes and trace elements, start them on PPI and TPN, treat diarrhea with lomotil, and try to start enteral feeds. If there is < 60 cm of small bowel, they will be TPN dependant. 60-120 cm of bowel can rehab to enteral feeds but it may take up to 2 years. More than 120 cm can be rehabbed to enteral feeds relatively easily. If the colon is still in continuity, then high complex carbohydrates can be used. If the colon is removed, then less carbohydrates and more fat should be used.

If you are unsuccessful at enteral feeds there may be bacterial overgrowth from the colon, requiring antibiotic treatment. Rapid transit through the small bowel can lead to diarrhea and may need a reversed segment to slow the transit time down.

Long term complications from TPN (most notably, liver failure) can be fatal. Therefore, small bowel transplant is a consideration.

(29) Colon and Rectum

(11) Diverticular disease*

H&P

Typical symptoms of diverticular disease are LLQ pain, fever, and constipation. Ask about pneumaturia, fecouria, weight loss, family history of colon cancer, and history of IBD.

Physical exam is of the abdomen and vital signs.

Diagnosis

Check the WBC to see if there is active inflammation. CT scan will rule out an abscess, show the diverticular disease and inflammation, and tell you if there is any perforation. Do not do a barium enema or endoscopy because you may perforate them.

Treatment

If this is an uncomplicated case (no abscess, fistula, bleeding, perforation, or obstruction) then admit them, put them on clears, and start oral ciprofloxacin and flagyl. Once they resolve their pain, they can go home and follow up in 6 to 8 weeks with a barium enema or colonoscopy. If they have another episode, offer an elective sigmoid colectomy. For severe cases, they should be made NPO and started on IV antibiotics. Wait until they are clinically improving to start a diet and put them on po antibiotics. If they do not improve, repeat the CT scan. If the episode is severe enough and the patient is young, then the chances of them having another recurrence is very high, and you may consider resecting the colon before a second episode.

For complicated cases, resection will need to be done at some point. For an abscess collection, percutaneous drainage is done and once the patient is improved, elective sigmoid colectomy should be done (after 6 weeks).

Emergent operation may be required if the patient is septic. It is suggested that ureteral stents be placed and that the mass/phlegmon be removed en bloc because of the possibility of malignancy. If there is a perforation, they should be resected and given an end ostomy.

If there is a fistula, do an en-bloc resection because it may be cancer. If there is an obstruction, resect and give them an end colostomy. Colovesical fistulas should undergo barium enema (once the inflammation has resolved) and cystoscopy. CT and colonoscopy is done to rule out cancer. Colovaginal fistulas are more common in women who have had a hysterectomy. Methylene blue tampon test, barium enema, and colonoscopy/CT scan is done pre-operatively.

80% of bleeding from diverticular disease will stop on its own. Rarely, bowel preparation and elective resection of the bleeding section of bowel is indicated.

Additional Therapy

Bowel preparation is still a routine, although the data is showing that this is not necessary. Fleets phosphasoda preps can cause hyperphosphatemia in some patients and should be avoided.

Cefazolin and flagyl are standard antibiotics to be given preoperatively. Cipro is used for PCN allergic patients.

Example Case

A 47 year old obese female presents to the emergency department for left lower quadrant pain. She had a similar episode of pain like this once before that her internist treated with antibiotics, and it got better. She has no medical problems except that she is a little overweight.

Sounds like she has had and is having again, a bout of diverticulitis; however, I still want to rule out gynecologic problems, hernia, or bowel obstruction. I am assuming that she may have been running a little low grade fever, maybe her bowel movement have been normal or a little loose, but no blood in the stool, she has not been vomiting, the pain is localized and has been so, and she has no pertinent history of cyst or ovarian pathology. Her vitals I hope are normal, and I would make sure she is not febrile now. I would examine her to rule out hernia and peritonitis, and do a rectal exam to make sure there is no blood or pus. I would also do a pelvic exam to rule out PID or pelvic mass.

This should lead me toward the diagnosis of diverticulitis, and I would start IV fluids, make her NPO, send labs for a WBC (which I expected to be elevated), and check electrolytes for abnormalities, amylase and lipase to rule out pancreatitis, and liver functions to rule out gallbladder disease.

She has not been that ill, in fact just this pain for the last 2 days. As I mentioned, there is no other medical history. She is currently afebrile, her abdomen is soft, tender LLQ but no peritonitis, and her WBC is 12,000, but the rest of the labs are normal.

Still sounds like diverticulitis. I would get abdominal films and chest x-ray to rule out a bowel obstruction and pneumonia, respectfully. This will not be diagnostic, but I would go ahead and start her on IV cipro and flagyl to cover the colon flora, and get a CT scan of the abdomen.

Ok, abdominal films are normal, and the chest x-ray is normal, but the CT scan shows fat stranding and diverticulum around the sigmoid colon.

So that confirms my suspicion. I would admit her and keep her on the IV antibiotics because this is her second episode and would like to watch her. Assuming that there is no abscess seen on CT, she should improve over the next 48 hours, at which time I would slowly advance her diet. She can go home when she is tolerating oral intake, but I would continue the antibiotics for 10 days total.

What if there was a focal fluid collection.

If the fluid collection is more than a couple of centimeters, then I would suggest that interventional radiology do a percutaneous drainage. I would continue this drain until the patient improved, tolerated food, and repeat CT showed resolution of the fluid collection

Ok, let's say she got worse; you took her to the operating room and resected the involved segment of the colon. There is contamination. What would you do?

I would give her an end colostomy.

The colon will not reach the abdominal wall.

That is a problem. Assuming that because she is obese, I cannot get this colon to come out even though I have fully mobilized the splenic flexure and left colon, I have two options. I can do the anastomosis in a contaminated field, which is not a great option; or, I can leave the abdomen open, leave the colon stapled off, come back the next day and wash her out again and again until the abdomen is clean, then do an anastomosis. I would tend to do the later. Another option is to do the anastomosis and divert her proximally with transverse colon that should reach up or even terminal ileum if I had to.

(1) Ulcerative Colitits*

H&P

Diarrhea, rectal bleeding, fever, and abdominal pain characterize the symptoms of ulcerative colitis. They may also present with extra-colonic manifestations including iritis, stomatitis, and pyoderma.

On physical exam, do a rectal and check the abdomen for acuity.

Diagnosis

Abdominal x-rays can rule out free air and demonstrate colonic distension. Send off basic labs to check the electrolytes and WBC and rule out anemia. Sigmoidoscopy allows you to send stool for C&S, C. dif, and take mucosal biopsies to rule out Chron's.

Treatment

Make the patient NPO, given them fluids, insert a Foley, and start broad spectrum antibiotics. Indications for operation are toxic megacolon that fails to improve with medical treatment, perforation, or hemorrhage.

If there is toxic megacolon but no perforation, admit them to the ICU and do serial abdominal exams and x-rays. Failure of clinical improvement in the next 48 hours as noted by persistent colonic distension, perforation, or sepsis requires that you go to the operating room for subtotal colectomy with end illeostomy.

If the patient is hemorrhaging, then stabilize them, T&C blood and correct their coagulopathy. If they continue to bleed, then go to the operating room for subtotal colectomy with end illeostomy. 12% will continue to bleed in the rectal stump but usually stops on its own, if not, do a proctocolectomy.

For perforation, take the patient to the operating room and perform a subtotal colectomy with end illeostomy.

Additional Therapy

Chronic ulcerative colitits has a risk of adenocarcinoma of 20% after 20 years with the disease and increases 1% per year after that. These patients require annual colonoscopy. Elective colectomy can be done to eliminate the risk of cancer. These options include total proctocolectomy with end illeostomy, subtotal colectomy with illeorectal anastomosis (still need yearly surveillance of the rectum) and total proctocolectomy with illeoanal pouch anastomosis.

Example Case

You have a 40 year old woman who has a ten year history of mucous and bloody discharge from her rectum and she has been treated by her local doctor with 6MP and azathiprine and she is still not getting any better. She is currently on 60 mg of prednisone and he asked you to see this patient because he does not know what else to do.

It sounds like she has UC.

Well, that's the thinking, but no one is quite sure.

Then I would do a colonoscopy on her and take some biopsies and cultures to rule in or out inflammatory or infectious colitis, and rule out a mass or cancer.

You see linear ulcerations along the transverse colon and friable mucosa and bleeding. You take some biopsies and see no granulomas or crypt abscesses.

Then this sounds like UC, and she has not responded well to medical management, is on a lot of steroid, and she is very symptomatic. So I would discuss surgical options with the patient. I would include in the discussion the fact that since she has had this disease for ten years, she has about a 10

% risk of cancer and a 1% increase in that risk every year. I would recommend that she undergo a total proctocolectomy with ileoanal pouch. This would essentially cure her of her disease.

She would like to know what the risks are.

There is a risk of anal incontinence, she will certainly have several bowel movements a day, there is a risk of injury to the pelvic nerves that may cause sexual dysfunction and bladder incontinence, and there is always a very small risk of developing cancer in the very small piece of the rectum that we sew the pouch to.

Are there any other options for her to consider?

She can certainly consider continuing medical therapy. She could have a total proctocolectomy with end illeostomy. This would decrease her chance of developing any cancer in the rectal pouch, and eliminate the diarrhea, but this will leave her with a permanent bag on her side; finally, she can consider a total abdominal colectomy with illeorectal anastomosis, and this will give her better function in terms of bowel movements, but she will have to undergo yearly screening with flex sigmoidoscopy to rule out the development of cancer.

(0) Chron's Colitits

H&P

These patients present with crampy abdominal pain, diarrhea, weight loss, and anemia.

Physical exam is of the mouth, abdomen, and rectum/perineal area.

Diagnosis

Colonoscopy on these patients will show a "rake-like" or "Bear-claw" ulcers with rectal sparing. Biopsy can confirm the diagnosis. Rule out infectious causes by sending stool for O&P, and C&S.

Treatment

Medical treatment is the initial management of Chron's colitis. These are the same meds as for small bowel disease: prednisone, 5-ASA, 6-MP, and TNF-α.

Surgical therapy is used to palliate symptoms, emergencies (IHOP), intractability (UC>Chron's to develop cancer), and fulminant or toxic colitis.

If there is toxic megacolon but no perforation, admit them to the ICU and do serial abdominal exams and x-rays. Failure of clinical improvement in the next 48 hours as noted by persistent colonic distension, perforation, or sepsis requires that you go to the operating room for subtotal colectomy with end illeostomy.

If the patient is hemorrhaging, then stabilize them, T&C blood and correct their coagulopathy. If they continue to bleed, then go to the operating room for subtotal colectomy with end illeostomy. 12% will continue to bleed in the rectal stump but usually stops on its own, if not, do a proctocolectomy.

For perforation, take the patient to the operating room and perform a subtotal colectomy with end illeostomy.

Once disease has been present for more than 10 years, they should undergo yearly colonoscopy and biopsy any areas of know previous involvement. If there are any areas with dysplasia, they should be offered a segmental resection.

Additional Therapy

The options are the same as for UC for elective cases: total proctocolectomy with illeostomy, total abdominal colectomy with ileo-rectal anastomosis, but **no** total proctocolectomy with IPAA.

(1) Large Bowel Obstruction*

H&P

Patient with large bowel obstruction present with obstipation, abdominal pain, distension, nausea, vomiting, and fever.

On physical exam, look for peritonitis, previous scars on the abdomen, hernias, or masses. Check the rectum for a mass or impaction.

Diagnosis

Abdominal x-rays reveal a dilated colon, no air in the rectum, "bent" inner tube sign (volvulus?) and cecal diameter.

CT scan can show you associated masses, colonic distension, metastatic cancer, and volvulus.

Gastrograffin enema is very helpful because it can define the level, type, and degree of obstruction. Rectal cancer may show an "apple-core" lesion, and colonic volvulus shows a "bird-beak" tapering.

Treatment

Initially, you have to resuscitate the patient, hydrate them up, place a NGT, correct the electrolytes, check for anemia and WBC, and insert a Foley.

If you find a right colon cancer, then do a right hemicolectomy with illeocolic anastomosis if the patient is stable.

For a left colon cancer, you have several options. Best option is left hemicolectomy with end colostomy. Intraoperative lavage with resection and primary anastomosis is possible. If there is a synchronous lesion, do a subtotal colectomy with illeostomy. If there is a cecal perforation, do a subtotal colectomy with illeostomy. Sigmoid perforation/gangrene needs a resection with end colostomy. Finally, if the patient has poor nutrition or is immunosuppressed, then resect with an end colostomy.

Example Case

An 84 year old woman is brought to the ER from her nursing home with abdominal distension.

Abdominal distension makes me think of some sort of bowel obstruction. In the elderly population I lean toward large bowel obstruction more commonly and you have to think about pseudo-obstruction as well. So I would start by making sure that this lady is stable, has a good blood pressure and is not tachycardic. If she appears stable, I will ask her about the onset of the distension to give me an idea if this has been a chronic problem that may suggest constipation or impaction. I would ask for a medication list to see if anything on that list could precipitate pseudo obstruction. Assuming this is an acute issue; I would like to know if she is having pain and where, and move quickly into what may be causing this. Adhesions, hernias, and cancer are the top three causes. Assuming she has had no surgeries to cause adhesion, I would ask her about a personal or family history of cancer. This will probably be unrevealing, so I would move on to physical exam, make sure she does not have peritonitis, see if I can localize tenderness, assess the abdomen for tympani and listen for high pitched bowel sounds, and do a rectal exam to rule out a low obstruction or impaction.

She has CHF and is on a diuretic and beta blocker. Her abdomen is diffusely tender, but there is no peritonitis. She has no hernias. Her rectal examination reveals an empty vault and trace heme positive stools.

So, there is not much information here so far, and I am still dealing with an obstruction of sorts. I would have routine labs drawn to assess for leukocytosis, electrolyte imbalances, kidney function, and hydration status. Because of her age, I would get a baseline EKG. I would then get abdominal films, and this should be very informative about the area that is obstructed. Assuming I see dilated large bowel with little small bowel dilation or air in then rectum, then I know I am dealing with a large bowel obstruction. If this is the case, then I may get an idea if there is a volvulus, proximal or distal obstruction, or pseudo obstruction if the entire colon is dilated.

Labs are normal, but the abdominal series shows a predominately dilated colon without free air.

So now I suspect the colon is the issue, but I still don't know where. I should mention that I had not put in an NGT, but this is certainly something I would want to do early in the workup. I don't expect a whole lot to come out with a large bowel obstruction, but if she has been vomiting, this may help.

I have to find out where the problem is in the colon, so I would get a water soluble contrast enema. This will delineate if there is an obstructing mass and where it is. Assuming this shows a mass, then I will want to take a look at this with a scope.

The enema shows the sigmoid colon tapering off into a bird's beak and then obstructing. What do you think is going on there?

Sounds like a sigmoid volvulus. So I would want to take a rigid scope or a flexible scope if available and go up the colon to try and detorse the volvulus. This is usually successful, and I can leave a rigid tube, like a chest tube, in the rectum to stent it open long enough to prep the colon because I will need to resect this sigmoid to keep it from happening again.

Well, you are successful, but you see the area of the mucosa that is purple on endoscopy.

Hmmm…that makes me worry that there could be some ischemia of this part of the colon. As long as her white count is normal, and her abdomen decompresses well and she becomes more comfortable (and there is still no peritonitis), I am comfortable just watching this for the next 24 hours. I would place her in the ICU, on a monitored bed, and repeat the scope the next day to look at this area. Hopefully it has improved; I can start my bowel prep, and take her to the OR in a semi-urgent fashion.

Well you place her in the ICU and, a couple of hours later, her tube falls out.

I would rescope her and put the tube back in.

What if you could not get her to decompress again?

Then I would take her to the operating room, resect the sigmoid colon, leave a rectal stump and fashion an end-colostomy.

Ok, what if you find an obstructing mass?

Then I would take her to the operating room and either decompresses her with a loop colostomy if she is unstable, or resect the mass and give her an end colostomy is she can tolerate it.

What about stenting her?

There is no good data about this; there is a risk of perforation. It is possible to stent her, prep her, and then stabilize her for elective operation and primary anastomosis.

(0) Ogilvie's Syndrome

H&P

This is painless colonic dilation. Patients have abdominal distension, obstipation, constipation, diarrhea, nausea, and/or vomiting. Ask about precipitating medications such as narcotics, tricyclic antidepressants, clonidine, and anti-Parkinson medications.

On physical exam, they may have peritonitis. Do a rectal exam to rule out mass or impaction.

Diagnosis

Flat and upright abdominal films and chest x-ray are used to rule out free air, obstruction, and evaluate the dilation of the colon and the presence of air in the rectum. The size of the cecum should be taken (>10 cm is concerning for perforation). Routine labs should be sent to correct underlying electrolyte abnormalities and check the WBC.

Treatment

Initially the patient should be made NPO and put on fluids. A rectal tube may be placed to help decompress the colon. Hold all narcotics and anticholinergics. You should perform serial abdominal examinations and repeat the abdominal films in 12 hours.

If the patient is asymptomatic and the cecum is < 10 cm, then you can manage this condition conservatively. If there is no improvement in 24 hours after the above initial management maneuvers, then move to a monitored bed and give neostigmine (2 mg over 3 minute, be aware of bradycardia and have atropine ready). Erythromycin my stimulate motilin receptors and help the colon move.

If there is no improvement or the cecum is > 10 cm then you should perform colonoscopic decompression, leaving a rectal tube in. Obtain a post procedure x-ray.

If this fails, the patient develops peritonitis, the cecum is >10 cm after colonoscopy, or there is gangrene seen on colonoscopy, then operative management is indicated. The preferred treatment is right hemicoloectomy with end illeostomy and mucus fistula. A loop colostomy with endoscopic decompression is an option. In severely ill patients without evidence of cecal necrosis, a cecostomy tube can be used.

(1) Colonic Volvulus

H&P

Signs and symptoms of lower GI obstruction is the typical history. There may be feculent vomiting if there is an incompetent illeocecal valve.

Physical exam is of the abdomen and rectum, and assess the vital signs.

Diagnosis

Flat and upright abdominal films will reveal the classic "bent inner tube" or "omega" sign of the counter clock-wise sigmoid volvulus verses the "coffee bean" shape of the clock-wise cecal volvulus. Check the labs.

Treatment

NPO, IVF, Foley, antibiotics, and NGT are the initial steps in management of this problem.

Definitive management for the sigmoid is flexible or rigid endoscopy to reduce the twist. Leave a rectal tube behind to prevent recurrence and the patient can be bowel prepped in anticipation for a semi-elective sigmoid resection with primary anastomosis. If you are unable to reduce with endoscopy or there is evidence of ischemia, then you should go straight to the operating room. In the presence of gangrene or un-prepped colon, the safest thing to do is a sigmoid resection with an end colostomy.

For a cecal volvulus, resuscitate the patient and go straight to the operating room. If there is gangrene or the patient is ill or frail, then a right hemicolectomy, end illeostomy and mucus fistula is in order. If the cecum is viable, then a right hemicoloectomy and primary anastomosis should be done. Do not do a cecopexy because the recurrence rate is up to 40%

and the distended, thin walled cecum is not suited for this kind of procedure. Do not place a cecostomy tube either as it has a high recurrence (2-14%) and mortality (14-30%).

Example Case

You are asked to see an 84 year old nursing home resident who has been transferred to the emergency room with a 16 hours history of diffuse abdominal pain and distension. She has not had a bowel movement in over a week.

There could be several things going on with this woman. It sounds like she has an obstruction. Assuming she probably has some history of constipation, and she has not been vomiting, then this is likely to be a large bowel problem. Off the top of my head, I am thinking about a volvulus, cancer, stricture, pseudo-obstruction, adhesions, or impaction. I would get her medical history and medication list to make sure none of these medications could cause the problem. I would examine the patient to make sure that she does not have peritonitis. I would look for scars on her abdomen that would make me concerned about adhesions. Assuming she is only distended and tympanic and has no peritoneal signs, I would do a rectal exam. An empty rectal vault would rule out impaction. I would make sure her vitals are normal, and then start IV fluids on her. Send a complete blood count on her and get abdominal x-rays.

She has Parkinson's disease and hypertension, no surgical history, takes sinement and a diuretic. The abdominal film reveals that she has a massively dilated bowel, probably colon.

I am very suspicious that this is a volvulus, so I would place an NGT, give her a little sedation and pass a rigid or flexible sigmoidoscopy up the rectum. If this is a sigmoid volvulus, then I can hopefully reduce this with the scope, decompress her and leave a rectal tube to keep it from torsing again long enough to bowel prep her for a definitive operation. If this is not the case, then I would get a CT scan of the abdomen or a gastrograffin enema to give me more information about where the obstruction is.

You are able to detorse the sigmoid colon, and get a rush of air and stool. The rest of the colon appears normal to the transverse colon. You start the bowel prep, but she begin to vomit, and becomes distended again. The nurses tell you that the tube fell out.

I would put it back in and try again.

Same result again.

Then I would have to take her to the operating room with un-prepped bowel and plan on doing the sigmoid resection, leaving a rectal stump and maturing an end colostomy.

(0) Rectal Prolapse

H&P

Patients have a history of constipation, chronic straining, incontinence, bleeding, sense of incomplete evaluation, and urinary obstructive micturation.

Physical exam is focused on the rectum, showing protrusion with valsalva. There may be mucosal bleeding/ulceration.

Diagnosis

Examination is used to diagnose this problem.

Treatment

Initial management should be conservative. For internal rectal intussception and paradoxical puborectalis (functional resistance to defecation), high fiber diet and laxatives are used.

Operative management is used for complete rectal prolapse. If the patient is low risk, no constipation, then an abdominal rectopexy is done. If the patient is low risk with constipation, then rectopexy and resection is done. For high risk patients, a perineal (Delorme) proctosigmoidectomy is performed.

For mucosal prolapse in low or high risk patients, a Delorme is used.

(0) Radiation Injury to Small and Large Bowel

H&P

These patients may present with crampy abdominal pain, diarrhea, bloody bowel movements, and weight loss. Ask specifically about a history of vascular disease, atherosclerosis, diabetes, or HTN.

No particular physical findings, except they maybe heme + on rectal exam.

Diagnosis

History is the main method of diagnosis. Endoscopy can show large bowel radiation changes of scaring, fibrosis and stricture. UGIS with SBFT can show the extent of the disease and the presence of any fistulas. CT scan of the abdomen and pelvis may show any associated abscesses or recurrent malignancy.

Treatment

Emergent operations are needed for perforation and obstruction (after failing conservative therapy). Patients are given fluids and antibiotics. Otherwise, try to manage conservatively with low residual diets, low fat, lactose free, and gluten free. Steroid may be used.

Radiation proctitis can cause inflammation, non-healing ulcers, strictures, fistula, and bleeding. In general, this is treated with conservative measures and medical therapy, if that persist then they should have endoscopy to rule out malignancy. Bleeding is treated with argon beam coagulation and formalin treatment, and cystoscopy is used to rule out fistula formation. If all else fails, surgery is performed.

Additional Therapy

Sucrulfate enemas are the most effective medical therapy. Argon beam coagulation can improve symptoms in 90% of patients but requires multiple treatments. Topical formalin is done in the operating room or under local. A 4% solution is used and left in contact with the mucosa for 30 seconds, followed by saline irrigation.

If there is a fistula, a colostomy should be brought out. If there is good sphincter tone, a resection with coloanal J-pouch anastomosis can be done. Resection with end ostomy is another option (especially if the patient has incontinence).

(0) Solitary Rectal Ulcer

H&P

These patients present with rectal complaints of bleeding and passage of mucus. They may give you a history of rectal trauma or anal sex. They may have constipation or diarrhea. These ulcers are associated with paradoxical puborectalis contraction and rectal prolapsed.

Diagnosis

The diagnosis is made by colonoscopy, which is done to rule out malignancy. The ulcer is found and multiple biopsies should be taken at this time. It is usually 5-10 cm above the anal verge and is a red and friable patch on the rectal wall. You have to suspect cancer in this situation and rule it out.

Treatment

If the patient has rectal prolapsed, then they should have a rectopexy with or without resection or a Delorme (see rectal prolapsed section).

If the ulcer is symptomatic and there is no cancer, have the patient eliminate suppositories, anal sex, and home remedies. Put them on a high fiber diet (>30 gms/day), and have them increase their water intake.

(2) Colon Carcinoma*

H&P

We have all taken a history on a patient with a history of colon cancer and this should seem natural to you. You want to know if they have had any weight loss (suggestive of metastatic disease), change in bowel habits (obstructing?), change in stool caliber, blood in their stool, constipation, and so on.

The physical examination is limited to the abdomen and rectal exam, but it is usually negative.

Diagnosis

The patient may be sent to you with the diagnosis of cancer, or may be in your office with complaints of vague abdominal pain. The diagnosis of colon cancer is usually made by finding a lesion in the colon on a contrast enema or colonoscopy. Biopsies must be obtained and the diagnosis of adenocarcinoma confirmed.

Stage 0	Tis, N0, M0
Stage I	T1, N0, M0
	T2, N0, M0
Stage IIA	T3, N0, M0
Stage IIB	T4, N0, M0
Stage IIIA	T1, N1, M0
	T2, N1, M0
Stage IIIB	T3, N1, M0
	T4, N1, M0
Stage IIIC	Any T, N2, M0
Stage IV	Any T, Any N, M1

Treatment

Once the diagnosis is confirmed, a CT scan of the abdomen and pelvis is usually done to look for metastatic disease and basic lab work is performed (especially looking at LFTs, alk phos, and a CEA level).

For FAP patients, proper surveillance is crucial, and they should proceed with a proctocolectomy with IPAA if malignancy is found.

For HNPCC, you do the same as for FAP.

Synchronous lesions are usually treated with a subtotal colectomy with ileo-rectal anastomosis (IRA). Metachronous lesions are found within 6 months of the primary operation and the surgery is the same as for synchronous.

Locally advanced tumors are treated with en-bloc resections to get histologically negative margins.

For stage IV tumors look for signs of IHOP and go to operating room if found. If there is no IHOP, then give preoperative chemotherapy. If there are positive liver mets, then do the liver resection later.

If the tumor has perforated, do the resection and primary anastomosis or Hartman's procedure. Postoperatively, they will need chemotherapy and radiation therapy. Mark the site for radiation in the operating room.

If there is ovarian involvement, resect them.

Local recurrence happens about 4% of the time. There is a poor survival. If possible offer resection.

Additional Therapy

After colonoscopy, if there were no polyps found, then it should be repeated in 5 years. If there are small hyperplastic polyps, then repeat the scope in five years. Small adenoma warrants repeat scope in three years, and if negative then every 5 years. If there is a malignancy, no risk factors, polypectomy is adequate (<1% chance of cancer) and the scope is repeated in one year. If they have risk factors, there is a 33% chance of cancer, and a colectomy is done. Polypectomy is not the treatment of choice for sessile polyps.

Principles of colectomy include taking the lesion with two major vessels, associated mesentery, and harvesting at least 12 nodes.

Post-operative surveillance requires an H&P every 6 months for the first three years, then yearly after that. CEA levels are taken every 3 months for three year, then annually after that. Finally, colonoscopy should be repeated after 6 months, and if that is negative, then every year for three years. If they are all negative, then repeat every three years for life.

Chemotherapy regiments are given to stage IIA with risk factors (poorly differentiated, perforation or obstruction, lymphatic or vascular invasion, and <12 nodes harvested on resection) or stage IIB and higher. This includes 5-FU, oxaliplatin, and low dose leucovorin for 6 months post-operatively. Radiation therapy is considered for T4 lesions, perforation, or positive/ close and indeterminate margins of resection.

Example Case

A 60 year old man presents to you with a history of prior sigmoid colon cancer several years ago now with a cecal mass proven to be malignant on biopsy.

I would start with a little history of his previous colon cancer and if he had received any adjuvant therapy for that. Assuming that was an early stage cancer and he did well, then I would be focused on his current functional status and begin to focus on the abdominal and rectal exam. Of particular interest to me would be the rectal examination because if I resect this tumor he will likely get a total colectomy and I will have to consider an illeorectal anastomosis. If he has poor sphincter tone or is incontinent, then I would not do this. I would review the pathology reports and send basic lab work to get him ready for surgery. I would have him see a cardiologist for clearance if there was any abnormality on his preoperative EKG, and I would get a CEA level to see if this high. It would be nice to compare this to one they got from his previous cancer if they did it. Finally, since he has a history of cancer already, I would get a CT of the abdomen and pelvis to see if there are any liver mets. I don't think this is necessary, but if I knew there are mets going in, then I could have the ultrasound available and perhaps get a liver surgeon in there with me to do a resection if needed.

Well, his history is otherwise unremarkable; he has good rectal tone; his heart is in good shape; his CEA level is high, and the CT is normal. How would you do the illeorectal anastomosis?

I would mobilize the small bowel up to the duodenum and get as much length on the SMA as I can. Then I would fold the bowel on itself for about 10 cm and make an enterotomy at the end of it so that I could fire 45mm staplers inside this to create a pouch. I would then place the anvil in this enterotomy and purse string it in and use the EEA stapler to make the anastomosis. I would test this with an air leak, and give him a temporary diverting illeostomy.

Why divert him if your anastomosis is good?

He is older, been through a lot already, don't want a complication.

What if you notice a mass in the left lobe of the liver when you are in the operating room?

If it was at the edge of the liver and could be wedged out easily, then I would do that. If it were deep, I would leave it alone and have him follow up with a liver surgeon.

Ok, he spikes a temperature on POD#3 and has some mild abdominal pain.

I would culture his blood and urine, and check the chest x-ray to look for routine causes of infection. Of course I would go see him and look at the IV sites and examine the wounds. If all this looks ok, I would start him on broad spectrum antibiotics and get a CT of the abdomen and pelvis because I am concerned about an abscess or leak.

CT shows that there is a fluid collection in the pelvis that is about 10 cm in size. What do you want to do with this now?

That is large, but hopefully it is accessible to radiology for percutaneous drainage. I would have them leave the drain and send the fluid for culture. Then I could tailor my antibiotics to the specific organism(s).

(5) Rectal Cancer*

H&P

These patients have a history of rectal bleeding, rectal pain, changes in stool caliber, bloody bowel movements, weight loss, and fecal incontinence. They may have a history of colon cancer, ulcerative colitis, Chron's disease, FAP, or HNPCC.

Physical examination may reveal an abdominal mass, inguinal adenopathy, or a rectal mass. You should note the location of the mass, is it fixed or ulcerated, and are there palpable lymph nodes.

Diagnosis

Colonoscopy is the best way to find the mass, measure the distance from the anal verge, and biopsy it for definitive diagnosis. At the same time, you will be able to rule out synchronous lesions that can occur in 5% of cases.

While CT scan after the diagnosis of colon cancer may be questionable, there is no doubt that it should be used for rectal cancer. This will allow you to diagnose not only metastatic disease, but also the size of the tumor, extent of local invasion, and its orientation to other structures.

EUS is quickly becoming standard of care for staging of rectal cancer that is not obvious T3 or T4 lesions on CT and allows you to determine the depth of invasion, visualize adenopathy around the tumor, and perform FNA on suspicious adenopathy that may change your treatment for that patient.

PET scanning may be used to assess for distant metastatic disease.

Primary Tumor (T)

T_x	Primary tumor cannot be assessed
T0	No evidence of primary tumor
Tis	Carcinoma in situ: intraepithelial or invasion of lamina propria
T1	Tumor invades into the submucosa
T2	Tumor invades into the muscularis propria
T3	Tumor invades through the muscularis propria into the subserosa or into nonperitonealized pericolic or perirectal tissues
T4	Tumor directly invades other organs or structures, and/or perforates visceral peritoneum

Regional Lymph Nodes (N)

NX	Regional lymph nodes cannot be assessed
N0	No regional lymph node metastasis
N1	Metastasis into 1 to 3 regional lymph nodes
N2	Metastasis into 4 or more regional lymph nodes

Distant Metastasis (M)

MX	Distant metastasis cannot be assessed
M0	No distant metastases
M1	Distant metastases present

Stage	TNM	Dukes
0	Tis N0 M0	—
I	T1 N0 M0	A
	T2 N0 M0	A
IIA	T3 N0 M0	B
IIB	T4 N0 M0	B
IIIA	T1-T2 N1 M0	C
IIIB	T3-T4 N1 M0	C
IIIC	Any T N2 M0	C
IV	Any T Any N M1	—

Treatment

Neoadjuvant therapy is offered to any patient with a T3 (subserosal/perirectal fat) or N1 (1-3 nodes positive) and T2 lesion in the lower rectum.

The regiment is 5-FU and 4500 rads of radiation for 6 weeks, rest 6 weeks, then go to surgery, followed by leukovorin for 4 months. The benefits for this treatment is decreased local regional recurrence rates, increases overall survival, increase the chance of sphincter preserving surgery, downstages the rectal cancer in 80% cases (with complete response in 30%), and increases the chances of obtaining negative margins.

Patients with stage IV disease (M1) may chose to undergo resection and metastectomy with 5-FU and leukovorin, have a resection and chemorads with FULFOX or FULFURI, or have just palliative chemotherapy without resection.

Local resection is determined by the accessibility of the lesion (<6cm from the anal verge), size (<4 cm tumor), circumference, mobility (T1), node negative by DRE or EUS, well differentiate, and medical need for local resection (elderly, frail patient). Patient is positioned so that the tumor is located posteriorly. A circumferential anal block is performed with local anesthetic and the lone star retractor is placed. 1cm marks are scored around the lesion circumferentially and the rectal wall is excised, full thickness down to the perirectal fat. The defect is closed with 3-0 PDS. If the pathology shows anything worrisome (>T2, poorly differentiated, vascular or lymphatic invasion, etc), then you should go back for a LAR or APR. Recurrence after this procedure is a death sentence.

You should be able to describe a LAR in your sleep. Indications to place a diverting illeostomy after an LAR include difficult anastomosis, repair of leaks, transfusions, and previous XRT.

APR is done the same as an LAR, but you have to do a perineal dissection as well. Dissect posteriorly outside of the external sphincter muscles toward the tip of the coccyx. You will then have to free rectum laterally on both sides. Anteriorly the posterior wall of the vagina or prostate is kept anterior to rectum. The specimen is freed and removed via the perineal opening and is closed in layers. Close the perineum over a drain that comes out through the perineum. Omentum is placed in the pelvis. Finally, mature the colosotomy.

Additional Therapy

Complications after these procedures include perineal wound complications, leaks, presacral bleeding, pelvic nerve injury, and mortality.

Unresectable disease may require a palliative LAR or APR for pain, bleeding, or incontinence in order to improve their quality of life. Colostomy and stenting are other options that may be employed in this setting.

H&P is done every 6 months for the next three years, then yearly after that. LFT's and CEA level is drawn every 3 months for three years, then annually. Colonoscopy should be done every year for three years, then every three years after that; and CT scan/bone scans are only done as needed.

Example Case

A 55 year old man is referred to you from his PCP for a mass that was felt on routine rectal examination. He has no significant past medical history, takes no medications, never had any surgeries, and has no family history of cancers. His physical exam is otherwise unremarkable except for this mass on rectal exam.

Well, he sounds pretty healthy and I will not go through all that again, but I would definitely get a better appreciation for this mass in the rectum. I am assuming that it is a relatively small mass that I can feel just inside the rectal vault and it does not feel fixed or rigid.

Yes, it is small, but you cannot feel proximal to it. It seems to be about 4 cm from the anal verge.

Ok, then I would have the patient take bowel prep and come in for a colonoscopy so that I can look at this mass and, in addition, look at the rest of the colon to make sure there are no other synchronous lesions.

The rest of the colonoscopy is negative. The mass itself is about 3 cm in size and mobile. The biopsy results come back villous adenoma.

I guess the mass is not amendable to endoscopic removal because it is broad based.

Yes.

Well, I would tell the patient that this is a premalignant lesion and it needs to be removed. Since I did not find a cancer in it, I think we can go after this with a trans-anal approach. However, there is a chance that there is a cancer in it, and if that is the case after excision, he may need further therapy. Also, because of the chance that there could be more to this, I would get a little more information.

I would get a CT scan of the abdomen and pelvis to rule out any metastatic lesions and make sure there is not more local invasion then suspected. In addition, I would have an EUS performed to look at the tumor and the depth of invasion. If there are any large nodes seen with this, FNA can be performed. I would also send a CEA now as a baseline, in case this is a cancer.

OK, you do all this, the CT is normal, the EUS shows that the mass is confined to the mucosa. His CEA is normal.

Then at this point I would do the trans-anal resection. I have never done this procedure before, but my understanding is that a lone-star retractor is used for exposure, the cautery is used to mark around the lesion with 1 cm margins, and then the lesion is removed with full thickness down to perirectal fat. The defect is then closed with interrupted, full thickness sutures.

What if you cannot close the defect?

Then I would leave a preacral drain, keep him NPO and watch for pelvic sepsis. If he got sick, I would divert him with a loop transverse colostomy.

Let's say that the biopsy came back as adenocarcinoma and the EUS shows that it invades up to the submucosa.

Since I am not comfortable with the entire trans rectal excision technique, I do not use it for cancer. It this is a known cancer and they are candidates for trans anal excision, then I would refer them to a colorectal surgeon or offer them a LAR/APR.

Let's say this rectal mass was quite large, adenocarcinoma by biopsy, and the EUS showed positive nodes that were FNA'ed and came back as metastatic carcinoma. What would you do with that patient?

This is more advanced rectal cancer and he will need primary systemic therapy. Assuming that the CT scan has already been done and stage IV disease is ruled out, then the patient should receive six weeks of 5-FU and 4500 rads of radiation therapy. He is given 6 weeks to rest from this and let it work. The tumor will hopefully have shrunken a lot, and the nodes are sterilized, so that we can now go in and do a LAR with clear margins and get a good node dissection. The primary systemic therapy makes the resection easier, decreases the recurrence rate, and helps us increase the overall survival of these patients.

What do they get after surgery?

They get another four months of leukovorin and oxaloplatin.

(0) Inherited Colorectal Polyposis Syndromes

H&P

These patients should be asked about their colon cancer risk factors and symptoms; that is, you want to know if they have had any weight loss (suggestive of metastatic disease), change in bowel habits (obstructing?), change in stool caliber, blood in their stool, constipation, and so on.

Physical exam is focus on their abdomen and rectal examinations.

Diagnosis

Colonoscopy is the diagnostic test that will give you the diagnosis. Essentially, you will find 1000's of gross polyps for FAP. In HNPCC, there are <100 smaller polyps.

For patients that you suspect have HNPCC, they should fit into the Amsterdam criteria: "3-2-1, 50-25-5," 3 relatives with HNPCC associated cancers, 2 successive generations, 1 relative under 50 years old, start colonoscopy at age 25 or 5 years earlier than age of diagnosis in relative. These polyps are very aggressive and can become cancer within two years of developing.

For those that have FAP, they should have an upper endoscopy or UGIS with SBFT to rule out upper GI tract polyps as well.

CT scan for FAP patients should be routine because of the possibility of retroperitoneal desmoids tumors.

Treatment

Colonoscopy is performed in patients with history of FAP starting at age 12. Colectomy is generally deferred in FAP until the patient is 17 to 18 years of age; however, they should have a prophylactic colectomy once polyps appear. The goal here is to minimize death from colon cancer.

These patients are offered a total colectomy with IRA. There is no stoma, decrease chance of injury to nerves, but the pouch that is left is still at risk for cancer and needs surveillance every 5 years. If cancer develops then they with need proctocolectomy with IPAA or end illeostomy.

HNPCC patients should have a colonoscopy every year, starting at 25 years of age or 5 years younger than the youngest affected family member. Surgery is indicated when adenomas form at an early age, adenomas with satellite instability, and patients who cannot adhere to surveillance. The surgery of choice is a TAC with IRA or total proctocolectomy with IPAA. If this is a female patient who is finished with child bearing, a hysterectomy should be done at the same time (increased risk of uterine cancer)

Additional Therapy

Patients treated with colectomy for FAP should still have CT scanning every 6 to 12 months to rule out formation of desmoids tumors (leading cause of death after colectomy for these patients). Also, they should have surveillance for duodenal polyps every 6 months to 3 years. Sulindac and COX-2 inhibitors may prevent the development of these polyps.

Patients with the Lynch II subtype of HNPCC are at risk for extra-colonic cancers such as stomach, ovary, kidney, biliary, and small bowel. Most common extra-colonic site is the uterus.

(0) Hemorrhoids*

H&P

Patients will present with bleeding per rectum, pain, thrombosis, and/or constipation.

Diagnosis

Physical examination and proctoscopy make the diagnosis. Grade I are internal and do not prolapse. Grade II come out, but spontaneously go back in. Grade III come out and need to be pushed back in. Grade IV will not go back in.

Treatment

Different management strategies exist based on your experience, and they include: conservative management, surgical management, banding, and laser therapy.

Grade I hemorrhoids are usually found because of bleeding, and banding is less effective here.

Grade II and III hemorrhoids are candidates for rubber band ligation.

Grade IV disease generally extend below the dentate, and banding is too painful. These patients need a formal hemorrhoidectomy.

Example Case

A 36 year old female presents to you because she is having trouble with constipation and has notice some blood on the toilet paper when she wipes.

Sounds like she has hemorrhoids, but I want to make sure there is no other anal pathology. Assuming she is otherwise healthy, and has no history of Chron's disease, pain with defecation to think this is a fissure, family history of colon cancer, recent anal/

rectal surgery, and this is a new problem, then we are headed toward hemorrhoids. Physical exam may reveal external, but not necessarily internal hemorrhoids if they are grade I or II. Certainly a DRE may reveal any unexpected masses, fluctuance, or tenderness. I would look for fistula and fissures.

Now what?

Now I would want to get a good look inside. I am most comfortable taking her to the endoscopy suit, using sedation, and doing a sigmoidoscopy.

You see 2 internal hemorrhoids and 3 large external hemorrhoids.

That's pretty bad, I would discuss sitz baths and bulking the stool and this may help a little, but probably will fail over the next year. I would discuss the risk and benefits with the patient and let her decide. If she wants surgery (I would), I would schedule her for excision of 2 of the external hemorrhoids, as this is most likely causing her symptoms. I would not try to remove all of them or too much at once to avoid removing too much anoderm that can cause stricture.

Are there any other options for this patient?

Banding and phototherapy have been used with good success for internal hemorrhoids, so that is an option in this case.

(6) Appendicitis*

H&P

Patients present with the typically signs and symptoms here. Peri-umbilical pain that radiates to the RLQ, anorexia, low fever, nausea, and watch for unusually presentation (like delay of medical treatment, HIV, young females, etc).

You should examine the abdomen and do a rectal exam. In females, do a pelvic exam to rule out PID or pelvic mass.

Diagnosis

CBC will show a leukocytosis, examine will show a fever. Abdominal films are not very useful unless it shows a fecalith. CT scan with PO and IV (+/- rectal contrast) contrast is the test of choice and is very sensitive and specific. The false appendectomy rate has decreased from 20% to 10% over the last 10 years because of this modality (offsetting the cost of the scan). In addition, it can diagnose the appendiceal abscess that should be drained instead of operated on.

Treatment

IV antibiotics should be given on suspicion of acute appendicitis.

For the straight forward appendix, laparoscopic or open appendectomy is the treatment of choice.

If there is a phlegmon in the right lower quadrant, then antibiotics, NPO, and serial abdominal exams and CT scan are a better way to go. If the patient becomes ill, then you should abandon this treatment plan and take them to the operating room unless CT now reveals an abscess.

Peri-appendiceal abscess should be treated with percutaneous drainage, and antibiotics are given until the patient improves. They are made NPO and can begin to eat once their pain is gone and leukocytosis is resolving. If they get sicker despite drainage, then they should be taken to the operating room.

Look for the changing scenario. This could turn into carcinoid of the appendix, PID, ovarian cyst or abscess, cholecystitis, cancer of the cecum, ectopic pregnancy, etc...

Creeping terminal illeal fat, do nothing but appendectomy. If pus coming from an inflamed tube, then incise and drain, do the appendectomy and place the patient on cefriaxone and doxycycline. For a big abscess, you may need to take the ovary and tube. Ovarian cyst less than 5 cm should be observed with US over the next few cycles, but if it is more than 5 cm then you should do an oopherectomy and get peritoneal washings and biopsies, omental biopsies, and colonic gutter biopsies (the ovarian cancer routine). If you find bilious fluid, then there is a perforated gallbladder and you will have to take this out. How you do that is based on the incision you have already. These changing scenarios are a good reason to do you appendectomies with a laparoscope, especially in the female patient. It is like a box of chocolates.

Additional Therapy

Interval appendectomy is now a debatable subject. A large portion of people who come in with a phlegmon or an abscess and successfully complete conservative therapy will not go on to have any other problems from the appendix. Recurrence rates can be about 4%. You should have the discussion with the patient about the risk and benefit of surgery and help them decide what they think is the right retort for them.

Example Case

You are asked to evaluate a patient in the ED with known HIV and cocaine use. He presents with progressively worsening abdominal pain. His WBC is 14k. He has a chest x-ray which shows patchy infiltrates.

So I am already thinking that he has some kind of infection right now base on his WBC, and the lungs and the abdomen are the suspected source or sources. In addition, he is an HIV patient and this could be atypical infections like pneumocystis carini, histoplasmosis, or CMV. To make thing even more confusing, his cocaine use could be contributing to mesenteric ischemia.

I would go see the patient and start with a history of presentation of the abdominal pain. I am expecting that this is the acute onset kind of pain you get with perforation or ischemia (if it is related to his cocaine use).

No, it has been lingering for 2 days now and getting worse.

Ok, so it may not be related to cocaine, and I think that this is probably not too acute if it has been going on for two days. I would go through his pulmonary review of symptoms to get an idea of how long he has been having symptoms.

I would examine the abdomen, looking for peritonitis or localized pain, and the chest…

The abdomen is tender in the RLQ.

In this case, I am concerned about pneumonia, and now, maybe appendicitis. I would do a rectal exam to look for blood, masses, tenderness, flucuance, and to get a stool sample to send for O&P and C&S. I would start him on broad spectrum antibiotics, like Zosyn and flagyl. I would then get a CT scan of the chest, abdomen, and pelvis.

CT shows a well organized RLQ abscess consistent with a perforated appendicitis with abscess.

Assuming that the chest doesn't look like pneumonia then, and the WBC is likely coming from the abscess, I would have the radiology percutaneously drain this and continue the antibiotics. I would make him NPO, give him IV fluids, and admit him to may service so that I could do serial abdominal exams and labs to make sure he improves with this therapy.

The following day, he becomes more short of breath and spikes a fever to 103F, what do you do?

If his abdominal exam has not changed or improved, then I am worried that it is the lungs. Obviously, I am not covering something with my antibiotics. I would add antifungal medication, and try to get a sputum sample. I would check an ABG to see if he was very hypoxic. If I need to, I will move him to the ICU setting and start him on CPAP or even intubate as needed.

His abdominal pain is actually a little worse today.

As long as he is stable and maintain his airway…I was going to say repeat the CT; however, I don't see any use in this now that I say it. I just did it yesterday. If he is not improving, his abdominal exam is worse, still having fever, I have to believe that either I don't have source control with that drain, or that drain has injured something else. I still think he has a bad pneumonia brewing and something strange will come of that, but at this time, I will have to operate on him by putting in a laparoscope and taking a look.

What is your plan in the operating room?

I expect this to be really bad looking, and I prefer to get in the abdomen with a laparoscope in the left upper quadrant, then look around and wash out the abdomen, opening the abscess and washing it out, trying to keep it contained. The plan would be to take the appendix if I could, but I might not even see it. I just want to see the percutaneous drain, make sure it did not injure anything, washout the abscess, make sure there is nothing else going on in the abdomen, leave another drain of my own, get some cultures in the process, and get out. If I cannot complete these tasks with a laparoscope, then I will open with a midline incision.

Let's say you have a different patient, 25 year old healthy male, you go in to do an appendectomy for typically symptoms of acute appendicitis and you find a 7 mm carcinoid at the tip of the appendix.

My general approach to these tumors is that anything less than 2 cm, then I must get a clear margin. If it is larger than 2 cm, it starts to act malignant, and it should be treated as such with a formal right colectomy. So in this case, I would just perform the appendectomy, and that should be adequate.

What if this 7mm tumor was at the base of the appendix?

Then I would wedge it out of the cecum with a stapler if that was safe. If I could not do this anatomically, then I would do a cecectomy and primary anastomosis.

How would you follow him up?

Most of these tumors don't secrete 5-HIAA; chromogranin A is probably high in about 80%, so this could be used. CT or octreotide scans may be used. Death from carcinoid tumors in individuals who had no evidence of metastasis at their index operation is very rare, so intensive follow up is hard to justify and is controversial.

(1) *C. dificile* Colitits*

H&P

Patients that develop colitis from *C. dificile* are usually inpatients or have recently been treated with oral antibiotics (like clindamycin). In addition, bowel preps and enemas that can change the colon flora can cause the colitis.

The patients present with abdominal distension, leukocytosis, fever, and diarrhea. Abdominal pain may be present and is usually mild.

Physical examination is used to rule out peritonitis. Do a rectal examination and send a stool sample.

Diagnosis

Stool cultures for the toxin are the most reliable way to make the diagnosis. However, clinical suspicion should be high based on the history and physical exam findings and empirical therapy should be started.

Sigmoidoscopy/colonoscopy can be used to visualize the pseudomembranes associated with this colitis. They are whitish in color and can be pulled off when taking biopsies.

Treatment

Flagyl can be given PO or IV, and the dose is 500 mg every 6 hours. Vancomycin must be given po and is 500 mg every 12 hours.

Surgical therapy is offered for those patients that do not respond to medical therapy. They may develop peritonitis from colonic perforation and ischemia as a result of the colitis. Increasing WBC and fever despite medical therapy is concerning. Fulminant colitis is a lethal problem if not treated quickly. Total abdominal colectomy is the surgical treatment of fulminant *C. dificile* colitis.

Example Case

You do a right hemicolectomy for cecal cancer. He does well post-operatively until day 4 when he begins to have some abdominal distension. He is mildly febrile at 100F and his WBC is 14k. He has been having diarrhea for 2 days.

I am sure that this patient got antibiotics recently from his surgery, and anytime a post-operative patient has abdominal distension, fever, leukocytosis, and diarrhea, you have to worry about *C. dificile* colitis as the possible cause. I believe in really getting on this early, and in this situation, I would send a stool sample for *C. dificile* toxins and empirically start flagyl. I am assuming that his wound looks good, chest x-ray (I would order as a fever work up) is clear, and he has no peritonitis on physical exam.

He does not have any peritonitis. What dose of flagyl would you start and would you do anything else?

I would give him 500 mg flagyl, IV or PO, depending on what he was tolerating. I would consider getting CT scan of the abdomen. His case seems pretty mild, and I don't routinely do this, but if he had any significant abdominal pain that may make me think there could be something else going on (like an intra-abdominal abscess), then I would get a CT. It can be helpful in *C. dificile* colitis because it can show you the extent of the colitis and any significant dilation.

Would you continue to feed him?

If this is a very mild case, then yes.

He does ok for the next 2 days and then seems to get worsening of his abdominal pain and WBC stays the same.

This would be a good reason to CT him now. If the *C. dificile* came back positive by this time, and I knew I was at least dealing with this, I may consider changing antibiotics regiments to PO vancomycin. But I would see what the CT scan shows first.

CT just shows some thickening of the transverse colon and changing him to oral vancomycin doesn't work. What are your indications for operating on a patient with C. dificile *colitis?*

I would not let the patient continue to deteriorate. Fulminate *C. dificile* colitis is extremely mortal and should be aggressively treated with a total colectomy, which is not without its own mortality. So, like anything else we do, we have to weigh the risk and benefits. If the colon becomes significantly dilated so that perforation is becoming a concern, the patient fails to respond to a week's worth of adequate medical therapy, he begins to look more septic, or he develops peritonitis, then I would take him to the operating room.

What does the colon look like in these cases?

I have never had to operate on a patient with this problem, so I can say that I fortunately don't know.

(1) Anus

(0) Anal Incontinence

H&P

Patients with a history of Chron's, radiation, proctitis, anal surgeries, or fistulotomies are at risk for anal incontinence. So ask about these things. Ask about trauma to the anus, hard vaginal deliveries, or hemorrhoid surgeries.

On physical exam, put your finger in the rectum and have the patient squeeze down on your finger so you can get an idea of how much tone they have, look for prolapse (nerve injury) and look for fistulas (that may cause soilage, confusing the picture). Make sure there is no rectal mass.

Diagnosis

History and physical are about all you need in order to start conservative management. Before considering surgery, however, you want to get sphincter manometry, anal ultrasound, and a pudendal nerve latency test. If any of these are positive, then surgical treatment will help,

Treatment

Initial treatment should be conservative. Drug therapy, bio-feedback, and avoiding food intolerances are the mainstay of conservative treatment. Advise them to increase the fiber in their diet, and schedule for colonoscopy to rule out inflammatory or neoplastic problems. Send stool cultures and *C. dificile*.

If this fails, and you have a positive manometry, ultrasound, or nerve latency test, then plication sphincteroplasty is done. Order a mechanical bowel prep pre-operatively, place the patient in prone jack-knife, make a curvilinear incision anterior to the anus and elevate the anoderm and rectal mucosa. Find the external and internal sphincters and overlap and wrap

(1) Anus

them. The scar of the transverse perineum and muscles are re-approximated. The skin is closed over a Penrose drain.

Complications of this procedure include anal stenosis, local sepsis, and fecal impaction.

(O) Anal Stenosis

H&P

Patients may have a history of an inflammatory process or previous anal surgeries.

Physical exam is focused on whether there is stenosis of the mucosa, muscle, or both.

Diagnosis

Physical exam is the diagnostic test here.

Treatment

Conservative treatment includes patient intervention (high fiber, stool softeners, mild laxatives, and increased po intake), doctor intervention (dilatation), or surgical intervention.

Surgical intervention involves flap advancement if there is mucosal stenosis or a lateral internal sphincteroplasty if there is muscle stenosis.

Complications include flap necrosis, re-stenosis, hematoma, abscess, fistula, and incontinence.

(1) Anal Cancer

There are several things that can be called anal cancer. To clarify, anal cancers include epidermoid carcinoma (squamous, transitional, and mucoepidermoid), sarcoma, and others (adenocarcinoma, melanoma, and carcinoid). Anal margin tumors can be malignant (SCC, BCC, verrucous, and Kaposi's) or pre-malignant (Bowen's disease, Paget's disease, condylomata acuminata).

H&P

Certain people are at risk for anal cancers, including those who have anal sex, HPV infections, HIV, herpes, chronic anal fistulas, Chron's disease, prior XRT, syphilis, Hodgkin's disease, and smokers. They may present with complaints of rectal bleeding, weight loss, and fecal incontinence.

On physical examination you should exam the anus and rectum to get an idea of the size and location of the tumor, check for abdominal masses, and feel the groin for adenopathy. Tumors at the dentate line and below metastasize to the groin.

Diagnosis

Colonoscopy and proctoscopy are used to visualize the lesion and take biopsies. The exact location and orientation of the tumor, whether it is fixed or mobile, and if there are palpable nodes, should be documented.

If the biopsy is positive for cancer, EUS should be done to determine the depth of invasion

CT scan is then performed for staging and to rule out distant metastasis.

If any groin nodes are palpable, an FNA should be performed to diagnosis metastatic cancer.

Treatment

Squamous cell carcinoma of the anal canal is treated with the Nigrol protocol with 5 year survival and local control in up to 90% of patients. This includes 4 weeks of 5-FU, mitomycin C, and radiation (3000-4800 rads), then a 6 week rest, and then a re-evaluation of the area and re-biopsy. If this is negative, then start surveillance, but if it is positive then they get a second dose of chemo-radiation therapy. After the second dose, another 6 weeks, and biopsy positive again, they are offered an APR as the only chance for cure.

If the inguinal region is positive for cancer cells, then inguinal radiation is included in the protocol. There is equivalent efficacy when compared to inguinal node dissection, but the morbidity is much lower.

Liver, lung, and bone mets are treated with local conservative surgery or systemic chemotherapy with 5-FU and cisplatin.

SCC of the anal margin is treated like any skin SCC (i.e. WLE with 1 cm margins).

BCC of the anal margin are rare, but these should be excised with clear margins.

Cloacogenic, transitional, and basaloid cancers (epidermoid cancers) are all treated the same as SCC.

Melanoma of the anus is treated with WLE if the depth of invasion is only to the submucosa. XRT is added to save the sphincters. If any gross disease is left behind or local control is not achieved, then APR should be done. For distant mets (60% with diagnosis), the 5 year survival is dismal. Question of whether systemic therapy is helpful at all.

Adenocarcinoma that is not invading the sphincters is treated with wide local excision; otherwise, you should treat it with Nigrol protocol.

(1) Anus

Anal sarcoma is considered malignant if there is > 5 mitosis per 50 HPF and should be treated with APR. Any residual tumor is treated with radiation therapy.

Bowen's disease is intraepidermal SCC, and it is treated with topical 5-FU, cryoablation, laser or argon ablation or WLE (treatment of choice) with 1 cm margins.

Paget's disease is intraepidermal adenocarcinoma and is treated with WLE with 1 cm margins.

All anal margin tumors (SCC, BCC, Bowen's disease and Paget's disease) are all treated with WLE except Kaposi's sarcoma. Kaposi's sarcomas are treated with radiation therapy.

Additional Treatment

After successful treatment with the Nigro protocol, surveillance includes a proctoscopy with biopsy every 3 months for 2 year, then every 6 months for 3 years, then annually after that.

Bowen's and Paget's disease is followed up with a proctoscopy every year and colonoscopy every 3 years.

(27) Liver/Gallbladder
(1) Liver Nodule

H&P

Patients may present with the finding of incidental nodule found by ultrasound for another reason. You should ask about oral contraceptive use (OCP, contribute to adenomas or focal nodular hyperplasia), history of other cancers (metastatic disease), foreign travel or fevers (abscesses), abdominal pain, or history of hepatitis.

Physical exam is focused on abdominal exam and palpation of the liver.

Diagnosis

LFT's, alpha-fetoprotein (>400 is diagnostic for HCC), hepatitis panel, CEA, and CA 19-9 should be sent off. Ultrasound of the liver will confirm if the mass is solid or cystic. If it is cystic, then follow the cystic work up (see liver cyst section).

For solid lesions, a tagged red cell scan is ordered to rule out hemangiomas. If this is positive then observe unless they are very large or symptomatic.

If the scan is negative then get a CT scan with triple phase contrast to visualize the liver mass better. This will give you pretty good idea whether this is an adenoma, focal nodular hyperplasia (FNH), or malignancy. On CT scan, hemangiomas are well defined, hypo dense lesion with early peripheral, nodular enhancement.

If you suspect that this is FNH by the central scar and spoke-wheel appearance, then get a sulfur-colloid nuclear medicine scan that will show a cold nodule. You can stop here.

Treatment

Adenomas have a hypervacular rim and no biliary ductules on CT scan. These are prone to bleed. For any liver lesion that bleeds, assess the stability of the patient. If the patient is unstable then go to the operating room to control the bleeding. Think about controlling the bleeding now and resect later. Pack all 4 quadrant, do a Pringle maneuver, selectively ligate the appropriate branch of the hepatic artery or suture ligate the tumor vessel that is bleeding. Resect them later. If they are stable, then go to angiogram and embolize the tumor and do surgery later.

Most of the time, a patient can be taken off OCP and repeat the scan in 6 months to see if the adenoma has decreased in size. If it is deep or they are not on OCP, then 2 out of 3 adenomas will become symptomatic and should be resected.

Focal nodular hyperplasia (FNH) will have a contrast enhanced center with a spoke wheel appearance, distorted biliary ductules, and are associated with OCP as well. Observation for these tumors is prudent. Repeat CT can be done in 6 months. Any symptomatic tumor or those that grow should be taken off estrogen and repeat the observation period. If they continue to give pain (or patient not on estrogen), then embolize the main large feeding artery or surgically remove (non-anatomical resection).

Malignant tumors have high CEA (if metastatic) or AFP (primary hepatocellular) levels. Colonoscopy and PET scan should be done on these patients. They are very vascular on CT scan, but wash out very fast to become hypo vascular on venous phase. Need to rule out mets to the lung with chest CT, and an angiogram with venous phase are done to plan resection.

(0) Liver Cyst

H&P

Usually these are found incidentally; however, typical history and physical exam is done. You should ask about oral contraceptive use (OCP, contribute to adenomas or focal nodular hyperplasia), history of other cancers (metastatic disease), foreign travel or fevers (abscesses), abdominal pain, or history of hepatitis.

Physical exam in is focused on abdominal exam and palpation of the liver.

Diagnosis

Ultrasound and CT scans are usually the first tests that are done on these lesions. Ultrasound typically delineates that you have a cyst in the liver.

Simple cyst are defined as well demarcated, no nodularity in the wall, not septated, and negative for immuno-electrophoresis for echinococcus.

Hydatid cysts are suspected by history of recent travel abroad and findings of calcification or septations on imaging studies.

Treatment

For the simple cyst, you can just observe them if they are asymptomatic. If they are symptomatic then a percutaneous aspiration is done first.

If there is no bile in the fluid, no bacteria, and the pain is relieved, then you can aspirate it again and inject with alcohol to ablate the cyst. This is done by aspirating 25% of the cyst fluid and replacing it with 95% ETOH solution, repositioning the patient every 10 minutes in the supine, left lateral, right lateral and prone position, then fully aspirating the cyst dry. This should cause scarring to prevent the cyst from recurring. You can recheck this with ultrasound and repeat if it recurs.

If the cyst is infected, then perform a CT guided percutaneous drainage and antibiotic treatment.

If the fluid is positive for CEA, CA 19-9, or cytology, then resect it.

If the cyst has bile in it, then alcohol ablation is contraindicated (could cause biliary sclerosis). An ERCP is done to locate the connection to the biliary system. Surgery is done if they are symptomatic. Unroof the cyst, find the communication and ligate it. Methylene blue can be injected into the cystic duct to locate the communication. Fill the defect with omentum and do a cholecystectomy. If you cannot find the site of biliary leak, then do a roux-en-Y cyst-jejunostomy.

Hydatid cyst is confirmed by serology and the patient is started on albendazole (10 mg/kg/d), ERCP is done to make sure there is no communication with the biliary system, and you proceed to surgery. The bowel is packed away with moist laparotomy pads and the cyst is aspirated and injected with hypertonic saline. Avoid spillage which may causes anaphylaxis. Unroof the cyst, pack with omentum, and suture ligate any biliary leakage. Continue the anti-helminthes drugs for 2 weeks postoperatively.

(1) Liver Abscess*

H&P

The differential diagnosis can be calculus cholecystitis, viral hepatitis, or liver abscess; and your questions are centered on ruling in or out these diagnoses. Patients may have a history of traveling abroad, immunocompromised patients, tired, low grade fever, RUQ pain, repeated infections; and, most commonly, a recent history of appendicitis or diverticulitis.

Physical exam is of the abdomen and rectum.

Diagnosis

Send a CBC, LFT's, and get a US to show fluid collection in the liver. Send stool off for ova and parasites. CT scan is used to further evaluate the abscess. Indirect hemagglutination test/ELIZA will rule out echinococcus. Compliment fixation test to diagnose entamoeba histolytica. You need to rule out Hydatid cyst and mycobacterium. Complicated abscess may be large (>5cm), located in the left lobe of the liver, and will likely fail medical therapy. Fungal abscess can present in immunocompromised patients.

Treatment

Diagnostic and therapeutic aspiration is done, and the fluid is sent for culture and sensitivity. Change antibiotics as results are available.

Fungal abscess is treated with amphotericin B. If medical therapy fails, then you should percutaneous drain. If drainage fails, then go to surgery.

Mycobacterium abscess is treated with anti-TB meds: isoniazid, rifampin, pyrazimamide, and ethambutal.

Amebic abscess is treated with flagyl (and chloroquine if no improvement in the first 3 days). If the patient does not get better after 1 week, then you should aspirate the abscess to rule out secondary infection. If this aspiration fails, percutaneous drainage is done; and if this fails, surgical drainage is done.

Bacterial abscesses (usually in right lobe) require antibiotics (Zosyn) and drainage. CT guided percutaneous drainage is done first. If this fails after 3 weeks, then open drainage through the 12th rib. You should always biopsy the abscess wall to rule out cancer.

Example Case

A 34-year old woman comes to your office with a 2-3 cm week history of right upper quadrant pain and generalized fatigue. Her internist has done an ultrasound, which shows a normal gallbladder and ducts and a 4 cm mass in the right lobe of the liver.

So this young woman with a mass in the liver associate with pain and fatigue is concerning for an abscess. She has probably noticed some night sweats and low grade fever and that would point toward an abscess also. Assuming that ultrasound shows fluid and not a solid mass, this would be more consistent with this diagnosis. If she had been traveling abroad lately, I may think of some strange causes of abscess like ameobic or echinococcus, but hydatid cyst are possible. Most common cause of liver abscess is from an intra-abdominal infectious process like appendicitis or diverticulitis.

She has not had any fever and the ultrasound is hard to tell if this is cystic or solid.

In that case, a CT scan would be very helpful.

That shows a 4 cm pyogenic abscess. Now that you mentioned it, she did have some crampy abdominal pain and diarrhea about 6 weeks ago, which resolved.

Her diarrhea and abdominal pain really doesn't clear things up for me. Could this be amoeba, may be. Diverticular disease more likely, but she is young. We need to treat this abscess by starting her on a broad spectrum antibiotic like Zosyn and I would include anaerobic coverage too, like flagyl (which would treat ameobic abscess as well). I am paranoid about aspirating a hydatid cyst, so I would send off electrophoresis and antibody studies to rule that out. If that is negative, I would aspirate this abscess and send it for culture and sensitivity so that I could narrow my antibiotics to a specific treatment and get a better idea where this came from. If there is E. coli, bacteroides, B. fragilis, etc, then I suspect colon, and I would follow her up with a colonoscopy after she got over her liver abscess.

(0) Malignant Liver Tumors

H&P

These patients may have abdominal pain, weight loss, or jaundice. You should focus on a history of cancer, hepatitis, cirrhosis, OCP use, steroid use, Wilson's disease, hemochromatosis and α-1-antitrypsin.

Examine the abdomen, liver, and rectum.

Diagnosis

Check the CEA and AFP levels. Colonoscopy is done to rule out colon cancer, CT scan of the abdomen and pelvis is done to evaluate the hepatic and extra-hepatic extent of disease. PET scan is done to rule out distant disease.

MRI is useful to delineate the tumor and its relationship to major vessels and extent of biliary involvement. This modality also lets you predict how much resection you will need and how much liver will be left afterwards.

Rule out Cirrhosis and calculate the Child-Pugh classification (or some other method to determine the function of the liver). Predictors of poor outcome include positive lymph nodes, tumors more than 5 cm, less than 12 months disease free from primary tumor resection (like colon cancer), more than one tumor, and CEA >200. Any of these factors makes the 5 year survival about 40%.

Treatment

Ideally the lesion is < 5 cm, no gross invasions, and not metastatic cancer. If the patient is a Child's B or C, they may not be good candidates for resection, and may be considered for transplantation. If there are more than 4 lesions, vascular invasion, lymph node invasion, or metastatic tumors, then the patient is not a transplant candidate.

Laparoscopy should be done first to determine the extent of extra-hepatic disease which could indicate unresectability and save the patient from a laparotomy. If this is negative, the abdomen is opened through subcostal incisions, mobilize the liver, and palpate the entire thing. Get inflow control by placing an umbilical tape around the hepatic duodenal ligament (Pringle maneuver); perform a cholecystectomy and tract the cystic duct to the CBD and the right and left hepatic ducts. Ligate the hepatic ducts, ligate the hepatic artery, and ligate the portal vein on the appropriate side of resection. Once the parenchymas demarcates, score the peritoneum with the bovie, crush the tissue with Kelly clamps and clip and dived all small exposed vessels. Sutures ligate all ductules. Paint the raw surface with fibrin glue after hemostasis.

Additional Therapy

For those patients that are not resectable and are not transplant candidates, then you can consider RFA or ETOH injection if the lesion is < 5cm and is a single lesion. If there are multiple lesions then try trans-arterial chemo-embolization (TRACE) with cisplatin, adrimycin, mitomycin C, and gelfoam.

(13) Post-Cholecystectomy Jaundice*

H&P

Usually these patients have an uneventful surgery and come back one week later with jaundice. Ask about pain, fever, when they became jaundice, dark urine, and clay-colored stools. Focus the H&P around the problems that you think about (cystic duct leak, CBD leak, liver bed leak, CBD clipped, retained stone, pancreatitis, etc).

Rule out peritonitis.

Diagnosis

Send off a CBC and LFT's, get an abdominal x-ray and start broad spectrum antibiotics.

RUQ ultrasound or CT of the abdomen can show biliary dilation, CBD dilation, stones, and fluid collections.

HIDA will show you if the CBD is occluded or not.

Treatment

If the CBD looks occluded (dilated ducts, and HIDA is suggestive), then get an ERCP to determine the location of the obstruction and possibly remove an impacted retained stone if that is the case. If this fails, or if a clip across the CBD is suspected, then go to the operating room for exploration and repair of the CBD (with a T-tube or choledocho-jejunostomy).

If there is a biloma present on US or CT, then get a CT guided percutaneous drainage , and then get GI to do an ERCP to stent the leak and determine if it from the cystic or common duct. If the cystic duct is leaking, leave in the drain and the CBD stent and follow. Most will close within 1-2 weeks. If GI or ERCP is not available in your institution for the purpose of the board exam, then you will have to get PTCA.

If the CBD is injured and the patient is stable, then let thing cool down, continue the drainage, and come back in 4-6 weeks to repeat the ERCP. If it continues to leak, then go in and repair it over a T-tube or do a choledocho-J. If the patient is septic, then you will have to go sooner.

If you get in the abdomen and the RUQ is all scared in so that you cannot dissect anything out, then locate the CBD by aspirating it with a 25 gauge needle and do a side-to-side choledochojejunosotmy.

Example Case

You perform an uneventful laparoscopic cholecystectomy on a 34 year old healthy female for acute cholecystitis and she returns 4 months later to her PCP complaining of RUQ pain and jaundice. He notices that you have done her operation and sends her to your office.

With her being 4 months out, I am concerned that there is a retained stone, a primary stone, or an injury to the common duct that resulted in a stenosis of the duct. This would cause her symptoms. So I would admit her to the hospital, make her NPO, start fluids on her, check vitals to make sure she is not febrile to suggest possible cholangitis, and start broad spectrum antibiotics. I would send off labs to check her WBC and her LFTs to see if the alk phos is elevated to suggest biliary obstruction. I would check and correct any other electrolyte problems. I would get abdominal x-rays and an ultrasound for the RUQ to look at the CBD, see if there is biliary dilation, maybe if there is stone there, and if there are any drainable fluid collections in the RUQ.

Her WBC is normal, bili is 18, and LFTs are elevated. There is intrahepatic biliary dilation on the US but not fluid collection.

Then I would ask GI to do an ERCP for me.

They are not available.

Then radiology could do a PTC for me. I am trying to evaluate the common bile duct for a stone or stricture or injury.

Yes, I know what you are doing. The PTCA shows a narrowing of the mid-CBD and about 10 clips all around the area.

She has a stricture of her CBD. This is a complication from the operation. I would advise her that she will need surgical reconstruction of this area. Stents and balloons are available for this problem, but I have no experience in this area, and I would recommend transferring her to a hepato-biliary surgeon at this time.

She wants to know what kind of reconstruction.

I would explain to her in detail what a choledochojejunostomy is.

If you were doing this operation, how would you identify the duct?

I would thoroughly explore the porta and try to dissect above the clips. If I had any doubt about what I was doing, I would aspirate it with a 22g needle.

What would you do if the US showed a fluid collection?

Then I would be concerned that there is a biloma, hematoma, or abscess. First thing I would do is get a CT guided percutaneous drainage of this fluid. I would send it for gram stain and culture. Furthermore, depending on the nature of the fluid, I would have a good idea how to proceed. If this is bile that I get out, then there is a leak from the cystic duct, the gallbladder fossa, a duct of Luschka, or an injured CBD (maybe the duodenum). In order to determine where it is coming from, I would get an ERCP and if it was coming from the cystic duct, I would have them leave a stent in to decompress the system and the cystic duct will likely heal in 1 to 2 weeks.

Now let's say she is 9 years out from her surgery and presents with intermittent RUQ pain, fever, chills, and nausea.

This scenario is more concerning for primary or retained stones. I would start with a RUQ ultrasound and if this sounds intrahepatic and CBD dilation or CBD stones, I would order an ERCP.

There is a duodenal diverticulum and they can't do it.

Then I would get a PTC.

So you find a lot of distal CBD stones.

I would take her to the operating room for a CBD exploration.

How do you do that?

I make a right upper quadrant incision along the costal margin, get exposure to the porta hepatits, find the CBD, aspirate it with a 22 g needle to confirm that this is the duct, make a vertical 2 cm incision in it and give the patient glucagon to relax the sphincter. I then forcibly flush the duct with saline on an olive tip, followed by serial passes with a #4 Fogarty. Hopefully I can retrieve all the stones until the Fogarty passes into the duodenum, then I would pass a choledochoscope down to ensure the duct is clear.

You can not get all the stones. There is one impacted in the ampulla.

I wanted to stay away from the duodenum because of the diverticulum, but I would like to remove that stone, so I would go transduodenal and do a sphincterotomy to extract this stone.

Still can not get the stone out.

Then I will close the duodenum in two layers and fashion a hepatico jejunostomy.

Anesthesia says she is getting unstable as you are closing the duodenum, and they want to get her out of the operating room now.

Leave a T-tube and get out, but why is she unstable....

(0) Post-Cholecystectomy Syndrome

H&P

This is papillary stenosis or inflammation due to CBD stones, ERCP, pancreatitis, or PUD. They present with continued pain after cholecystectomy.

Physical exam is unremarkable.

Diagnosis

Try to rule out non-biliary causes with UGI (reflux), EGD (PUD), and amylase (pancreatitis). Also get an US or ERCP (retained stone), HIDA scan (rule out dyskinesia), and IBD as a diagnosis of exclusion.

Treatment

ERCP with stent placement may relieve the pain. If this works, then sphincteroplasty could be done. Alternative is trans-duodenal sphincteroplasty.

(3) (Post-Cholecystectomy) Cholangitis*

H&P

Patient will present with fever, pain and jaundice (Charcot's triad). They may have a history of cholecystectomy and a retained stone, stricture (benign or malignant), or primary biliary stone is the cause of the cholangitis.

You want to check the vitals and make sure that they are not in septic shock.

Diagnosis

You should have a high suspicion of the diagnosis just from the presentation. Check the LFT's to confirm the bilirubin is elevated, and the WBC is usually elevated as well (leucopenia is an ominous sign). An US will show dilated biliary ducts and possibly a stone or mass in the distal CBD.

Ultimately, the diagnosis is a clinical one and based solely on physical exam findings (they have RUQ pain, they are yellow, they have fever, they are obtunded, and they are in shock)

Treatment

Stabilize the patient with fluids and antibiotics. Admit them to the ICU. You have to drain the biliary system ASAP.

Emergent ERCP is the procedure of choice because they can do a sphincterotomy, remove the stone and/or leave a stent to drain the system.

If ERCP is not available or unsuccessful, then percutaneous trans-hepatic cholangiogram can be done by interventional radiology to decompress the biliary system behind the blockage. Surgery can be done later.

If neither of these can be done, then you are going to have to operate on the patient and do a CBD exploration to remove the stone and/or decompress the biliary system. First, explore the duct and get the stone out. If you can not get the stone out, then place a T-tube and close if the patient is in extremis. If the patient is stable, you can permanently drain the biliary system with a choledochojejunosotmy or choledochoduodenostomy. If the portahepatis is very scared in, then you can do a duodenotomy and sphincteroplasty with stone extraction. Bottom line, drain the system some how, and get the stone if you can.

Example Case

You are asked to see an 80 year old patient from the nursing home who presents with abdominal pain, jaundice and a fever of 40C, pulse of 110. She was found by the nursing staff to be increasingly confused. She was also discovered by the ER physician to have a-fib.

This lady seems to have ascending Cholangitis (though, with a-fib I have some concern about a clot causing mesenteric ischemia; however, these people don't get jaundice), and she seems to be septic. I am assuming that she is probably hypotensive as well. I would begin by given her a couple of liter of normal saline boluses to begin resuscitating her and monitor that by placing a Foley catheter and get her urinating about 50 ml and hour. She needs some broad spectrum antibiotics started (like Zosyn or primaxin). I would assess her airway at this time and make sure that she is protecting it well. If she is severely decompensated, she may need to be intubated. I would draw lab work on her, expecting to find either a very high or very low WBC, and check her LFTs, which should show the elevated bilirubin and alk phos. I would get a stat bedside ultrasound of the right upper quadrant just to show the dilated biliary radical, and that would be enough for me to call the GI doctors to get in here and do an ERCP for this patient.

WBC is 21K, bilirubin is 5, LFTs are elevated, and US shows dilated biliary radicals with no mass in the head of the pancreas. There are some stones noted in the gallbladder. She goes for her ERCP, all goes well, they leave a stent after removing some impacted stones, but when she returns her blood pressure is still 90 and her pulse is 110. The urine output is good.

So I don't know the status of the a-fib and there is no evidence of acute MI. I would get an EKG to make sure this is a-fib, and send labs for cardiac enzymes to rule out an MI. Also, I like the fact that she is making good urine and it tells me that she is perfusing well, but she is hypotensive and I don't know why. I would place a PA catheter to tell me a little more about her heart function and her vascular resistance. Since she is making good urine at this time, I am not willing to start any kind of pressors.

Her wedge pressure is 4.

I have not done a very good job resuscitating her, and I would bolus her 500 ml boluses, watching her CI and wedge pressure. I want to get her to wedge around 12-14, as long as the CI does not fall.

What if the wedge is 16 and the BP is still 90?

Then you have plenty of fluid on board and I would look at the SVR and CI. Depending on which one is low, she could be in cardiogenic shock or septic shock.

What if the heart rate was 140 and the wedge was 12?

Sound like unstable a-fib and I may consider synchronized cardioversion.

(1) Acalculus Cholecystitis*

H&P

Commonly this is an inpatient who is S/P CABG, Aorta, "big surgery" who is on TPN, NPO and in the ICU.

On physical exam they are found to have fever, RUQ pain, high WBC, and increased LFT's.

Diagnosis

RUQ ultrasound shows a thickened gallbladder wall, pericholecystic fluid, but no stones. HIDA is not good choice in a patient that has acute inflammation and is NPO.

Treatment

The patient is started on antibiotics. If they can tolerate surgery, then optimize them and do a laparoscopic cholecystectomy. In critically ill patients, you can have IR place a percutaneous trans-hepatic cholecystostomy tube under US or CT guidance. This is 95-100% successful. If there is no IR available, then you can do an open cholecystostomy tube at the bedside under local anesthetic.

Example Case

You are asked to see a 70 year old man 3 days out from a mitral valve replacement. He is on the floor and complains of RUQ tenderness. What do you want to do?

I assume that everything has gone well from his valve surgery, and I would find out from the chart if this was a tissue valve (would make more sense at his age) and if not, is he anticoagulated already. My concern is that he has cholecystitis, and I don't want his valve infected. If he has not already started running a fever that would be good, and I would check labs to make sure he does not have a leukocytosis. I would send of LFT's as to check his bilirubin.

I did get a bit ahead of myself; I certainly would like to meet the patient and ask him about a history of gallbladder disease or stones, or problems like this in the past, and examine the abdomen for peritonitis. I would check his vitals and make sure he is doing well.

Well he has never had problems with his gallbladder before, he seems quite well, but he is tender in the RUQ. He has had some low grade temperature, however, and his white count is 16 k. His alk phos is slightly elevated as well.

I would get an US of the gallbladder to look for stones or signs of infection, and I would empirically start antibiotics to cover gram negatives and anaerobes.

The GB US shows slight dilation of all the ducts and gallbladder without any stones. There is no wall thickening or pericholecystic fluid.

I would expect some thickening if this was his gallbladder, you did not tell me if the bilirubin was elevated, but I would assume that it is if his ducts are dilated and alk phos is high. This makes me worry about a stone in the CBD. Since the patient is stable, I would get a MRCP.

Well, they cannot get to him until tomorrow and his pain gets worse now. What do you want to do for him?

Based on these symptoms and lab findings, I think his gallbladder is bad, he has acalculus cholecystitis and I would take him to the operating room and perform a laparoscopic cholecystectomy with IOC.

Do you do an IOC on all your laparoscopic cholecystectomies?

No, only in those people who I have a reason to believe may have a stone in their ducts by evidence of elevated bilirubin or dilated ducts, or if they have had a recent episode of gallstone pancreatitis.

(1) Primary Sclerosing Cholangitis

H&P

This is a rare problem and patients have increased LFT's, pain, jaundice, and purities. They may have a history of UC, cholangitis, and cirrhosis.

Physical exam is normal. They may be jaundice or have stigmata of cirrhosis.

Diagnosis

Get LFT's to document their liver function. And ERCP will show you the strictures of the biliary tract. Note the intra- and extra-hepatic disease. A liver biopsy should be done to determine the stage of the disease. Stage I is portal inflammation, stage II is portal and peri-portal inflammation, and stage III is bridging fibrosis.

Treatment

Medical therapy is ineffective. Anti-inflammatory and immunosuppressive like corticosteroids; ASA, colchicine and azathiprine are all worthless. Ursodeoxycholic acid relieves symptoms and decreases LFT's, but does not prevent progression of disease.

Non-operative maneuvers include balloon dilation. This can help the symptoms but does not stop the disease and may increases the risk of cholangiocarcinoma

Percutaneous stenting may be of some benefit to assist in dissection of hepatic ducts during operative intervention, and it can assist in the exchange for larger silastic stents.

Operative therapy for those without intrahepatic disease includes a near total ductal excision and a hepatico-jejunosotomy over silastic stents with 0000-PDS and a retro colic Roux-en-Y. Closed suction drainage is appropriate. This will postpone transplant.

If the patient has cirrhosis, they need a transplant.

(0) Choledochal Cyst

H&P

People with this problem have a history of RUQ pain, jaundice, acute pancreatitis, acute cholangitis, or biliary cirrhosis

Diagnosis

Ultrasound and CT can give you the diagnosis and define the anatomy reasonably well. ERCP is diagnostic and clearly defines the anatomy of the cyst, location of the pancreatic duct and can be therapeutic if sphincterotomy or stent is needed.

Type	Description	% of All Cysts
Type I (chole-dochal cyst)	Cystic, fusiform saccular extrahepatic biliary dilatation	50%–80%
Mixed type I and II	Fusiform dilatation of the extrahepatic biliary tree in combination with a separate diverticulum, mid-portion of the common bile duct, with cystic duct entering in the right of the diverticulum	1%
Type II	Extrahepatic biliary diverticulum	2%–3%
Type III (chole-dochocele)	Dilatation of extrahepatic intraduodenal biliary tree	<10%
Type IVA	Intrahepatic and extrahepatic saccular/cystic dilatation	30%–40%
B	Multiple extrahepatic cysts	<5%
Type V (Caroli's disease)	Intrahepatic biliary cyst	<10%

Treatment

Treatment is surgical excision if possible. If it is too close to the portal vein, then a portion of the cyst must be left behind.

For type I, cyst excision or choledocho-J.

The type II cysts require excision and primary closure over a T-tube.

Type III requires cyst excision (leaving intrapancreatic portion) and a choldocho-J or hepatico-J (malignant potential is low).

Type IV cysts are treated with lobectomy and Roux-en-Y hepatico-jejunostomy (RYHJ) if intrahepatic, or if diffuse then they need a transplant. Excise all extrahepatic cysts and do a RYHJ.

Type V cyst get actigall to reduce biliary sludge and reduce stasis. You can do a lobectomy for localized disease in one lobe or transplant for diffuse disease in bilateral lobes.

(0) Biliary Cancer

H&P

These patients will have symptoms similar to symptomatic cholelithiasis.

Physical is normal.

Diagnosis

You do a cholecystectomy and the path report comes back cancer. You have a diagnosis. Ultrasound findings that may suggest cancer include a mass >1cm, calcified gallbladder wall, discontinuous wall layers, and loss of interface between the GB and liver.

Treatment

Treatment is based on T stage.

T:Primary Tumors	
Tx	Primary tumor cannot be assessed
T0	No evidence of primary tumor
Tis	Carcinoma in situ
T1	Tumor invades lamina propria or muscle layer
T1a	Tumor invades lamina propria
T1b	Tumor invades muscle layer
T2	Tumor invades perimuscular connective tissue, no extension beyond serosa or into liver
T3	Tumor perforates serosa (visceral peritoneum) or directly invades the liver and/or one other adjacent organ or structure, e.g., stomach, duodenum, colon, pancreas, omentum, extrahepatic bile ducts
T4	Tumor invades main portal vein or hepatic artery, or invades two or more extrahepatic organs or structures

For early staged tumors (Tis and T1a), simple cholecystectomy is enough.

For T1b and T2 lesions, resection of the tumor, 2 cm of the gallbladder fossa and lymphadenectomy is done. Lymphadenectomy consists of dissection of the lymph node beds in the porta hepatis, gastroduodenal ligament, gastrohepatic ligament, and a Kocher maneuver with removal of the lymph nodes along the posterior duodenum,

For T3 and T4 lesions, metastatic disease should be ruled out radiologicaly and then by placing a laparoscopy in before laparotomy. The tumor should not be resected if it can not be completely removed because there is no survival benefit to debulking the tumor. If any other adjacent organs are involved (colon, stomach or duodenum), they should be resected as well to get negative margins. Large segments of the liver (e.g. segments 4-8) may need resection if involved. The most important factor for survival is resection of the tumor with negative margins, preferably greater than 2 cm.

Para-aortic lymph node involvement has an equal survival rate as gallbladder cancer with distant metastasis and therefore should be a contraindication to operation.

(0) Extra Hepatic Biliary Cancer

H&P

Risk factors include PSC, choledochocyst, radiation, and clonorchis. They present with painless jaundice, weight loss, fatigue, abdominal pain, and biliary colic.

Diagnosis

PTC and ERCP with biopsy or washings is the best way to make the diagnosis. You want to rule out non-malignant causes like choledocholithiasis (US), extrinsic compression from lymph node at porta (colon cancer colonoscopy, breast cancer MMG, or lymphoma), and PSC.

CT san should be done to see the extent of the tumor, if there is vascular invasion or lymphadenopathy, and if there is any distant metastasis. It will also tell you if this is a proximal, middle, or distal CBD tumor.

MRI or angiogram is used to assess any vessel invasion. The lesion is unresectable if it is multi-focal hepatic disease, portal vein involvement, or hepatic artery involvement.

Treatment

At the time of operation, use laparoscopy to determine if the lymph nodes are involved, liver mets, peritoneal implants, and the extension of the tumor. If the patient is not resectable, then drain the biliary system with either a stent via ERCP/PTC or biliary-enteric anastomosis.

For resectable proximal tumors (Klatskin), you do a distal to proximal dissection, en bloc resection to include cholecystectomy, resect to healthy right and left ducts, resect the caudate lobe if needed and perform a RYHJ.

For middle lesions, resect the GB and CBD to the intra pancreatic portion and hepatic ducts, and then create the RYHJ.

For distal lesions, or intrapancreatic extension, the patient needs a Whipple.

Additional Therapy

Palliative therapy goals include biliary drainage and prevent cholangitis. This may involve PTC catheters changed out every 3 months or with malfunction. Unresectable cancer has a 10 month median survival. There is no adjuvant chemotherapy.

(1) Miscellaneous Gallbladder

Indications for CBD exploration: multiple stones, primary CBD stones, benign CBD stricture, prior surgery, no GI available, stones >1.5cm, unsuccessful lap CBDE, impacted stone.

Contraindications include portal HTN, severe periportal inflammation, cholangitits with septic shock, and CBD <5mm (high risk of stricture)

CBD exploration is done through a right subcostal incision. Perform an IOC. If there are just a few small stones, give glucagon and flush. If the stones persist, do a Kocher maneuver, trace the cystic duct to the CBD and aspirate it to ensure that it is the CBD. Place 5-0 vicryl suture as stay suture and make a 1.5 cm longitudinal incision in the duct. Flush it with saline via a 10Fr red rubber catheter. Place a flexible choldochocscope and pass a 4 Fr Fogarty or use a basket to retrieve stones. Leave a T-tube in after you are done. Perform a completion cholangiogram to ensure the stones are gone, repeat this in 3 weeks. If there are retained stones, wait another 3 weeks and try to extract stones via the tube. If it is normal, then remove the T-tube.

Indications for an open cholecystectomy include gallbladder cancer, cirrhosis, severe pulmonary disease, low cardiac output, pregnancy in the third trimmest, and part of another open procedure.

Intra-operative recognition of common bile duct injury requires that you assess the situation. Do not open if you are not prepared for the dissection and reconstruction or you will make the situation worse. If no expert is available, place closed suction drains and transfer to a high volume center. Type A injury is a cystic duct leak or a liver bed leak. Suture ligation and closed suction drainage is adequate. Type D injury is lateral injury to major ducts. Closure of the defect over a t-tube and closed suction drainage should be done. If there is an avulsion of the cystic duct, same as above. If there is more than a 50%

circumferential injury or complete transection of the duct, you will need to do a RYHJ.

Post-operative recognition of injury may be recognized early, in which case you should do PTC/ERCP with stent, percutaneous drains, antibiotics and wait 3 months for inflammation to calm down before repair. Type B injury is a clipped aberrant right hepatic duct. This will require a RYHJ (or hepatic resection if an anastomosis is not possible). Type C is a leaking cut end of right aberrant hepatic duct. If it is a small duct (< 1mm), then ligate it. If it is a large duct, then place pre-operative catheters via PTC and perform a RYHJ.

(1) Gallstone Illeus

H&P

Patients will present with 1-2 weeks of crampy, intermittent abdominal pain (tumbling obstruction), nausea, vomiting, history of gallstone, and postprandial colic.

Diagnosis

Flat and upright x-rays of the abdomen may reveal a small bowel obstruction, pneumobilia, or you may see the gallstone in the right lower quadrant. CT scan may show the same if it is not obvious on plain films.

Treatment

Hydrate the patient and start antibiotics. They are made NPO and given an NGT. Correct electrolytes. Patient has a small bowel obstruction and will need an operation to fix it, so get them ready for the operating room. 65% of the time, the stone will be lodged in the ileocecal valve.

On exploration, examine the entire GI tract to look for other stones that may need to be removed. Milk the stone back to healthy proximal small bowel, perform an enterotomy and extract the stone. If there is any bowel ischemia, it should be resected and a primary bowel anastomosis is done. Do not go for the cholecystectomy.

Additional Therapy

After 8 weeks, when the inflammation is decreased, go back for the open cholecystectomy, excise the fistula, and close the defect. I would only do this in a young patient in which the lifetime risk of recurrence (4.7%) or cancer is significant. In the elderly or frail, I would not do this.

(5) Portal Hypertension and Shunts*

H&P

Patient may have a history of ETOH abuse, present with massive UGIB, have cirrhosis, or hepatitis.

Physical exam may reveal stigmata of liver failure. If they are bleeding, assess their stability.

Diagnosis

For those presenting with an upper GI bleed, diagnosis is made with an emergent EGD to determine the cause (gastric or esophageal varicies, PUD, etc.).

Ultrasound may show refractory ascites. These patients may be on nephrotoxic meds (NSAIDs, aminoglycosides) which can worsen the ascites. Check the fluid for cell count, culture, total protein, and total albumin.

Spontaneous bacterial peritonitis is diagnosed by 250 PMNs/mm^3 with a positive culture for one organism.

Encephalopathy is diagnosed by confusion, and you can document an elevated NH$_3$ level.

Child-Pugh Classification of Cirrhosis

Parameter	1 Point	2 Points	3 Points
Albumin (g/dl)	>3.5	2.8–3.5	<2.8
Bilirubin (mg/dl)	<2	2–3	>3
INR	<1.7	1.7–2.3	>2.3
Ascites	None	Slight	Moderate
Encephalopathy	None	1–2	3–4

Child-Pugh classification is calculated by summing the points per parameter to arrive at a total between 5 and 15. *INR,* international normalized ratio.

Grade A = 5–6, grade B = 7–9, Grade C = 10–15.

Treatment

EGD will allow you to perform sclerotherapy or banding to control the bleeding. Octreotide and vasopressin drips can help control the bleeding from varicies. A PPI drip should be started.

Up to 95% of the time, endoscopic maneuvers are successful. Banding is better than sclerotherapy because there is a lower complication rate, lower recurrent bleed rate, lower stricture rate, and sclerotherapy is not effective for prevention.

If all else fails, place a SB (Minnesota) tube for 48 hours. If they still cannot be controlled after the SB tube, and they are a transplant candidate, then consult IR for TIPS. If the patient is not a candidate for transplant, then get a duplex study to evaluate the portal and splenic vein patency.

If they are both patent, and they do not have risk factors that make TIPS a better option (major abdominal surgical history, significant cardiopulmonary impairment, irreversible encephalopathy, sepsis on pressors), then do a mesocaval shunt.

If the PV is patent, but SV is thrombosed, then do a splenenctomy.

If the PV is thrombosed and SV is patent, find out if there is ascitis. If yes, then splenorenal interposition graft is used. If no, then do a Warren's (spleno-renal) shunt (see procedures).

If both are thrombosed, then do a gastric devascularization procedure.

Once they are controlled, continue to stabilize them, B-block then to decrease venous pressure, and counsel them to quit ETOH.

Indications for TIPS include: esophageal bleeding refractory to meds or endoscopic maneuvers, intractable ascitis, non-surgical candidates to surgical shunts, bridge to transplant, and portal HTN secondary to Budd-Chiari syndrome. These patients should have a base-line duplex and LFT's prior to TIPS and every 6 month for one year, then yearly. Any re-bleeding or worsening ascitis repeat the dilation and place additional stents.

Additional Therapy

Ascitis should be treated with low Na diet, spironolactone, and lasix. If this does not help, check a 24 hour urine Na. If there is >78 meq/24 hours, then the patient is non-compliant. If it is < 10 meq/24hours, then they are compliant.

Other treatments include therapeutic paracentesis (up to 5L per session, every other week) and TIPS.

Spontaneous bacterial peritonitis (SBP) is treated with empirical antibiotics (ofloxacin, cefotaxime, and cipro).

To treat encephalopathy, rule out other causes (UTI, peritonitis, acute liver failure, GI bleed, etc). Restrict the diet to 1 gm/kg/day of protein. Start them on lactulose. Neomycin by mouth can kill off the colonic flora that produces urea and decrease the NH3 level.

Example Case

You are asked to consult on a 42 year old alcoholic woman who has been on the medical service for two weeks after being admitted for bleeding esophageal varicies. The bleed has resulted in a two unit transfusion and had resolved spontaneously. She has a bilirubin of 2, albumin of 3, and no obvious ascitis. She is now stable and ready for discharge, and you are asked to render a surgical opinion.

Well this lady is a Childs A or B cirrhotic (depending on her INR), has had a bleed that spontaneously stopped, and I am assuming that they want me to decide if a shunt should be done. Normally, I would not consider a surgical shunt in a patient unless it is the last option or he has intractactable bleeding, but I would work her up in the event she needs one soon for re-bleeding. The next thing to do is to verify with the endoscopist that there were no gastric varicies or ulcers and it was esophageal varicies that were bleeding, get a biopsy of the liver to confirm the diagnosis of cirrhosis, you told me she has no ascites and I will assume that is documented with an US or CT scan, asses the patentency of the portal vein and splenic vein with a duplex US (assuming all is patent), and confirm that there is a high portal wedge pressure (>20). If all this is the case, then she is a good candidate for a TIPS or distal spleno-renal shunt. However, she should be treated medically first with beta blockers and get her to some AA meeting to help her stop drinking. I would recommend that the gastroenterologist begin banding or injecting these varicies on an outpatient basis

She fails to follow up with the enterologist, and two months later they call you from the ER where this same patient is having a massive hemorrhage and is hypotensive and frankly jaundice. What do you want to do now?

I would go to the emergency room, make sure she did not need to be intubated, get some IV lines in her and start giving her some boluses to get her blood pressure up. I need to start a blood transfusion as well. I would have the nurses starting getting a PPI, octreotide, and vasopressin drip ready for the patient. I would send of hemoglobin and get a gastroenterologist in there PDQ for a therapeutic endoscopy. Assuming he can control…

Nope, he can't see a thing, and she is continuing to bleed. She remains hypotensive.

I have never place a SB tube before, but this sounds like a time to use it. I would place an NGT to suction; rapid sequences induce her, and then place the tube down to tamponade the bleeding.

How do you put that tube down?

You insert in the mouth until you think you are in the stomach, then inflate the balloon to 50 cc and get an x-ray. You confirm it is in the stomach and then fully inflate it to 500 ml and pull back. Check the proximal port and if there is still bleeding, then you inflate the esophageal balloon to 30 mmHg pressure and secure it the patient. I would leave this in for 24 hours, and the plan will be to take it out and put a scope in immediately to make sure the bleeding stopped and try any endoscopic therapy.

Well it doesn't stop, and endoscopy doesn't work again.

Then I would put the SB down again, the same way, and call IR to do a TIPS procedure.

IR performs TIPS. What is this?

It is a shunt between the portal vein radicals in the liver and the hepatic veins.

She bleeds again the next day.

I would get a duplex ultrasound of the TIPS.

It's obstructed.

Then I would take her to the operating room. I have never been in this situation, or seen this situation, before in my training; however, if I am the only surgeon around to do this, then I would try to save her life by doing a side-to-side mesocaval shunt to decompress the esophageal varicies through the short gastric and splenic veins. If she is really unstable, I could open the stomach anteriorly and ligate the varicies directly or fire an EEA circular stapler to completely divide and reanastomose the esophagus.

(10) Pancreas

(2) Acute Pancreatitis*

H&P

This is a serious infirmity. Ask them about their biliary history, ETOH use, current medications, recent ERCP, infections, or trauma. Think about the differential diagnosis and use this to formulate the H&P (MI, reflux, AAA/dissection, Boorhave's, gastric volvulus).

Physical exam involves auscultation of the heart, vitals, "eye-ball" sign, abdominal exam for peritonitis, check the monitor and rhythm, etc.

Diagnosis

Amylase and lipase is usually elevated and will lead you to the diagnosis. You need to rule out the other causes, so get cardiac enzymes, chest x-ray, US of the abdomen (focused on RUQ to look for stone because it will change your management, see below), and check WBC. CT scan is the best test to get because it will show the inflammation around the pancreas, and it will be able to tell you what portion of the gland is necrotic (or ischemic), establishing a base line.

Calculate Ranson's criteria: glucose, AST, LDH, WBC, age. CRP>150 may indicate increased severity.

Treatment

Based on the severity, the patient is admitted to the floor or ICU (lean toward the ICU) and place them on IVF, NGT if vomiting, antibiotics if significant necrosis is seen on CT or CRP is >150 (primaxin and diflucan), DVT and GI prophylaxis, hydration is a big deal, place a Foley and keep their output >50 ml/hr (they may need a lot of volume), and give them pain medication.

Follow serial labs and calculate Ranson's after 48 hours: calcium, hematocrit, PaO2, BUN, base deficit, and fluid sequestration.

The treatment of pancreatitis is conservative at first. 80% will resolve spontaneously. You have to consider the presence of gallstone in the management.

If the pancreatitis is mild and there are no stones, then continue supportive care and follow serial abdominal exams, labs, and symptoms. If they are progressing by 48 hours, then advance diet slowly.

If it is mild with stones, then continue supportive care and serial exams. If mild, do a lap cholecystectomy with IOC within 4 days. More severe disease; you may wait a couple of weeks for the inflammation to go down.

Severe disease with gallstones needs ICU supportive care. Get an ERCP for evacuation of stones if no improvement in 24 hours. If they do not have gallstones, then repeat the CT in 48 hours to look for necrosis, pseudo cyst, abscess, phlegmon, or fluid collections if not improving.

At this time, I would get an FNA with gram stain and cultures. If the fluid is sterile, then continue aggressive supportive care. Continue this for 3-4 weeks, but consider going to the operating room if it last longer than this, or the patient is worsening, in order to debride and place a feeding J-tube. The reasons to wait are to allow demarcation of necrosis, avoid the pro-inflammatory mediators, and avoid converting a sterile fluid collection into an infected one.

Infected fluid collections need large percutaneous drains. If the drains fail to help the patient within 24 to 48 hours, then take them to the operating room for surgical debridement and feeding J-tube placement. Don't mess around with percutaneous drains too long on the boards (this is not the IR oral exam!).

Infected necrosis needs to go to the operating room immediately for debridement and feeding J-tube. Mortality here is 50%.

Additional Therapy

Debridement involves a midline incision, enter the lesser sac, blunt finger dissection suction all loose material, irrigate with copious amounts of warm saline, leave two large sump drains above and below the pancreas at the tail and head, and place a feeding J-tube. Leave the abdomen open and re-explore every 48 hours until no further debridement is needed.

Other options include open packing and continuous lavage.

Complications of debridement include pancreatic fistula (treat with ERCP and percutaneous drain or pancreatic resection/ enteric drainage), intestinal fistula (gastric-excised, duodenal-drainage/TPN, and small bowel or colon- resection and ostomy), hemorrhage (angiography and embolization), and pancreatic insufficiency (pancreases and insulin).

Example Case

You were called by the ER doctor to evaluate a 55 year old man with abdominal pain. He states that he is swamped and the patient is in the other room and asks you to take care of it. What are you going to do?

I would go see this man and get an idea of when this pain started and what type of pain it is. I would be interested in what started the pain, what makes it worse or better.

He states that he was fine until last night, after he had a few drinks, the pain started and it is radiating into his back.

Sound like pancreatitis. I would ask him more about his drinking history and ask him if he has any history of pancreatitis. I would also be concerned about PUD with perforation, AAA dissection, gastric volvulus, bowel obstruction, or gallbladder problems as well, and focus a history on these subjects. Given an otherwise negative history, I am still concerned for pancreatitis; so, I would examine the abdomen and make sure there is no peritonitis, pulsatile masses, and check the rectal vault for masses or blood.

He has a negative past history. He has some rebound tenderness in the middle of the abdomen, but that is it. Now what?

I would start IV fluids on him and send labs to include a CBC to check his white count, LDH may be elevated in pancreatitis, amylase and lipase may be high, and LFTs (in particular the AST) will be high in pancreatitis, send off chemistries and check the glucose. I would order an upright chest x-ray to rule out free air from a perforated DU, and get a flat and upright of the abdomen to see if there are any air fluid levels.

After I have given him a couple of liters of fluids and his labs come back, I would make sure his renal function is normal, and if this looks like pancreatitis, then I would get a CT scan to get an idea of how severe it is and if there is much necrosis of the pancreas.

His amylase is 1500. How do you want to monitor his fluids?

I would place a Foley catheter and based on the labs I send, I would determine how severe the pancreatitis is (using Ranson's criteria) and place him in the ICU if it is very severe.

It is severe and he is only making 5 cc/hour of urine. What are you going to do?

I am going to continue to give him fluids at a very good rate and bolus him. I would place a central line now, and monitor the CVP to ensure that I am giving him enough volume and get the CVP up to 10-12.

You get it up to 8 and the nurse is calling you because he is very short of breath now. What do you think?

I think I am flooding his lungs, but he needs the fluid to prevent dehydration, renal failure, and pancreatic necrosis. So I would go see him and electively intubate him if I have to; however, I would continue to fluid resuscitate him.

What ventilator setting do you want?

I would put him on an IMV mode, with an 8-10 cc/kg tidal volume and PEEP and PS at 5, and I would give him 100% FiO2 as need to keep his saturations >92%. I would wean down that O2 ASAP.

He still is not making much urine, and he is a little hypotensive. What are you going to do now?

I am missing something here, because I am pounding him with fluids, he is on the ventilator now and he is dying in front of me. I assuming I never got a chance to get that CT scan.

No, do you want it now?

If he is stable enough, then yes I would get it. Something is not right here.

Ok, the patient is pretty pale at this point and you take him down to the scanner and see a large retroperitoneal hematoma along the pancreas.

So he has hemorrhagic pancreatitis. I would send for a stat T&C and check a Hgb.

His Hgb is 3.

I would begin transfusing him PRBCs and FFP in a 1:1 ratio until I could get his Hgb above 7.

How many units would that take?

It will probably take about 4 units or so.

What if he does not respond to the blood like you think he should?

Then he may be actively bleeding and I would ask for an angiogram and possible embolization of the bleeding vessels. If this could not be done, or they could not successfully stop the bleeding then I would take him to the operating room, get proximal and distal control of the aorta and open the hematoma to find the bleeder. This would be a desperate attempt to save his life with a poor prognosis.

(0) Chronic Pancreatitis

H&P

Patients are often thought to be drug seekers, they have a history of acute pancreatitis, and most commonly ETOH abuse is the cause. They complain of chronic abdominal pain, weight loss, steatorrhea, exocrine and endocrine insufficiency, and malnutrition. They can present with anatomical complications like CBD stricture (symptoms of biliary obstruction, duodenal obstruction, SV thrombosis).

Physical is generally unremarkable.

Diagnosis

Plain x-rays of the abdomen may show calcification in the pancreas, and this is a unique finding of chronic pancreatitis. US, CT, ERCP are utilized to image the anatomy and rule out malignancy and duct stricture.

Treatment

Basic treatment goals are mainly palliative, rule out malignancy, long term pain relief, and preserve the exocrine and endocrine function of the pancreas.

Initial treatment should be non-surgical with analgesics, enzyme replacement, and insulin replacement. If this is successful, then continue. If this fails, then they may need surgery.

Indications for surgery include intractable pain, frequent relapse, decreased quality of life, narcotic addiction, SV thrombosis, pancreatic fistula, obstructive symptoms, or suspected malignancy.

For patients with intractable pain with proximal disease, you need to rule out cancer and then proceed with a Whipple, Frey or Begar. Frey is coring out the pancreatic head and doing a longitudinal pancreatico-jejunostomy (PJ). Begar is coring out the head with a roux limb to drain the head and tail.

For intractable pain with localized distal disease, then do a PJ if there is a dilated duct (duct must be > 7mm) or distal pancreatectomy.

If the duct is < 4mm, bilateral thoracic splanchniectomy is offered.

If there is biliary obstruction, you must rule out CBD stones, get and ERCP, sphicnterotomy and stenting. If this does not help, then do a choledocho-J.

(0) Pancreatic Divisum

H&P

10% of people have this and they present with recurrent acute pancreatitis.

Diagnosis

RUQ US may be suggestive. ERCP is diagnostic because they will be able to rule out cancer, and they will not see the ventral duct (which normally drains the head and neck of the pancreas). CT scan is used to rule out a mass in the pancreas.

Treatment

If the patient is having chronic pancreatitis, you have to rule out other etiologies like biliary stones or ETOH abuse. They must be severely symptomatic before surgery is offered. If gallbladder is present, remove it and do IOC. An ERCP is done and shows dilated duct do a Peustow. If there is stenosis, do a distal pancreatectomy.

If the patient is having recurrent acute pancreatitis or recurrent pain and hyperamylasemia, then usually this is associated with a stenotic dorsal duct opening and responds well to dorsal duct sphicnterotomy.

US the pancreas with simultaneous secretin injection and observe the dilation of the duct. This will cause pain. Do an ERCP and stent the duct, and if this relieves the pain, then sphicnterotomy will help.

Intra-operatively, if the duct is healthy, do the sphicnterotomy; however, if the duct is fibrosed and dilated do a PJ. If it is stenotic do a distal pancreatectomy.

(0) Pancreatic Pseudocyst

H&P

Patients can present with early satiety, gastric outlet obstruction (GOO), jaundice, abdominal pain, acute pancreatitis, pancreatic trauma, or chronic symptoms. Ask about history of pancreatitis, biliary symptoms, ETOH use, medication list, recent ERCP or infections, weight loss, diabetes, or fever.

Physical may reveal jaundice, abdominal mass or peritoneal signs.

Diagnosis

RUQ ultrasound is done to rule out biliary cause and usually finds the cyst. CT scan will demonstrate the number of cyst, size and location, and relationship to other structures.

Treatment

If the cyst is < 6 cm and asymptomatic, then observe them for symptoms and repeat the CT in 6 weeks to 2 months to see if it has decreased in size. Do nothing unless it is > 6cm or symptomatic.

If it is > 6cm, repeat study in 6 weeks, if it is smaller or stable and the patient is asymptomatic, then observe. Complications of observation include obstructive symptoms, portal HTN (SV thrombosis), hemosuccus pancreaticus, infection, fistula, or rupture.

If the cyst enlarges or the cyst is any size and symptomatic, then do an ERCP to see if it communicates with the pancreatic duct. If there is no communication then you can percutaneouly drain it and send the fluid for analysis (CEA, mucin, CA 19-9 and amylase). Complications of aspiration include recurrence (70%) and 15% fistula formation. If there is communication with the duct, then you should do surgical drainage.

If the cyst is suspicious for malignancy, do fluid analysis. Cystic neoplasms will have a low amylase (pseudo cyst have high amylase), and you may have positive mucin, CA 19-9, or increased CEA.

Transpapillary and transgastric endoscopic therapy are possible. Open techniques include cystgastrectomy by performing an anterior gastrotomy, aspirating the cyst on the posterior wall of the stomach, coring out a 5 cm section and sending it for pathology (rule out cancer), and doing a continuous running vicryl cyst edge to stomach. A 60 cm roux limb can be brought to the cyst and anastomosed in 2 layers.

(1) Pancreatic Ductal Disruption

H&P

This can lead to a fistula, ascitis, or pleural effusions. Pt will present with acute or chronic pancreatitis; therefore, ask about causes of pancreatitis.

Physical exam may reveal a fluid wave, suggestive of ascitis.

Diagnosis

Send basic labs (commonly find low Na and HCO3) and check a pre-albumin level. CT scan will show fluid and pancreatic inflammation. If you suspect disruption based on history and presence of ascitis on physical exam and US, then you may do a paracentesis and find a high amylase. Send the fluid for cultures. At this point, do an ERCP to identify the site of disruption (which will determine the surgical treatment) and place a trans-papillary stent to decrease the pressure and assist with spontaneous closure of the duct.

Treatment

For pancreatic ascitis, place a central line and start TPN and make the patient NPO. Start them on octreotide to decrease pancreatic output. Place percutaneous drains and/or a chest tube for external drainage.

If there is a dilated pancreatic duct (> 7mm), then do a pancreatico-jejunosotmy (PJ).

If the duct is dilated (> 7mm) and there is a pseudo cyst, then do a PJ with cyst incorporation.

If the duct is not dilated and there is tail disruption, do a distal pancreatectomy. For body disruption, distal pancreatectomy is done. Extended distal pancreatectomy is done for neck disruption, and operative debridement and ERCP with stenting is done for head disruption.

If the patient develops a cutaneous fistula, wait at least 6 weeks to give it a chance to heal unless there is a dilated duct. If it persists for more than 2 to 3 months, consider surgical resection based on ERCP findings.

Pleural effusions can present from a posterior disruption. Place chest tubes, TPN, and octreotide. Do an ERCP and stent. Evaluate with ERCP and consider surgical treatment based on these results.

(7) Peri-Ampullary Cancer/Pancreatic Cancer*

H&P

Patient will have painless obstructive jaundice. Ask about biliary colic, abdominal pain, weight loss, and ETOH and tobacco use. The patient may have blood per rectum.

Physical is focused on the abdomen, palpable gallbladder, ascitis, umbilical nodes, or supraclavicular adenopathy.

Diagnosis

Essentially, you are working up obstructive jaundice and thinking cancer. Check their LFT's, amylase, and lipase. Send a CEA and CA 19-9.

Get a GB US to rule out CBD stones.

CT scan will show you if there are any masses and assist you with staging (liver mets, peritoneal mets, invasion into the PV/common hepatic/SMV/SMA/celiac, ascitis).

You need to get an ERCP with stenting for relief, and they may be able to get you positive cytology on brushings or biopsy. EUS (with FNA) will assess the mesenteric vascular invasion, nodal involvement, provide biopsy for diagnosis, and may offer alternative diagnoses.

Treatment

There may be no local vascular invasion or metastatic disease. Maximize their nutrition and cardiopulmonary status and do a staging laparoscopy and rule out peritoneal or liver mets. You should biopsy areas as needed. 30% are upgraded here. If they are unresectable, palliate with gastric or biliary bypass. If they are resectable, proceed with a Whipple.

If there is vascular invasion, then do EUS with FNA or CT guided biopsy to confirm the diagnosis of cancer. Give neo-adjuvant chemo radiation and reassess in 3 months.

If there is metastatic disease, then do the same as for vascular invasion. Palliation therapy may be warranted.

Additional Therapy

Palliation may include gastro-J bypass or duodenal stenting, hepatico-J, and chemical splanchniectomy with 50% ETOH to the celiac plexus.

5-FU, gemcitabine, and external radiation may increase median survival to 12 months for unresectable cancer.

Example Case

A 60 year old man presents you with painless jaundice, blood per rectum, and weight loss. How would you like to proceed?

Since my first concern is that he has a malignancy given the bleeding and weight loss, and that it is around the bile ducts or involving them directly, I would proceed with a focused history about his timing around the jaundice, when the blood started and how much weight he has lost. I would assess his risk factors for colon cancer, pancreatic cancer, and biliary cancer. Assuming that it otherwise, unremarkable, then I would focus my exam on the abdomen and rectal exam. I may find lymph node disease that could be FNA'ed for a diagnosis. If I do not, then I would get CBC to assess how anemic he may be, chemistries with LFTs to assess his liver function and bilirubin, and an albumin to assess his nutritional status. In addition to these, I would send a CEA and CA 19-9. I would order a right upper quadrant ultrasound which may be able to show me a mass in the pancreas and if there is dilated biliary radicals and if he had not had a colonoscopy in the last 3 years, and then I would put him on my schedule for a colonoscopy this week.

His Hgb is 10 and bilirubin is 10. Ultrasound shows dilated intrahepatic biliary radicals, but nothing more than that could be seen. CEA and CA 19-9 are both a little elevated. Colonoscopy is negative.

That bilirubin is really high, and the dilated radicals tell me that it is post hepatic obstruction. At this time, I am thinking that the obstruction is in the biliary tree itself or is extrinsic compression. Since I am think that this is cancer, I would go ahead and get a CT scan pancreas protocol to see if there is mass in the pancreas and what involvement it has to other structures. In addition, I would consult GI to perform an ERCP to see where the blockage is, if there is a mass there, can they biopsy it, and can they place a biliary stent to relieve the jaundice?

There is a 2.5 cm, friable, mass at the ampulla that is obstructing them from cannulating the duct. They take some biopsied and this shows dyplasia.

That is a tough one, now I have this mass, the patient is symptomatic and needs it removed. If it were a cancer, she needs a Whipple, but dysplasia, may just need a local resection. This thing is so big, that I am inclined to treat this like cancer. I would assume that the CT scan did not show any evidence of liver mets, peritoneal mets, or vascular invasion.

No it did not show any of those things.

I would get a chest x-ray to make sure there are no mets to lungs. Assuming that is negative, I would consider the patient a surgical candidate. I would assess his cardiac and pulmonary status with a stress test and PFTs, respectfully. Assuming that these are fine, I would consider his nutritional status. If his albumin is less than 3 or he has lost more than 10% of his total body weight, then I would place him on a high calorie diet and start TPN as well to get his prealbumin above 15. This may take a couple of weeks. In the mean time, I could have radiology place a biliary catheter percutaneously to give him relief.

So you would offer this man a Whipple?

Yes, for the reasons I said before. He is anemic, jaundice, losing weight, the mass is big and friable, and I think it is cancer.

So how would you proceed with your operation? He is healthy and fit for it. Carry on.

I would insert a laparoscope to initially assess the liver and peritoneum. If there are any suspicious lesions, I would biopsy them and send it to pathology to rule out metastatic disease, making this unresectable. If no such lesions are found then I would proceed with bilateral subcostal incisions for exposure and assess the abdominal cavity for any metastatic disease. Finding no such disease, then I would fully kocherize the duodenum and mobilize it such that I can feel behind the pancreas and make sure this mass is not encasing the SMA and SMV. Then, I would open the duodenum longitudinally at the level of this mass on the antimesenteric border and biopsy this mass, sending a big chunk for the pathologist to give me a tissue diagnosis.

Good, it comes back as adenocarcinoma. It is resectable, you remove the specimen, how do you do your anastomosis?

It has been a long time since I have been in on a Whipple, but my recollection is that the pancreatico-J is created by sewing the mucosa of the duct to the mucosa of the jejunum with 5-0 PDS over a stent (5 Fr pediatric feeding tube) and then created a second layer to invaginate the pancreas into the jejunum. Then I would create an end to side hepatico-J with 5-0 PDS, and finish with a side to side gastro-J in two layers of Vicryl. I would place a distal feeding J-tube, NGT, and leave closed suction drains next to the pancreatico-J and hepatico-J.

On day three, He is putting out clear fluid through the drains. What would you do now?

Assuming the patient is doing well otherwise and he is stable, I would send this fluid for an amylase level, expecting that it will be high because this is a pancreatic leak.

It is very high, in the thousands. Your patient looks just fine though.

Good, then I would continue the drain to control the pancreatic fistula, and I would certainly keep him NPO. I would start TPN for the time being and begin the J-tube feed. When I was at goal with the tube feeds, then I would stop the TPN. I would put him on somatostatin to decrease the pancreatic secretion, and hope that it will close. I would give him a good 2 months to close this before I would consider having to go in and fix this. Fortunately, most of these leaks will stop on their own.

(19) Thyroid/ Parathyroid

(3) Hyperthyroidism*

H&P

Patients may present with anxiety, nervousness, palpitations, heat intolerance, weight loss, and/or excessive sweating.

Physical may reveal tachycardia, a-fib, exopthalmus, goiter, hyperreflexia, gynecomastia, and pretibial edema.

Diagnosis

The diagnosis depends on the TSH, T4, and radio-active iodine uptake (RAIU). So these are the test to get. Ultra sound may reveal masses in the thyroid.

High T4, low TSH and high RAIU indicate Grave's disease, toxic multinodular goiter, or solitary toxic nodule.

High T4, low TSH and low RAIU indicate subacute thyroiditis (see below), postpartum thyroiditis, factitious thyrotoxicosis, or stroma ovarii.

Low TSH and a normal T4 indicate subclinical hyperthyroidism, dopamine or glucocorticoid usage, or T3 toxicosis.

Treatment

Options include anti-thyroid medications (high recurrence, reserved for small glands, need to take for 1 to 2 years) such as PTU and methimazole, RAI (older patients, 2 doses needed, 90% success in Grave's, slow acting, high incidence of hypothyroidism, small risk of cancer in children), or near total thyroidectomy (done in children, young women, non-responsive or refuse RAI, failure of anti-thyroid meds, compressive symptoms, thyroid nodule unable to rule out cancer, thyrocardiac patient, severe hyperthyroidism or significant Grave's disease).

Grave's disease is treated with near total>RAI>anti-thyroid meds.

Toxic solitary nodule is treated with lobectomy>RAI

Toxic multinodular goiter is treated with subtotal thyroidectomy>RAI

Additional Therapy

Preoperative therapy includes PTU for 2 weeks, lugol's for 10 days pre-op, and propanaolol to control heart rate. Postoperatively, 0.125 mg synthroid (10-15mcg/kg) replacement is given

Hyperthyroid crisis presents with fever, tachycardia, respiratory arrest and coma. Treat it with NS bolus, versed, lugol's, PTU, hydrocorisol, propanaolol, O2 therapy, and Tylenol.

Example Case

A 30 year old woman is referred to you by her endocrinologist because she has been non-compliant with her medical regimen for Grave's disease. Otherwise, she is completely healthy and has no other medical problems, takes no medications and no surgeries in the past.

So, I am assuming that this referral is to discuss the options of subtotal thyroidectomy. I think it is a good choice for this young patient. You have given me the history, and I am assuming that her thyroid gland is unremarkable, has no nodules or masses, and she has no compressive symptoms. I will also assume that since she is non-compliant with her medications that she is probably hyperthyroid and has symptoms of such.

Yes, she is tachycardic and hypertensive. The thyroid has no nodules in it.

Well I would explain to her that we can take out her thyroid to take care of this problem; however, I need her to at least get her hyperthyroidism under control before the surgery. I would do this by starting her on PTU and a beta blocker. This may take up to two weeks to get good symptomatic control, and then I would take her to the operating room to perform a subtotal thyroidectomy.

Does she have any other options?

Yes, medication is one option, but she is non-compliant. RAI is another option, but in a young woman of child bearing age, I would not think this is a good option. Plus, 90% of these patients will develop hypothyroidism and that means she will have to take medication for the rest of her life. Again, we have a patient with compliance problems and making her hypothyroid would be a problem. So that leaves surgery.

Anything else you would do right before surgery?

I would just make sure that her hyperthyroidism is under good control with PTU and her heart rate is normal with beta blockers if needed. I do use Lugol's solution because I believe that it reduces the vascularity of the gland, but I know a lot of my colleagues would argue with me about this.

How do you do a subtotal thyroidectomy?

I like to leave a little bit of thyroid tissue at the upper and lower poles around the thyroid vessels because this decreases the chance of injuring the RLN and the parathyroids. On occasion though, I have left a bit of tissue on top of the trachea by going through the substance of the gland with small hemostat, curved side up down avoid injuring the RLN.

(0) Thyroiditis

H&P

Hyperthyroid and hypothyroid symptoms may be present.

Physical may reveal tender thyroid, goiter, erythema, or adenopathy.

Diagnosis

Hashimoto's is mostly asymptomatic. 20% of patients are hyper- and 5% hypo-thyroid at presentation. Test for thyroglobulin antibodies, thyroid microsomal antigen antibodies and thyrotropin receptor antibodies are present.

DeQuervain's thyroiditis presents with muscle aches and fever. 70% present with thyrotoxicosis, then euthyroid, then hypothyroid, finally euthyroid. The gland is tender and nodular. ESR is high, RAIU and TSH are low, and the serum thyroglobulin is high.

Postpartum presents like DeQuervain's, but have elevated antithyroid antibodies. Suppuritive thyroiditis present with infection from bacteria, fungus, TB, parasites, or AIDS.

Reidel's thyroiditis is extensive inflammation and fibrosis. Have to rule out malignancy and lymphoma.

Treatment

Treatment for Hashimoto's is non-surgical. Symptomatic treatment is given. Possibility of thyroid lymphoma requires work up of suspicious nodules.

Acute treatment for DeQuervain's thyroiditis is for thyrotoxicosis if present. Hypothyroidism is treated with synthroid, and pain is treated with NSAIDs.

Postpartum thyroiditis is treated like DeQuervain's.

Suppuritive thyroiditis treated with I&D, culture, and antibiotics.

Treatment of Riedel's is high dose steroids and perhaps tamoxifen. If they develop compression symptoms, an isthmustectomy may be in order.

(4) Thyroid Nodule*

H&P

History of head and neck radiation (for breast or NHL) predisposes to papillary cancer. Ask about family history of goiter, MEN, or isolated familial medullary cancer. They may have symptoms of hyper- or hypothyroidism, hoarseness, dyspnea, stridor, hypercalemia, or pheochromocytoma symptoms.

Physical exam is of the size, characteristics, multiplicity, and adenopathy.

Diagnosis

US and FNA are the main tests employed for diagnosis. If you suspect toxic nodule, then first get a TSH so you don't cause thyrotoxicosis.

US shows if it is cystic or solid, borders, vascular markings, calcifications, looks for nodes (FNA and suspicious), and FNA guidance if needed.

FNA is the gold standard and provides cytology but not architecture.

Treatment

If it is clear fluid, then aspirate, and send for cytology. Continue to do this up to twice more 6 months apart. Do a lobectomy if it does not resolve, has follicular particles, or cytology is concerning. Bloody fluid, send for cytology, then do a lobectomy.

For solid masses, the risk of cancer is 10% (50% in children). AMES stratifies the risk based on age (younger better), presence of suspected metastatic disease, extent of tumor (within the gland is better), and size (< 2 cm is better). The masses can also be benign, suspicious, or indeterminate.

Benign include non-toxic goiter which is treated with thyroxin suppression. If it enlarges, do a lobectomy.

Toxic Goiters and toxic multinodular goiters are treated per hyperthyroid algorithm.

Indeterminate get a repeat FNA in 6 months.

Suspicious or malignant should have surgery. Psammoma bodies (papillary), spindle (medullary), follicular, highly cellular (anaplastic) and monoclonal (lymphoma) can be seen on FNA.

For thyroid cancers, see the following section.

Example Case

A 42 year-old woman with no past medical history is referred to you because of a mass in her right neck. You examine her and find a 2 cm right thyroid nodule, but the rest of the exam is normal.

A thyroid nodule may be benign, malignant, functioning, or non-functioning. Since you told me she has no past medical history I will assume that she has no history of head and neck cancer or radiation, and there is no adenopathy. My plan at this time would be to begin the work up by sending a TSH and T4 to ensure that she is chemically euthyroid, CXR to rule out a metastatic lesion, US of the lesion to determine if it is solid or cystic and if there are any other nodules in the gland, and an FNA of the lesion to get a better idea of the pathology.

Thyroid functions are normal. Normal thyroid tissue on the FNA and the US shows a 2 cm solid mass, no other lesions.

So this is a 2 cm, non-functioning nodule of the thyroid, and FNA is normal thyroid tissue. I would ask myself if the nodule was really sampled by the FNA. My concern is that this could be a cancer (maybe a 10% chance). 90% of the time this is just a benign non-toxic goiter. So I would get a thyroid scan to make sure that this is non-functioning and get a TRH stimulation test to make sure that this is not a cold nodule and this is functioning tissue. If that is the case, then we can try thyroxin suppression with 0.125 mg of synthroid to suppress the TSH to 0.1 to 0.5. I would give this a year to see if it shrinks or goes away. If it enlarges at all during this time, I would do a lobectomy.

OK, you are in the operating room because it enlarges over then next three months. You do a lobectomy and frozen section comes back as follicular neoplasm. Now what?

Frozen section cannot tell me if there is capsular or vascular invasion of the follicular neoplasm to suggest that it is malignant. This is a young woman, and I think that there is a low risk in her, so I would stop here and wait for final path. If it comes back as cancer, then I will have to go back and take out the other side as well. If she was high risk (i.e. she was older, had a history of radiation, or had nodules on the other side by ultrasound or physical examination in the operating room), I would have to consider removal of the entire gland at the first operation. Of course, I would have discussed all these possible scenarios with the patient pre-operatively...

Sure you would. She does well and the next morning she is very hoarse. What do you tell her?

Sometime the ETT can cause an acute injury to the cords, or there may be some neuropraxia to the recurrent laryngeal. If the later is the case, she may remain hoarse up to six weeks, but it should get better. If the nerve was transected, it may be permanent.

(4) Thyroid Cancer

H&P

Patients present in the same way as they would with a thyroid nodule, and you want to ask the same questions. Do they have a history of radiation to the neck, hyper or hypothyroid symptoms, etc…?

AMES criteria determine prognosis: **A**ge, **M**itosis (differentiation), **E**xtension of tumor, and **S**ize of tumor (> 2cm).

Physical exam is similar to a neck nodule.

Diagnosis

U/S and FNA, again, is the first step in evaluating any nodule in the neck. You want to get a TSH first if you think they may be hyperthyroid so that you do not precipitate a thyrotoxic storm. Any suspicious nodes by exam or US should be FNA'ed as well. If there is history to suggest a pheochromocytoma or hyperparathyroidism, think about possible MENII and medullary cancer. Calcitonin, Ca, PTH, and urine catecholamines may be diagnostic (an, if so, send for a RET proto-oncogene test. MEN IIA 100% expressed, IIB 50% expressed).

High resolution US is finding more lymph nodes involved with papillary carcinoma, and this is leading to a more aggressive treatment for papillary carcinoma.

Treatment

If you find papillary cancer on FNA, you need to know the risk factors of the patient (AMES). If they are low risk, small nodule, then a lobectomy and isthmusectomy is probably adequate. This offers 100% 10 year survival and < 5% recurrence rates. There is a good rational for doing a total, however, and that is there is a tendency for these tumors to be multicentre, you can then follow thyroglobulin levels afterwards, and I^{131} can be used as a diagnostic and therapeutic modality for post recurrence or mets.

There are variants of papillary cancer, including the follicular subtype of papillary and the tall cell variant. Tall cell is very rare, thought to be more aggressive, but age and gender are more important to determine the prognosis. You may consider total thyroidectomy for this variant.

If the patient is high risk or has a history of radiation to the neck, then she needs a total thyroidectomy with en bloc regional lymph nodes if positive. Any disease found in the nodes on FNA warrants a MRND on that side. Prophylactic neck dissection is not standard at this time.

Follicular carcinoma is diagnosed on final pathology by capsular or vascular invasion. If carcinoma is found after a lobectomy, a completion thyroidectomy is performed. One might offer total thyroidectomy at the first operation, especially if there is anything suspicious on the opposite lobe at surgery or the patient is high risk.

Medullary cancer is usually sporadic but can be familial. It spreads by hematogenous and lymphatic drainage. You are required to rule out pheochromocytoma and hyperparathyroidism. If found, pheochromocytomas are removed first, followed by the thyroid and parathyroids. Total thyroidectomy with central lymph node dissection is the treatment for medullary carcinoma of the neck. And nodal disease laterally is treated with a MRND on that side. Prophylaxis thyroidectomy is offered at age 6 for MEN IIA and in infancy for IIB.

Anaplastic thyroid cancer is rapidly expansive with a 5 year survival of < 5% (median survival is 4 months). Treatment is multi-modality. Adrimycin, XRT for 3 weeks, debulking surgery, and maybe tracheostomy is all palliative, but does not increase survival. Surgery is usually not helpful.

Lymphoma can be found in the thyroid gland and is usually the NHL type (associated with Hashimoto's). There is a better survival if the lymphoma is intrathyroid (80% vs. 40% 5 year survival). Treatment is XRT and doxorubicin for extrathyroid lymphoma, and thyroidectomy for intrathyroid lymphoma.

Additional Therapy

Post op follow up for follicular and papillary cancer includes following the thyroglobulin levels. The patient is started on synthroid to keep the levels suppressed to 0.1 to 0.4. When the synthroid is stopped, the TSH will rise. If thyroglobulin does not rise too, there is no cancer. If the thyroglobulin rises, then there could be cancer. This prompts a radioactive iodine (RAI) scan.

All patients should have iodine scan at 6 weeks post op. This is done by holding the synthroid for 4 weeks (or cytomel for 2 weeks) in order to elevate the TSH > 30 mu/ml. The whole body scan is preformed with 3 mCi of I^{131}. If there is remnant tissue in the thyroid bed, give 30 mCi of I^{131} and repeat the scan in 6 weeks. If there is distant mets found, then give 150 mCi I^{131} and repeat in 6 weeks.

Patients are kept on synthroid long term. If there is metastatic disease that is treated, you want the TSH suppressed < 0.1 mu/ml. They should undergo, thyroglobulin levels, PE, and RAI scan every year for 5 years. After that, only thyroglobulin levels every year.

The follow up for medullay cancer is the pentagastrin stimulated calcitonin level. After a total thyroidectomy for medullary cancer, this level should be < 10 pg/ml. This level should be check every year for 5 years. If the level is greater than 10, get a neck ultrasound, CT the chest and abdomen, and get a bone scan, looking for mets.

After a total thyroidectomy, calcium should be drawn on the next day. Most patients are sent home on oral calcium, especially if you think that the glands could be in danger. In general, 1 gm of calcium per day is sufficient. You should to council the patient on symptoms of hypocalcaemia.

(0) Non-Toxic Goiter

H&P

These present as a painless enlargement of the thyroid gland and fullness of the neck on physical exam. They may have thyroid symptoms; ask about risk factors for cancer and compressive symptoms. Look for signs of fixed nodules, hyperthyroidism and adenopathy.

Diagnosis

Check the thyroid function test and make sure this is not a functioning nodule. Get a thyroid scan as a baseline test. Ultrasound is used to rule out any other nodules, and FNA is done to rule out cancer.

Treatment

Because most of these are caused by slow T4 production, this causes high TSH and thus an enlarged gland. Suppression with thyroxin is usually done. However, you should test the TRH stimulating test to make sure they respond. If there is no response to TRH, then thyroxin is contraindicated.

Small sized goiters that are TRH responsive are given synthroid 0.125 mg per day with a TSH goal of 0.1 to 0.5. RAIU goal is < 5%. 50% of nodules will decrease in size and 10% should disappear.

Total thyroidectomy or subtotal thyroidectomy is done for diffuse multinodular goiters that are TRH nonresponsive, failed treatment with thyroxin for 1 year, have compressive symptoms, have malignancy on FNA, or for cosmesis.

Finally, RAI can be used. It takes weeks to work, and it only works in functioning tissue. Most multi-nodular goiters (MNG) are not functioning. RAI is not used for patients with acute respiratory symptoms. You can develop problems with extra thyroidal cancers in young patients. Ideally, this modality is used in the elderly, nontoxic goiter with significant cardiopulmonary disease.

(8) Hypercalcemia/Hyperparathyroidism*

H&P

You have to be concerned about a malignancy with boney mets, primary and secondary hyperparathyroidism, renal failure, sarcoidosis, thiazide diuretics, familial hypocalcinuric hypercalcemia (FHH), milk-alkali syndrome, and MEN I or II.

They may complain of renal stones, osteoporosis, arthralgia, myopathy, constipation, weakness and ulcers.

On physical, do a breast and neck exam. Look them over for neurofibromas or calcium deposits in the subcutaneous tissue.

Diagnosis

You will want to repeat the calcium, no matter what value they give you. A value more than 11 with bone disease, or symptomatic, is an indication to operate. PTH (>70), Cl/Phos ratio of >30 (PTH causes phosphorous excretion and Ca absorption from the kidney), 24 hour urine calcium (to rule out FHH), creatinine clearance (rule out renal failure), and maybe a bone scan should be done to find the cause of hypercalcemia. Calcitonin level should be sent to rule out medullary thyroid cancer in association with MEN II syndrome.

Treatment

Treatment is diagnosis specific. Most of the time, you are given hyperparathyroidism to deal with. 80% are adenomas, 10% hyperplasia, < 1% cancer, and 2% are multiple adenomas.

The traditional 4 gland exploration is always safe. This is done through a collar incision, split the strap muscles, and then ligate and divide the middle thyroid vein.

Along the inferior-lateral thyroid, identify the RLN cephlad and the inferior thyroid artery crossing it. The inferior parathyroid will be within 1 cm of this junction. If it is not, it may be inside the thyroid capsule or lower pole thyroid parenchyma, carotid sheath, and thymus/anterior mediastinum. Consider intraoperative ultrasound to look in the thyroid parenchyma for the gland.

Posterior-lateral to the superior pole, follow the RLN to the larynx. The inferior thyroid artery crosses it within 1 cm of the superior parathyroid gland. If you do not find it here, you should check retropharyngeal or retroesophageal planes, the posterior mediastinum, inside the upper or posterior thyroid capsule, and the carotid sheath.

Repeat on the other side.

The examiners can present you with a wide array of scenarios. Try to find all four glands before you start to remove any tissue. One adenoma and three normal glands will prompt you to remove the adenoma and biopsy of at least one of the normal glands to make sure it is normal too. If you have 2 adenomas, then remove them and biopsy the other 2 normal glands.

If there are three normal glands and a missing superior gland, then look in the usual places. If it is not there, then do an ipsilateral thyroid lobectomy and stop there. If it is the inferior gland that is missing, then look in the usual places, then thyroid lobectomy, then cervical thymectomy.

Four gland hyperplasia is found in secondary and tertiary hyperparathyroidism and MEN syndromes (so CT the pituitary or at least get a prolactin level, do a secretin test and check a fasting insulin to glucose ratio). Total parathyroidectomy and auto-transplantation in the non-dominant brachioradialis muscle is done. This way, if the gland hypertrophies, you can diagnose it by placing a tourniquet on the transplant arm and venous sample the PTH to distinguish if it the recurrence is in the neck or the arm. Furthermore, this can be done under local.

Parathyroid cancer is rare, but if presented to you, then you should do an en bloc resection of the tumor with an ipsilateral thyroidectomy, regional lymph nodes, and soft tissue resection.

Additional Therapy

If you are comfortable describing the minimally invasive parathyroidectomy, then go for it. Be cautious here and make sure they are going to allow you to do intra-operative PTH assays (or else bail and go for the 4 gland exploration).

You should inject the patient with radioactive material pre-operatively (about 2 hours before surgery) and use an intra-operative radio-probe to find the gland. Any gland with more than 20% background noise is considered positive. If you feel that you found the responsible gland, check a PTH and remove the gland. Check a PTH at 5 and 10 minutes, expecting a > 50% decrease in the level. If you don't get this (49.9% is not enough), then go to the 4 gland exploration.

Be prepared to discuss neck hematoma, persistent hypercalcemia, post-operative hypocalcaemia, and RLN injury. Most of the time, persistent hypercalcemia will have residual disease in the neck. Either you go back within one week, or you should wait 3 months. Repeat all the studies and labs. Localize it with all possible tests (venous sampling, sestamibi scan, CT, ultrasound, etc).

If there is any question about a parathyroid gland's vascularity, then re-implant it in the SCM or arm. 200-400 mg of hydrocortisone can cause an increased excretion of calcium (over 3-4 days), bisphosphanates (e.g. pamidronate 90 mg IV) can normalize calcium in most patients. Calcitonin acts quickly (within 24 hours) and should be used with glucocorticoids. Once the patient is stabilized, do a localization study and take out the parathyroid responsible, emergently.

Example Case

You are asked to see a 62 year old woman who was operated on for hyperparathyroidism by another surgeon. The surgeon says that she had a Ca of 11 and a PTH that was abnormal and he was able to find three glands and couldn't find the left inferior gland so he closed without resecting anything. What would you do?

Well, I guess the first thing I would do is talk with this patient and get an idea of the symptoms that she was having before the surgery. Assuming that she was symptomatic from her hyperparathyroidism then, I would ask her if she was continuing to have these symptoms since surgery. If yes, then I would examine her neck and feel for any masses that may be an enlarged parathyroid gland. I would send calcium and a PTH level off, and check the Cl to Phos ratio. If the calcium is high, the PTH is high and the Cl to Phos ration is greater than 30, then I am convinced that she has hyperparathyroidism still and we should actively search for the missing gland.

Yes, it all still looks like hyperparathyroidism.

The other thing to consider is MEN syndrome, and I would focus a brief history on hypoglycemic spells, gastric ulcers, thyroid cancers, or unexplained hypertension. Assuming this is negative, I would do a sestamibi scan to see if there is a gland that lights up in the neck. It was the left inferior gland he could not find. So I would also be interested to read the operative report and see if the surgeon looked in all the usual places for the gland. For example, he looked in the trachea-esophageal groove and carotid sheath, and he did a thymectomy or thyroid lobectomy on that side? If he did, then I don't think I would offer anything to this patient and would refer her to an endocrine surgery specialist.

No, he just looked in the normal place, couldn't find it and closed up. The Sestamibi scan shows a gland behind the left part of the sternum.

I am not experienced with doing re-explorations for parathyroid glands. It would make me uncomfortable to do this procedure, but my understanding is that this gland may be in the thymus. I would explain to the patient that I could refer her to a tertiary care center where they do this all the time, or I could go in and look for it, perhaps pull the thymus up from behind the sternum, but I would not do sternotomy. If there is a thoracic surgeon willing to do the sternotomy for me and close the sternum for me and the patient was agreeable to this, I would be more comfortable.

How do you pull the thymus up without a sternotomy?

Sometimes, you can dissect out all the fatty tissue and thymus just behind the sternal notch. Ring forceps can be used to pull on the thymus up until all the tissue is removed in one piece or piece-meal if you have to.

Let's say they do a sternotomy for you and you find this 2 cm brownish looking mass in the thymic tissue.

That's a good size gland. I would biopsy this and send it for a frozen section. If it comes back as parathyroid adenoma, then I would remove this gland. I would then check the PTH levels intraoperatively and see if it decreases by 50% by 15 minutes. If it does not, then I would go looking at the other glands as a typical four gland exploration.

(6) Endocrine
(3) Pheochromocytoma*

H&P

Patient will present with refractory or paroxysmal hypertension, palpitations, and headaches. They may have a history of anxiety, sweating, family history of MEN.

On physical, see if they have an abdominal mass.

Diagnosis

Send 24 hour urine for VMA, metanephrines, and catecholamine. Check the electrolytes for elevated calcium or decreased potassium. Send a calcitonin to rule out medullary carcinoma. If these tests are equivocal, then do a clonidine test. Give 0.3 mg clonidine and check the metanephrines again three hours later. If they are <500, then there is no pheochromocytoma.

The tumor needs to be localized too. This is done several ways. CT scan is 90% accurate (no contrast as this could precipitate a crisis). MRI is good in the case of a pregnant woman. MIBG scan is I^{123} scan is 90% sensitive and shows extra-adrenal gland disease or non-localized disease. PET scan is used when not seen in the other modalities.

Treatment

So this tumor will need to be removed surgically. First, they have to be prepared for the operating room. This is done with the alpha blocker, phenoxybenzamine. You start with 10 mg po tid. It is given until the patient develops orthostatic hypotension. If they remain tachycardic, then they should receive a β-blocker as well (propanalol). In the holding area, make sure there are good central access and IV lines. You need to have nitroprusside, esmolol, neosynephrine, and lidocaine drips available.

Surgical approaches depend on the side and your preference. Most can be done laparoscopically unless the tumor is > 8cm, has local invasion (by CT or MRI), or may require en-bloc resection of other organs.

For the right gland, place the patient in the semi-left lateral decubitus; divide the lateral hepatic attachments to find the IVC and adrenal. The harmonic scalpel is then used lateral to the IVC to identify the short adrenal vein which is clipped and divided (or stapled). You then circumferentially dissect around the gland.

For the left side, the patient is placed in the semi-right lateral decubitus, the splenic flexure is mobilized and the spleno-renal ligament is divided. The spleen is rolled medially and the gland is identified. The harmonic scalpel is used to dissect the medial aspect. The left adrenal vein is usually small enough to be taken with the harmonic. Continue the circumferential dissection until the gland is removed.

Post-operatively, place them in the ICU and monitor them for changes in their blood pressure. Keep the blood pressure low.

Addition Therapy

Annual 24 hour urinary test are done to follow for recurrence, which can occur in up to 15% of patients.

Treatment of a malignant pheochromocytoma includes I^{131} MIBG for symptom palliation, shrinkage, and decreased catecholamine production. This can be repeated in 3 months if needed. If there is no response, then you offer chemotherapy.

Chemotherapy for malignant tumors is called Aurbuch protocol and includes cyclophosphamide, vincristine, and dacarbazine.

XRT is used on any boney mets.

Example Case

A 28 year old female otherwise healthy present to her internist with sever headaches and noted to have a blood pressure of 220/110 mmHg. The internist got an MRI that showed a mass on the top of the left kidney.

Well, I think that this is a pheochromcytoma based on the adrenal mass and blood pressure. I would see the patient and ask her about a family history of this or medullary thyroid cancer (worried about MEN II). Assuming that this is negative and she has no other medical problems, I would do a physical examination. I expect the exam to be relatively normal (except the blood pressure) and focus on the neck and abdomen to rule out any masses. Next, I would send a serum metanephrines, and if this is positive I would feel confident in the diagnosis (the false positive rate of *serum* is high, but when there is an adrenal mass with symptomolgy, it is a good test. If this is negative, I would send 24 hour urine). I would also check the K^+ in case this is an aldosteronoma, and a cortisol in the case of a cortisol producing tumor. Finally, I would check the calcium and calcitonin level to exclude the chances of hyperparathyroidism and medullary thyroid cancer, respectively, associated with MEN II.

You do all of this, it is all negative except the serum metanephrines, which is positive. Now what do you do?

Well this is a functioning adrenal tumor, and it has to be removed. She will need some preparation for the operating room. In particular, I will start her on phenoxybenzaprine, 10mg po bid, which is an alpha block to get her blood pressure under control. She should be on this, increasing it as needed, to obtain orthostatic hypotension. This usually takes about 2 weeks. If her heart rate is still high, then beta blockers could be added. Once her blood pressure is under control, I will bring her to the operating rom. I would make sure that the anesthesiologist has esmolol, nipride, neosynephrin, and dopamine ready to go in case we have hypotension or hypertension. Assuming that the mass is noted to be less than 4 cm on MRI, I would approach this laparoscopically. If it is any bigger than this, I would consider an open approach.

Let's say that when you check the calcium, it comes back 13. What now.

So, sounds like she has MEN II with hyperparathyroidism. The pheochromocytoma will need to be addressed first. After this, I would send serum to test for the ret protooncogene that is positive in people with MEN. If this is positive, then I would council the patient on her disease and explain to her the risk of developing thyroid cancer. She will need a total thyroidectomy and 4 gland parathyroidectomy with auto-transplantation in the forearm.

But you would take on the pheochromocytoma first?

Yes.

Even though she could have a cancer in her neck right now…

Yes, I cannot operate on someone with a functioning pheochromocytoma because that would be dangerous and could precipitate a hypertensive crisis. Furthermore, there was no neck mass on physical examination of the neck to suggest that she does have a cancer at this time. My order for taking care of these problems is pheochromocytoma, then medullary cancer, then parathyroid.

How would you follow her after this operation?

Assuming she did not have any cancer in the thyroid, then I would see her annually and test her with 24 hour urinary catecholamines and serum clacitonin and calcium levels.

What if she did have medullary cancer and you removed this? How would you follow her for that?

Then I would follow her yearly with a pentagastrin stimulated calcitonin level.

(0) Aldosteronoma

H&P

Patients have hypertension, K^+ < 3.4 meq/L, and an adrenal mass. Ask about symptoms of renal disease, CHF, liver disease, diuretic usage, and multiple HTN meds.

Physical exam should include a BP in both arms

Diagnosis

Check the electrolytes. These patients generally have hypokalemia. Plasma rennin level (PRA) and plasma aldosterone concentrations (PAC) are checked.

High PRA is due to secondary aldosteronism. You have to rule out renal disease.

Low PRA and high PAC (ratio > 30) is primary aldosteronism.

To confirm the diagnosis, do an aldosterone suppression test. You give them 3 gms of Na per meal for 3 days. Send a 24 hour urine: Na level >200 confirms proper Na loading, aldosterone >12 mcg/day is consistent with primary hyperaldosteronism and K > 40 meq/day is consistent with primary hyperaldosteronism.

Alternative test is to give 2 liters of saline IV over 4 hours, then check the plasma aldosterone level. If it is > 8.5, then this is primary hyperaldosteronism.

Finally, you have to rule out bilateral hyperplasia. CT scan should be done with 3 mm cuts to identify the mass.

Postural stimulation testing can be done. If it is an adenoma then the 4 hour upright level is > 20 and decreases or stays the same with moving supine overnight to upright. For hyperplasia, it is < 20 and increases when moving from supine to upright.

Plasma 18-hydroxycorticol is > 100 in adenomas.

Adrenal venous sampling is done if you cannot find the tumor. The level is 5 times higher on the affected side if there is an adenoma. Aldosterone is compared to cortisol as a ration in order to standardize the two sides.

Finally NP-50 scan with dexamethasone suppression will show greater uptake on the side of an adenoma.

Treatment

Preoperatively, you should give the patient spironolactone (50 mg/day) and K supplements to correct their potassium. Start them on verapamil or lisinopril to control blood pressure. Amiloride may be used.

If the tumor is > 6 cm, then it is more likely to be malignant, and an open approach should be taken. Otherwise, approach this lapascopically as you would for any adrenal mass (like pheochromocytoma).

Additional Therapy

Management of bilateral hyperplasia is the same as preoperative therapy. There is no surgery done for this condition.

(0) Cushing's syndrome

H&P

Patients may have a history of a buffalo hump, moon facies, proximal muscle weakness, headaches, depression, striate, easy bruising, hirituism, acne, hyper pigmentation, hypokalemia, diabetes, osteoporosis, kidney stone, polyuria, immunosuppression, and menstrual changes.

On physical exam, look for the classic cushinoid appearance.

Diagnosis

Rule out Cushing's syndrome, determine if the cortisol production is ACTH dependant or not and the source of cortisol, and localize it.

Can be caused by and adrenal adenoma (15%) or carcinoma, pituitary gland adenoma (75%) or hyperplasia, or may be a paraneoplastic syndrome (10%). ACTH levels are the best place to start. ACTH < 5 pg/ml suggest adrenal, > 15 pg/ml suggest pituitary, and > 100 pg/ml suggest ectopic production.

A 24 hour urine cortisol over 300 mcg/ml is abnormal. Low dose dexamethasone testing is positive if the am cortisol level is > 5 mcg. If this is positive, then it is consistent with Cushing's syndrome.

The adrenal is ACTH independent, but the pituitary and ectopic sources are ACTH dependant. High dose dexamethasone test shows a low ACTH (independent) in adrenal pathology. For the pituitary source, the ACTH is high, but the cortisol production is suppressed. For ectopic tumors the ACTH is very high and the cortisol is not suppressed.

Localization studies include CT scan or MRI, NP-59 scans (to rule out bilateral hyperplasia, treated with mitotane), and venous sampling.

Treatment

If the tumor in the adrenal is < 6cm, no local invasion, and no mets, then it is safe to proceed laparoscopically. If the opposite is true, then you may need open en bloc resection. Mitotane is adrenolytic, aminoglutathione (ketoconazole and metyrapone, too) will inhibit the p450 corticosteroid production.

Pituitary tumors are lateralized with petrosal venous sampling and a trans-sphenoid hyposphysectomy is performed. If they fail surgery, then do bilateral adrenalectomies and replace both steroids.

Ectopic tumors may be found on CT scan of the abdomen (pancreas) or chest (small cell lung cancer or bronchial carcinoid). Treatment is resection if possible. If it is unresectable, then debulk or give chemotherapy (mitotane, aminoglutethione, ketoconazole, and metyrapone). You may consider bilateral adrenalectomies.

(2) Adrenal Incidentaloma*

H&P

Patient may have pheochromocytoma symptoms, Cushing's symptoms, aldosterone symptoms, and history of cancer (lung cancer metastasizes to the adrenals).

Physical exam is focused on the abdomen for masses and looking for cushingnoid appearance.

Diagnosis

Initially, the CT scan should be done or reviewed to make sure of the size, local invasion, and any other obvious primaries.

Determine if the mass is functional by sending 24 hour urine for catecholamines, metanephrines, VMA, 17-hydroxy ketosteroids, and cortisol. Plasma metanephrines are helpful for a mass on abdominal CT (false positive less likely in this situation). Check their electrolytes to see if there is a potassium abnormality, and take their blood pressure. May want to check a plasma aldosterone and rennin level if there is any doubt.

Tumors < 4cm have a 2% cancer of cancer, 4-6 cm have a 6% chance and tumors > 6 cm have a 25% chance.

MRI can give you information about an adrenal mass. That is, if the signal intensity of the mass compared to liver (as a ratio) is > 3, then it is a pheochromocytoma. If it is 1.4 to 3, then it is a carcinoma (metastatic or primary), and if it is < 1.4, then it is an adenoma.

Treatment

If this is a functioning lesion, more than 4 cm in size, confirmed metastatic cancer by FNA, or lesion less than 4 cm that changes with observation, including size (more than 0.5 cm over 6 months) or functionality (20% will become functional over ten years), then it should be surgically excised. Laparoscopic or open approached can be employed. If the tumor is more than 6 cm, then it should be removed with an open technique.

Example Case

A 4 cm adrenal mass is found on a 40 year old man who was getting a CT scan of the abdomen for another reason. He is sent to you for the work up. What do you want to do?

I think that some surgeons would just take out a 4 cm adrenal mass because there is a 6% chance of there being a cancer in a tumor that size and the risk of a laparoscopic adrenalectomy is relatively small. However, traditionally 6 cm is used for the cut off. Nonetheless, before you take it out or in the determination of whether you should remove it or not you have to know if this is a functional primary tumor, a benign adenoma, or a metastatic carcinoma. Lung cancer can frequently metastasize to the adrenals, so I would get a chest x-ray. An MRI can be used to give you a better idea it this is an adenoma, carcinoma or pheochromocytoma. So I think this would be useful to have. Finally, I would get 24 hour urine for cortisol level, VMA, catecholamines, and metanephrines. If his chemistries show low potassium, then I would consider an aldosteronoma. I would get a serum rennin and aldosterone level. Depending on these test, the patient and I would discuss the need to take out this tumor.

It is not functional but the patient wants it out. Describe your technique.

Assuming this is a left sided gland, I would approach this laparoscopically. Place the patient in the right lateral decubitus. I would expose the splenorenal ligament and take this sown with the harmonic scalpel, exposing the kidney and the adrenal gland. I would start the dissection by opening up the retroperitoneum laterally along the kidney and the adrenal to expose the adrenal vessels. The harmonic can be used to come around the gland without stopping because the vein on this side is small and usually can be taken with the harmonic. I remove the gland and take it out through the abdomen with a bag.

(0) Zollinger-Ellison Syndrome
(Gastrinoma)

H&P

Patients may present to you with recurrent PUD that is refractory to other treatments, abdominal pain, atypical ulcer locations, multiple ulcers, diarrhea, and hyperparathyroidism (MEN I, so ask about the family history of MEN).

Physical exam is unremarkable.

Diagnosis

Initial work up should include a gastrin level. Hold the patient's PPI for at least a week (and H2 blockers for 2 days). If the level is > 1000, it is positive for ZES.

Gastric pH analysis will show a pH < 2.5.

Secretin stimulation test is used when the fasting gastrin level is equivocal. You should check a baseline gastrin level, and then give 2 units/kg of secretin. Check gastrin levels at 2, 5, 10, 15, and 30 minutes. If the gastrin level is >200, then it is ZES.

Ca and PTH levels are drawn if there is a suspicion of MEN I. 75% gastrinomas are sporadic and 25% are associated with MEN.

Once diagnosis of gastrinoma is made, you must localize the tumor. Most of these tumors are located in the gastrinoma triangle: the CBD and cystic duct, duodenum, and pancreas. 50% are found in the duodenum and 25% are in the pancreas.

CT scan of the abdomen and pelvis and/or MRI may help. These tumors are usually multiple.

Somatostatin receptor scintigraphy and EUS are other options. ^{111}In-pentetreotid binds to receptors. It is more sensitive than CT scan. 85% of gastrinomas are found. EUS is good at finding tumors in the pancreatic head or duodenum (75% tumors in these two locations) and combined with somatostatin scan is > 90% sensitive.

Treatment

If the tumor is felt to be unresectable, then offer chemotherapy (ZAP-5): streptozosin, doxorubicin, PPI, and 5-FU.

If the tumor is resectable but you can not localize it, then open the abdomen, Kocherize the duodenum and feel the pancreas. Get an intra-operative US and do an EGD. If you still cannot find it, then open the duodenum and palpate the submucosa for any mass. If you still can find it after all of this, then do a P&V, keep them on somatostatin and PPI's, and give them ZAP-5.

If the tumor is resectable and localized, then it depends on the location: In the duodenum, do a full thickness resection and gastrin triangle lymphadenectomy. In the pancreas with no ductal involvement, enucleate it. If it is in the pancreatic head with ductal involvement then you will have to do Whipple, but only if solitary and there is no metastatic disease. If it is in the pancreatic body or tail with ductal involvement, then do a distal pancreatectomy.

If the primary is removed completely and there are hepatic mets, then debulk as much as you can if it is easy. If a lot of tumor is left behind, consider P&V. Consider radio-frequency ablation (RFA) and/or trans-arterial chemo-embolization (TRACE) with doxorubicin and streptomycin and interferon-alpha.

If the patient has had previous failed ulcer surgery and complications from his ulcer symptoms, then consideration to a total gastrectomy is given.

Additional Therapy

Post-operatively, if a resection was performed, the follow up with a fasting gastrin level for recurrent disease. If this is positive, then you have to go through the localization process again with secretin stimulation, Ca/PTH levels, CT scans, and somatostatin scans.

15 year survival without liver mets is 80%. 5 year survival with liver mets is 20-50%. Liver mets are worse than lymph node mets. Pancreatic tumors tend to be larger and tend to involve lymph nodes.

(1) Pancreatic Endocrine Tumors except Gastrinoma*

These tumors are very rare and include insulinomas, gastrinomas, VIPomas, glucagonomas, somatostatinomas, and nonfunctional tumors. These are associated with four genetic syndromes: MEN I, von Hippel Linau, von Reckling Haussen, and tuberous sclerosis.

H&P and Diagnosis

Generally you have to take a history and physical to diagnose the syndrome.

Insulinoma have Whipple's triad: symptoms with fasting/exercise, glucose < 50 and relief of symptoms with glucose administration. You have to rule out MEN I syndrome (pituitary tumors and hyperparathyroid). Insulin to glucose ratio is > 0.3, and the C-peptide is elevated (only with endogenous insulin). 10% are malignant

VIPomas have watery diarrhea, hypokalemia, and acholrhydria.

Glucagonomas present with migratory necrotizing erythema, diabetes, malnutrition, and venous thrombosis.

Somatostatinomas have gallstone, steatorrhea and diabetes.

Treatment

Medical therapy exists for these tumors. For insulinomas, diazoxide, propanalol, verapamil and IV glucose is given to stay the symptoms. Gastrinomas, glucagonomas, and VIPomas are relieved with somatostatin.

Bony mets and liver mets are contraindications to surgical therapy. Otherwise, make a midline incision, palpate the liver and do an exploratory laparotomy. Perform a Kocher maneuver and palpate the posterior head of the pancreas. Enter the lesser sac by dividing the gastrocolic ligament, expose the entire pancreas. Do an intraoperative ultrasound to find the lesion and see if there is an adjacent duct. Mobilize the pancreas above and below and rotate it medially with the spleen. Enucleate the tumor if possible. If there is ductal involvement, do a formal resection. If there are multiple insulinomas, you need to do a distal pancreatectomy. If you cannot find the tumor, do a limited distal pancreatectomy and send for frozen section to rule out islet cells hyperplasia or nesidioblastosis and close the abdomen. If there is hyperplasia or nesidioblastosis, a subtotal pancreatectomy is done.

Additional Therapy

If there is any metastatic disease, then treat with TRACE, octreotide, and/or ablation.

Example Case

You are seeing a 28 year old nurse who has weakness and sweating when she doesn't get a chance to eat. She is referred to you to rule out insulinoma.

I would get a history of her symptoms that you very well described, sounds like Whipple's triad. I would ask her about MEN I symptoms, including getting a calcium level and PTH level, and ask her about her family history of MEN I. Assuming that is all unremarkable, I would put her in the hospital and make her NPO. When she became symptomatic, I would draw her glucose and insulin levels, as well as a c-peptide level. If the c-peptide is high, then this is endogenous insulin. If the glucose to insulin level is >0.3, then this is consistent with an insulinoma. I would try to localize it with a CT scan and angiogram. If neither of these were successful, I would ask for selective venous sampling.

The tumor localizes to the distal pancreas. What do you want to do?

She is symptomatic and 10% can be malignant, so I would advise that we should excise this tumor.

How would you do that?

I would make a midline incision, go through the lesser sac, expose the anterior pancreas and feel for the tumor. If I could not feel it well then I would use intra-operative ultrasound.

You can't find it even with ultrasound.

It is in the tail of the pancreas, I would look at the CT again, and go through the surface of the pancreas until I found it, but I would not go too deep for fear of injuring the pancreatic duct.

You find it, now what?

I would enucleate it.

Anything else you want to do?

I would leave a drain and close.

Two days later there is clear fluid coming out of the drain. What do you think that is?

I think that is a pancreatic leak and I would confirm it with an amylases level.

It is 2000.

Then I would make her NPO, start TPN, and start somatostatin to decrease the pancreatic secretions. Most of these will heal on there own. If it continued to drain after 6 weeks with no signs of healing, then I would shoot an ERCP to confirm that the leak is in the tail of the pancreas and then do a distal pancreatectomy.

(0) MEN Syndromes

MEN I (PPP) includes: parathyroid hyperplasia, pituitary tumors (treated first), and pancreatic islet cell tumors (gastrinoma, insulinoma, VIPomas, and glucagonomas). Surveillance for these patients includes q 6 month blood work for calcium, prolactin, insulin, gastrin, VIP, and glucagon.

MEN IIA (PPT) includes: parathyroid hyperplasia, pheochromocytomas, and thyroid medullary carcinoma. They are screened every year with calcium level, calcitonin, and catecholamines. Prophylactic thyroidecotmies are done at 6 years old.

MEN IIB (PTM) includes: Pheochromocytomas, thyroid medullary carcinoma, and mucosal neuroma. Yearly screening for this population includes calcitonin and catecholamines. Do a prophylactic thyroidectomy in infancy.

(8) Miscellaneous Malignancy
(4) Melenoma*

H&P

Patient may have a suspicious skin lesion, history of sun exposure, history of skin cancer, xeroderma pigmentosum, giant congenital nevus, and family history of melanoma. Dysplastic nevus syndrome is autosomal dominant with a 100% chance of developing melanoma. They have > 100 moles, 1 mole > 8 mm in size, and 1 mole with atypical history.

Physical exam is the ABCDE of the lesion and check the nodal basin for adenopathy.

Diagnosis

You want to check their labs, including an LDH. Get a chest x-ray to rule out metastatic disease. You may consider getting a CT scan of the chest, abdomen and pelvis if needed.

You need to take a tissue biopsy in order to make a diagnosis. There is no intension to take margins at this time, just biopsy for diagnosis. So for lesions that are < 2 cm, take a full thickness excisional biopsy with gross margins. If the lesion is more than 2 cm, then use a 6 mm punch biopsy over the thickest area.

FNA any clinically suspicious nodes (decreased spillage of tumor compared to open biopsy).

Treatment

The treatment now depends on the diagnosis of melanoma, and its depth and node status. Factors of poor prognosis include depth, ulceration, male, proximal location, and BANS (back, arms, neck, and scalp).

Depth of the lesion is based on the Breslow classification. Thin is 0-0.75mm, intermediate is 0.75-4mm, and thick is > 4mm. Clarks is not used as much, but "I" is in situ, "II" into papillary, "III" thru papillary dermis, "IV" into the reticular dermis, and "V" is through all the layers.

If the melanoma is < 1mm then you need 1 cm margins and no SLNBx.

If the melanoma is 1-4 mm, get 2 cm margins and do a SLNBx.

If the melanoma is thick (> 4 mm), you can assume that the cat is out of the bag. Get a 2-3 cm margin, but SLNBx is not useful.

If the tumor is on the digit, take into consideration which digit and where on the digit it is. You want remove one phalanx proximal to the melanoma. If it is in the web-space between the fingers or toes, or on the proximal digit, then you have to do a soft tissue dissection with preservation of the tendon and bone and do a full thickness skin graft to that area.

Sole of the foot lesions require WLE to the plantar fascia and reconstruction with skin graft or rotational flaps/myocutaneous flaps (ideally innervated flaps).

Ear requires a wedge resection 2 times the diameter of the lesion. Amputate the ear if there is extensive involvement.

Breast melanoma requires WLE and ALND (I, II, and III).

Anal melanoma requires WLE. APR is offered only for massive bleeding or obstruction.

Additional Therapy

Stage IV melanoma requires specific treatment. If there are mets to the brain, lung, or liver, you should try to resect them. If the disease is disseminated then give IL-2, INF-α, and vaccine therapy. Boney mets get XRT for palliation.

Melenoma in transit is usually seen in intermediate thickness lesions and requires a full staging work up again, followed by WLE with 1 cm margins, local radiation, and isolated limb perfusion with melphelan and TNF-α.

Regional node recurrence requires a full staging workup, WLE of the recurrence, complete node dissection, and adjuvant radiation therapy.

Systemic recurrence has a median survival of 6 months. Systemic biochemotherapy is offered. Dacarbazine is the standard chemotherapy agent used. Biologic agents include IF-α and IL-2, which may improve disease free survival, but not overall survival. Symptomatic distant mets are resected for palliation only.

SLNBx specimens are sent for permanent (unlike breast cancer). A positive SLNBx on pathology means a return to the operating room for formal nodal dissection.

Radical lymphadenectomy for involved nodes improves regional control and improves survival. There is no survival advantage to doing a prophylactic node dissection over an elective dissection at ten years. Intermediate thickness lesions have a 30% of having positive node disease at the time of their diagnosis.

Axillary nodal dissections include all three levels. There is a 10% lymphedema risk.

The boundaries of the inguinal and iliac dissection includes 6 cm above the inguinal ligament superiorly, the pubic tubercle and adductus longus muscle medially, the lateral border of the Sartorius and anterior-superior iliac spine laterally, and the apex of the femoral triangle inferiorly. During the superficial dissection, you make a lazy "S" incision across the groin and raise flaps medially and laterally to the boarders, removing the nodes off the external oblique superiorly, the cord structures medially, including the GSV inferiorly, and the nodes on the Sartorius laterally, taking Cloquet's node underneath the inguinal ligament. This node is the lowest node on the iliac chain. Cloquet's node is sent for frozen as a separate specimen. If this node is positive, you will need to do a deep dissection

Illiac/obturator (deep) node dissection is indicated if Cloquet's node is positive, there are > 3 lymph nodes more than a cm in size in the pelvis on CT scan without evidence of para-aortic node enlargement, and/or there are > 4 positive nodes in the superficial dissection specimen.

The inguinal ligament is split medial to the femoral vein; find the ureter over the external illiac artery, and all the external iliac nodes are removed superiorly to the common illiacs and medially and inferiorly off the internal illiacs, bladder, and obturator nerve. Re-approximate the divided inguinal ligament and place a Sartorius muscle transposition graft.

There is a 23% incidence of lymphedema after this operation. Elastic stockings at night for 6 months and leg elevation may alleviate symptoms.

Neck dissection may include a radical neck dissection +/- superficial parotidectomy.

Example Case

A 50 year old man has a 1cm right temporal lesion and a palpable lymph node in the submental area.

That is concerning that this man could have a skin cancer that has metastasized to the neck nodes. I would begin by getting a history form the man that should include personal or family history of skin cancer, surgical removal of any lesions on his body before, sun exposure, and other risk factors like smoking or drinking alcohol.

Assuming all that is negative, and then I would examine this lesion for characteristics that may tell me if this lesion is melanoma, BCCA, or SCCA and how fixed is this submental node. I would look for other lesions as well, and examine the rest of the nodal basin.

Everything else is negative. It is a 1 cm pigmented lesion.

I am worried it is melanoma, so I would plan on excising this lesion with gross margins to get a diagnosis. First, I would FNA that node in the neck on his first visit to my office. If this is positive, then I know he has metastatic melanoma and is a stage IV.

The node comes back positive for melanoma.

So, he is a stage IV melanoma, I will have to get 2 cm margins for this lesion, it really does not matter how thick because this cat is out of the bag, and I would do a metastatic work up by getting a CXR, LFTs, bone scan if needed and CT of the abdomen/pelvis or brain is symptoms warrant it. Assuming I find no other metastatic disease, then I would take him to the operating room for excision of the forehead lesion and a modified radical neck dissection. I will admit, however, that I have little experience with radical neck dissection and plastic surgery. I would optimally have these consultants working with me to reconstruct the defect I have created and do the radical neck dissection.

Well, they could not help you on this day, it is the ENT/plastics golfing association welcome day.

I see, then I would excise the lesion with 2 cm margins, and the defect created here could be closed with a rotational flap, free flap, or full thickness skin graft from behind the ear. Then, I would start the radical neck, making my cranial incision a little higher and more posterior so that I could incorporate the superficial parotid in the specimen.

What! You are going to do a Parotidectomy too? Why?

This is the first nodal basin for drainage of lesions that are above the upper lip and lateral to the vermillion.

(8) Miscellaneous Malignancy

Is that so?

I am not a head and neck surgeon, but that is my understanding. Yes.

But the node is obviously in the submental region. Fine, describe your neck dissection.

Raise my flaps, dissect out the posterior triangle of the neck, remove all this tissue preserving the accessory and SCM if I can, working medially, preserve the juglar, work up the carotid sheath, remove all tissue in this area to the submental area, spare the hypoglossal and find the anterior belly of the digastic, remove all the submental tissue and work posteriorly now, find and spare the linguinal nerve, may have to remove the submental salivary gland and duct since this node is here, work to the posterior border of the SCM and lift all this tissue up superiorly. I would take the parotid by finding the facial nerve and working along the top of it to preserve the branches.

That's enough time on this, let's move on.

(1) Lymphoma*

H&P

B-symptoms of lymphoma include fever, chills and night sweats. They may present with weight loss, or history of adenopathy. The adenopathy may be from something else, so ask about HIV, URI, skin cancer history, tobacco, ETOH, head and neck radiation, and pain.

Physical exam should be done on the skin, nodal basins, and head and neck area.

Diagnosis

The diagnosis is made by working up the lymph node. US of the neck area with FNA may show lymphocyte dominant, lymphocytic depleted or nodular sclerosis type of cells. In this case, you have to excise the node and send it for lymphoma protocol in order to confirm the diagnosis.

Once the diagnosis is confirmed, they should be staged with a CT scan (of the chest, abdomen, and pelvis) and bone marrow biopsy (to rule out stage IV).

Treatment

Hodgkin's lymphoma is staged as stage I, one group; stage II, two groups on same side of the diaphragm; stage III, two groups on different sides of the diaphragm; and stage IV, positive bone marrow. A is asymptomatic, and B is symptomatic B-symptoms. Stages IA and IIA is treated with external beam radiation, but no chemo (50% sterility rate with chemo). Stages III or IV, or B-symptoms, are treated with CHOP therapy (cyclophosphamide, doxorubicin, vincristine, and prednisone).

Staging laparotomy may be needed to exclude stage III disease and save the patient from getting unnecessary chemotherapy. The procedure includes bilateral liver lobe biopsies, splenectomy, lymph node biopsy (from celiac, porta, splenic hilum, para aortic and para-iliac), and orchipexy to keep ovaries out of radiation field. Mark any enlarged nodes with clips for future radiation.

Non-Hodgkin's lymphoma is usually stage III or IV when diagnosed and is treated with MOAP therapy.

GI lymphoma is a B-cell lymphoma that is radiation sensitive, but it is not chemo sensitive. Resection offers a good cure rate.

Example Case

A 40 year old woman with a 2 cm mass above the left clavicle, asymptomatic:

I would get a history of this neck mass that may give me a clue as to what it is. So I would ask about recent infection that may point to infectious, is it tender, and ask about history of malignancy, family history of lymphoma, and B-type symptoms. If this is not helpful, then entire exam of the head and neck looking for a skin lesion, oral exam looking for a lesion in here (including a bimanual exam), and a breast examination looking for breast cancer would be my neck step. If that is negative, then I would get an FNA.

FNA shows some lymphocytes. Rest of the history and physical is not helpful.

I would perform an excisional biopsy, and then I would have a definite diagnosis and can proceed with the work up from there. If this suggests lymphoma, then she will need staging.

So it is lymphoma, so how would you stage her?

I would get a CT scan of the neck, chest, abdomen and pelvis looking for adenopathy elsewhere, especially on the opposite side of the diaphragm. She would also need a bone marrow biopsy.

It all comes back negative and her oncologist wants you to do a staging laparotomy.

If she didn't have B-symptoms, then I suppose that is reasonable if they want to avoid giving her chemotherapy and just use XRT. So I would do this laparosocpically and would biopsy both lobes of the liver, do a splenectomy, biopsy lymph nodes from the celiac, splenic hilum, para-aortic, iliac, and any other enlarged nodes.

What if she had B-symptoms?

Then I would give her chemotherapy, especially in a woman this age where fertility may not be of too much concern. I would have to discuss her family plans.

She's only 40! What chemotherapy are you talking about?

CHOP for Hodgkin's and MOAP for non-Hodgkin.

What if you found something on the other side of the diaphragm?

Well, since I think it is lymphoma, A CT guided percutaneous biopsy is a reasonable thing to do to confirm the diagnosis. If they could not do this, and oncology really wanted a sample before they decided on her management, then I would help them by obtaining a specimen laparoscopically.

(3) Soft Tissue Sarcoma*

H&P

You want to ask about a history of trauma (which usually brings attention to the mass but doesn't cause it). Ask about radiation history, time mass has been there, changes in size, etc.

Examine the mass. Notice if they have café au lait spots and feel the lymph node basins.

Diagnosis

You need to get some tissue in order to diagnosis this. You can either do a core (no FNA), incisional, or excisional biopsy. Make sure that whatever you do, you get good hemostasis so you don't seed the area and mark your biopsy site (tattoo if you core) so that you can excise it later if you have to.

Imaging after a diagnosis of sarcoma is needed for staging and to localize surrounding structures. MRI is excellent for soft tissue. CXR and CT scan of the chest should be done because sarcoma spreads to the lung. CT scan of the abdomen and pelvis can be done to rule out liver mets or retroperitoneal masses.

If retroperitoneal mass is found, only core needle biopsy when you suspect that it is lymphoma, germ cell tumor, tissue for diagnosis of unresectable disease, or suspected metastasis from another primary.

Treatment

Treatment is based off location. In the extremity, you need to resect with 2 cm margins, not in the plane of the psuedocapsule. You do not need to excise the entire muscle compartment. The skin and subcutaneous tissue is sent with the tumor (along with the biopsy site). Vessels can be resected and reconstructed or ligated if there is direct invasion; however, you can not take motor nerves (e.g. sciatic nerve). If vital structures are left intact with positive margins, then 6000 rads is provided to that area. The survival and recurrence rates are the same as with morbid resections.

In the pelvic region, they get hemipelvectomy. Shoulder region tumors require forequarter amputation. Popliteal or antecubital area required amputation. Hands and feet require local amputation because of the high recurrence rates (50%) with just excision.

Visceral sarcoma includes the esophagus (resection with 2 cm margins), gastric (resection with 2 cm margins), small bowel (resection), and colorectal (resection). The 5 year survival of these tumors is in the 80% range for low grade tumors vs. 5-15% for high grade tumors.

Retroperitoneal sarcomas are usually liposarcomas or leiomyosarcomas and require resection with 2-3 cm margins and en bloc with any other organs. Radiation therapy is limited by GI and kidney toxicity. There is no role for chemotherapy in these tumors.

Additional Therapy

Follow up after resection is a physical exam every 3 months, CXR every 3 months, and a chest CT every 6 months.

80% of the time, recurrence of disease occurs in the first 2 years. If there is disseminated disease, then treat with chemotherapy using ifosfamidie and adrimycin. Lung mets alone should be resected, even if they are bilateral. Local recurrence is treated with resection or amputation.

Example Case

A young man comes to your office with a new anterior thigh mass he noticed last week while he was playing football. He has no significant past medical history.

A mass in the thigh of a young man makes me worry about sarcoma, soft tissue tumor, but it could be just a hematoma or lipomas. I would ask him if there is any family history of unusual cancers or soft tissue masses. Assuming this is negative; I would exam the thigh and get an idea of the size. If this is a small, 2 cm mass in that anterior thigh that is mobile and seems rather superficial then it may be amendable to an excisional biopsy. Before I do that, however, I would complete a neurovascular exam and exam the groin lymph nodes as well. I would then get an ultrasound of the mass ass well to make sure that it is solid and not involving any other deeper or more significant structures.

What kind of structures?

Blood vessels or nerves

You can tell that on an ultrasound?

No, but if it is a real superficial lesion just under the skin, then it is not going to be involving major structures.

Let's say it is 5 cm and it's not that superficial.

In that case, I would get a CT or MRI to evaluate the soft tissue mass and its relationship to the other tissue.

CT or MRI, which do you prefer?

I think a good CT scan of the thigh is adequate, and I am better at looking at CT scans anyway. So, I would get a CT scan. Assuming there is no major vascular, nerve, or bone involvement, I would want a tissue diagnosis. 5 cm is a little too big for excisional biopsy, so I could do a core biopsy with a tru-cut needle or an incisional biopsy. Tru-cut is easier and can be done in the clinic. So I would do that.

How do you do that?

Well, I can feel the mass, so I would prep the skin over the mass with betadine, use local anesthetic to numb the skin, make a small incision with a #11 blade and insert the core needle into the mass and fire it. This should get me a good sample of tissue. I would hold pressure for a good five minutes to make sure a hematoma does not form (that could spread the tumor), and sometime I will inject a little ink under the incision to mark it in case I need to excise it; I want to remove the biopsy site.

It is a malignant fibro-histiocytoma (MFH.)

Assuming this is a low grade, the next thing I want to do is get a chest x-ray to make sure it has not spread to the lungs.

It is has 8 mitosis per 50 hpf. What does that tell you?

This is high grade. So I would get a CT of the chest. If that is negative, I would proceed with resection of this mass. I want to get 2 cm clear margins.

You shave this tumor off the sciatic nerve and your final pathology report comes back with positive margins. What do you tell the patient?

I tell him that I left clips around the margins that I took out, and in order to give him the best chance of this thing not coming back again, he needs radiation to the area.

Do you know how much?

I am not a radiation oncologist, but my understanding is that it is pretty high, about 6000 rads.

How do you follow him up post operatively?

I would see him in the clinic every 3 months for a physical examination and chest x-ray. I would also get a chest CT every 6 months.

18 months post-operatively, he develops a LLL lesion.

I would resect it with a wedge if it is peripheral and a formal lobe if it is central.

(8) Miscellaneous Malignancy

What if there is a lesion in the RUL as well.

I would go after it. Bilateral pulmonary mets is not a contraindication to resection for this tumor.

(3) Gynecology/Urology
(0) Vaginal Bleeding

H&P

Ask about the menstrual history, LMP, presence of an IUD (or anything else in there), recent pregnancy (hydatiform mole), prior ectopic, abdominal or pelvic pain, post-coital bleeding, history of HPV, or fevers.

Physical is focused on stability (vitals), abdominal exam, and pelvic exam.

Diagnosis

Check the labs, including H&H and B-HCG, get a Doppler if positive, and do a pelvic exam to check the cervix.

Treatment

If the HCG is positive, then you should Doppler the abdomen for fetal heart tones.

If the HCG is +, cervix is closed, and no FHT, then get an US. If the uterus is negative on US, then quantitiate the HCG in 48 hours. If <1500, expectant management. If >1500, this is an ectopic pregnancy. Ectopics need to be sized. If it is < 4cm then give methotrexate. If it is >4 cm, then do a salpingectomy (if they no longer want to get pregnant, have no risk of recurrence, or having uncontrolled bleeding) or salpingotomy.

If the HCG is +, cervix is closed, and + FHT, then order pelvic rest and consult an OB.

If the HCG is +, cervix is open, and no FHT, then it is an abortion or mole. They need a D&C and follow up HCG.

PID is treated with cefotetan and doxycyclin or clindamycin and gentamycin. Complications of PID include infertility, ectopic, and recurrent PID. Tubo-ovarian abscess are treated with PID antibiotics and drainage.

(O) Adenexal Mass

H&P

Menstrual history, GU and GI symptoms, pelvic pain, and abdominal pain are sought.

On physical, look for abdominal mass or tenderness, pelvic tenderness, and do a rectal exam.

Diagnosis

A pelvic US can rule out a solid mass vs. a cyst.

Doppler flow studies should be done if you suspect torsion.

Treatment

Simple cyst are treated with OCPs, repeat US in 6 months, and laparoscopic cystectomy if persistent.

Tubo-ovarian abscess is treated with drainage, rochephin, doxycycline, and flagyl. Let them cool off for 6 weeks, then go in and do a unilateral salpingectomy.

Endometriosis is treated with OCPs and NSAIDs. Danazol, GnRH analogs, and progestins may be used. A laparoscopic excision of the lesions and TAH with BSO with post operative estrogen is another option.

Adenexal Torsion is treated with laparoscopy and release of the torsion.

Carcinoma is treated with TAH with BSO, omentectomy, peritoneal and diaphragm biopsies, periaortic node biopsies, and peritoneal lavages.

Corpus luteum cyst deserves observation and repeat ultrasound.

(3) Gynecology/urology

Ectopic pregnancy < 4 cm is treated with methotrexate. If it is > 4cm, do a salpingectomy or salpingotomy.

(1) Ovarian Mass

H&P

Get history of their menstruations, OCP usage and bleeding. Ask about pain and fever.

Physical exams based on abdominal mass and pelvic exam.

Diagnosis

Check CBC, HCG, US and Ca-125. Get an ultrasound to see the mass, and get a CT scan if you suspect appendicitis or diverticulitis.

Treatment

Treatment is based on the age of presentation. The ovarian cancer routine is: peritoneal lavages, peritoneal biopsy, diaphragm biopsy, omental biopsy, and para aortic and pelvic node evaluation.

In a pre-pubertal girl, if the mass is cystic, then observe. If it is solid or complex, then do an ovarian cystectomy.

If the woman is pre-menopausal, there is a 10% risk of cancer. If it is < 5 cm then observe and repeat US in 6 weeks. If it is >5 cm or solid or complex, then an ovarian cancer routine and salpingo-oopherectomy is done. If it looks malignant, then full surgery is done.

Post-menopausal women are at 50% risk of it being a cancer. If it is < 5 cm, then observe. Anything other then this depends if the lesion is cystic or solid. Cystic lesion gets bilateral oopherectomy and TAH. Solid or complex cyst needs a TAH, BSO, omentectomy, peritoneal biopsies and lavages.

Advanced ovarian cancer with seeding requires the ovarian cancer routine, biopsy seeding nodules, and return later for formal ovarian cancer surgery.

Additional Therapy

The adjuvant therapy for ovarian cancer includes doxorubicin, cisplatinum and cyclophosphamide as chemotherapeutics and whole abdominal radiation.

(2) Testicular Tumor*

H&P

These patients may present with a lump or swelling in the testicle. It may be a mass. You want to know if it is painful. Physical exam is of bilateral testicles and metastatic sites: neck, lungs, abdomen, and nodal basins.

Diagnosis

Think about seminoma, non-seminoma, non-germ cell, other (like hernia, lipomas, etc). Get an US of any inguinal or scrotal mass. Send off an HCG, AFP, and LDH, and get a CXR (or CT chest if there is something on the CXR). Germ cell tumors include the seminoma and non-seminoma. Seminomas have a high HCG, and non-seminomas have both a high HCG and high AFP.

In order to diagnose a mass on the testicle, it has to come out. The excisional biopsy is an orchidectomy.

Before you can offer treatment, the tumor has to be staged. CT scan of the abdomen and pelvis to look for nodal disease is done. If the abdomen is positive, then scan the chest to see if there are mediastinal nodes.

Treatment

Seminomas are treated initially based on tumor markers. If you have removed the testicle (to make the diagnosis) and the tumor markers are still elevated, then you give them chemotherapy and radiation (this is cisplatinum, bleomycin, and etoposide; followed by 2500-3500 rads radiation). You have to know the CT results. If there are no para-aortic nodes involved, then irradiate the ipsilateral pelvic and para-aortic nodes. If there are positive para-aortic nodes, then do the above, but include the mediastinum and give them chemotherapy. Chemotherapy is given only for persistently elevated tumor markers or involved para-aortic nodes.

Treatment of non-seminomas depends on node involvement. If there are no para-aortic nodes, then do a deep pelvic and retroperitoneal lymph node dissection. This is followed by chemotherapy (non-seminomas are chemo-sensitive, but they are not radio-sensitive). If the para-aortic nodes are positive, then give chemotherapy, and then do the deep pelvic and retroperitoneal node dissection. This is followed by salvage chemotherapy if the tumor markers or CT remain positive. If the tumor markers remain high after orchidectomy, treat it like they have positive para-aortic nodes.

Example Case

A 25 year old man comes to your office complaining of a right testicular mass he has just noticed.

This is concerning for a testicular tumor, although things like torsion, epidydimitis, hernia, hydrocele and varicocele could present with this. So, I would begin by getting a history related to a recent onset, does it change with valsava, growing in size, non-tender mass, does it swell, etc. This leads me toward a tumor. On physical exam, I would note if it is tender or not, is it a hernia and reduces, is a hydrocele and does it illuminates. Once I have ruled these things out and feel like it is a solid tumor, I would confirm that with an US of the testicles, and get a CXR to look for adenopathy and send lab work for a HCG and AFP because these will be needed during the treatment algorithm.

It is a solid tumor on US and your tumor markers are pending.

A solid mass needs to be biopsied, and that is done with an inguinal orchidectomy.

A what?

The testicle is removed through an inguinal incision in order to make the diagnosis.

Let's say it comes back a seminoma.

These tumors can spread to the para-aortic and mediastinal nodes. Fortunately, they are chemo- and radiation sensitive. I would get a CT scan of the chest, abdomen, and pelvis and check the HCG and AFP again. If the tumor markers are elevated or there are positive para-aortic nodes, then he needs cisplatinum based chemotherapy and radiation to the mediastinum. If the HCG and AFP are normalized and there are no nodes, then he just needs radiation to the ipsilateral para-aortic nodes.

What if it is an embryonal cell cancer?

Then he will need a para-aortic node dissection and chemotherapy. Unlike seminomas, non-seminomas are not radiosensitive.

Can you describe a retroperitoneal node dissection?

I have never done that operation before, but my understanding is that you have to remove all of the lymphatic-bearing tissue along bilateral iliac arteries with extension of the dissection proximally along the para-aortic tissue

Why are you doing a lymphadenectomy if you are just going to give chemotherapy anyway?

The lymph node dissection is therapeutic...

Really, it is?

(0) Prostatism/Prostate Cancer

H&P

Patients may have an increase urinary frequency, increased urgency, and decreased urinary flow.

On physical exam, check the prostate for indurated nodules, hypertrophy and tenderness.

Diagnosis

Check routine labs, including urinanalysis and cultures, and alkaline phospahatase. Check the PSA level. If there is a nodule on the prostate, a TRUS can be done to get a core needle biopsy of the mass.

Treatment

5-alpha-reductase inhibitors (prazosin) can decrease the size of the prostate. LHRH agonist (lupron) can decrease the size, but causes a decrease in libido and impotence. TURP can be done if the gland is < 80gm. An open prostatectomy is required for any gland bigger than this.

Prostrate cancer is suspected with PSA >4 and a positive TRUS biopsy confirms it. If the patient has < 10 years life expectancy, many co-morbidities, and is older than 70 then watchful waiting may be in order. If the PSA increase >10, start them on lupron, bilateral orchidectomies, and radiation therapy

If they have > 10 year life expectancy, low risk co-morbidities and < 70 years old, the do a pelvic lymphadenectomy. If the FS is negative then do a radical prostatectomy, give lupron, and XRT. If the nodes are positive then a radical prostectomy is not done. They are given lupron, bilateral orchidectomy and XRT.

If there is a positive bone scan or mets by CT scan, then give lupron and bilateral orchidectomy and XRT.

(0) Renal mass

H&P

The patients may have hematuria, flank pain, UTI, or history of renal stones.

Physical exam is done on the abdomen to rule in a mass.

Diagnosis

Renal ultrasound of the kidney is done if you suspect a mass. This will tell you if it is cystic or solid. Follow up CT scan is often done.

If there is a solid mass, then get an MRI to evaluate the local invasion or renal vein/ IVC tumor thrombosis. Cystoscopy is done to get brush biopsies.

Treatment

Simple cysts are observed.

Complex cyst or abscesses are drained percutaneously and the fluid is sent for cytology and cultures.

Renal cell carcinoma is treated with a radical nephrectomy.

Transitional cell carcinoma is treated with a radical nephrectomy.

Angiomyolipoma is a fatty appearance on CT, and this is just observed.

Onocytoma is a central necrosis with spoke wheel appearance, and this is just observed.

(3) Pediatrics

(0) Tracheoesophageal Fistula/Esophageal Atresia

H&P

These are new born babies that are unable to swallow, pooling saliva, spits up feeds, coughs or chokes with feeds, and you can not pass an NGT. There may be a pre-partum history of an ultrasound that shows polyhydraminos and a small stomach bubble.

Physical will reveal wheezing, cyanosis and aspiration.

Diagnosis

Place a soft NGT as a far as you can and get a pediogram with lateral views. Look for air in the stomach.

If there is air in the stomach, then there is a TEF with EA.

No air in the stomach, then it is just an EA.

If the NGT is in the stomach, then there is a TEF without EA.

Echocardiogram is done to rule out cardiac anomalies.

Renal ultrasound is done to rule out renal anomalies.

Treatment

Preoperatively, you should keep the HOB elevated to 45 degrees to prevent aspiration. A repogle tube is placed on suction, start H2 blockers, and give antibiotics and vitamin K.

For TEF with EA do a right posterior lateral throacotomy, dived the TEF and close the tracheal opening with 5-0 PDS, anastomose the esophageal stumps, leave an NGT and chest tube. Postoperatively, give antibiotics until the CT is out, start tube feeds within 48 hours, get a gastrograffin swallow at 7 days, no leak feed, and remove the chest tube.

For EA, you should place a gastrostomy tube within the first 48 hours of diagnosis. Start tube feed in the stomach. If there is a long gap (> 3cm) then do daily bougie per mouth and Blake dilators via gastrostomy. Go through the right chest, mobilize the proximal esophagus and sew two ends together. Post op is the same as TEF with EA.

For TEF without EA, proceed to surgery unless there is pneumonia. In this case wait for 24 hours of antibiotics. In the operating room, do a bronchoscopy and place Fogarty catheter to prevent air from escaping with positive pressure ventilation and it helps with identification during exploration. Create a lower right cervical incision and divide the fistula, close the tracheal defect and the esophageal defects with PDS suture. Keep NPO for 48 hours, and then start tube feeds.

(0) Pyloric Stenosis

H&P

Usually present at 4 to 6 weeks of age with intermittent, non-bilious vomiting (projectile), and they are hungry after emesis. Physical exam demonstrates dehydration (sunken fontanels, dry mucus membranes, and poor skin turgor), palpable olive mass in the right upper abdomen, and gastric waves from left to right.

Diagnosis

Ultrasound will show a thicken muscle (> 4mm), long channel length (> 16mm) and increased diameter (> 14mm). UGI will show the elongated track (string signs), and labs will demonstrate a hypocholeremic, hypokalemic, metabolic alkalosis.

Treatment

Get them ready for the operating room by hydrating them up well. Give them D5$^1/_2$NS (15ml/kg/hr) until voiding and then add 15 meq of KCl to 500 ml bag. When the lytes are normal, you can go to the operating room. There you will make a transverse incision, split the rectus muscle, elevate the stomach and deliver the pylorus. Make a 3 cm longitudinal incision 2 mm proximal to the vein of mayo and 5 mm onto the antrum. The circular muscles are bluntly opened until the mucosa bulges out. Test for any leaks.

Post operatively, you start feeding 4 hours after the operation. Start with pedialyte and slowly advance to more frequent, larger volumes, high concentration of formula.

Additional Therapy

If there is regurgitation, assure the mother. Most of the time, this will get better. If it persist for more than 10 days, get an

UGI, if it is incomplete, then make a fresh myotomy on the other side of the pylorus.

(0) Neonatal Small Bowel Obstruction*

H&P

Baby will have emesis, feeding intolerance, abdominal distension, and no passage of meconium for more than 24 hours. The differential is huge: pyloric stenosis, duodenal atresia or stenosis, duodenal webs, annular pancreas, jejunoilleal atresia, intussusceptions, malrotation, colonic atresia, small left colon syndrome, meconium illeus, meconium plug syndrome, or imperforate anus. Think about all these when getting a history.

Physical exam concentrates on the abdomen.

Diagnosis

Get a pediogram after placing a 10 Fr NGT. You may find a double-bubble sign (dilated stomach and proximal duodenum with little or no air distally. This could be from malrotation, duodenal stenosis or atresia, or annular pancreas.

Free air suggests necrotizing enterocolitis.

Calcifications suggest meconium peritonitis.

Multiple dilated loops proximally suggest that there is jejunoilleal atreasia.

Diffuse small bowel loop dilation points more to a distal obstruction in the colon.

Get an UGI if you suspect malrotation or atresia. If you think the obstruction is more distal, then get a gastrograffin enema

Current jelly stool can be found in the diaper of a baby with intussusceptions and you may feel an abdominal mass.

Treatment

Pyloric stenosis has already been discussed.

Duodenal stenosis or atresia and annular pancreas are addressed by passing an OG tube to locate the obstruction. Make a duodenostomy and create a duodenojejunostomy.

Jejunoilleal Atresia is treated with short segment resection with primary anastomosis. Preserve the illeocecal valve.

Colonic atresia is treated with resection and anastomosis for the right and transverse colon. The sigmoid colon needs resection with an end ostomy.

Meconium illeus and plug (rule out CF with sweat test and Hirsprung's disease with suction rectal biopsy) is treated with hyperosmotic gastrograffin enemas. 50% will respond to this, repeat as needed. If you have to operate, make an enterotomy and irrigate with mucomyst and saline to evacuate the meconium.

Malrotation is repaired with a Ladd's procedure. This is done through a transverse supra-umbilical incision, reduce the volvulus with a counter clockwise rotation times three, divide the Ladd's bands and broaden the duodeno-colic mesentery. Perform an appendectomy, check the bowel viability, and tack the duodenum in the right upper quadrant and the cecum to the left upper quadrant.

NEC, Hirsprung's, and imperforate anus see respective sections.

Intussception is treated with a hydrostatic barium enema (3 feet, 3 minutes, 3 attempts). If it is not reduced like this, then go to the operating room and milk the bowel back or resect it if you can not reduce it.

Example Case

A nine month old boy is brought in to the ER with his parents with abdominal pain. His parents tell you that for the past several hours he has had episodic pains, draws up his legs and cries and rest. Why don't you take it from here?

It sound like this child has intussusceptions and I would start by asking the parents about the child's health and birth events. Assuming he has been a healthy baby, then I would proceed with physical exam, focusing on the abdomen, looking for peritoneal signs or abdominal masses, and I would perform a rectal exam to see if there is blood. Current jelly stool would be the classic finding.

Well he has passed some bloody mucus. The child is afebrile, and has a palpable mass in the right upper quadrant, but the abdomen is soft and nontender. There is a little blood on the physical exam.

To be complete, I would send some labs and make sure there is no leukocytosis, check his chemistries for abnormalities that should be corrected, and then I would take him to radiology to perform a 3 ft barium enema to diagnose, and hopefully treat, what seems to be intussusception.

Yes you find that, and the column of barium reduces the intussusception nicely. So you admit the child and he becomes symptomatic again over night.

I would repeat the enema.

This time it does not reduce.

I would give it at least three attempts.

It will not reduce.

Then I will have to take the child to the operating room and explore the abdomen. I would explore him through a lower transverse incision, find the intussusception and milk it back until it had been reduced.

Would you resect it?

Only if I could not reduce it or I injured it.

What if there were some large lymph nodes in that area?

309

(3) Pediatrics

Those are probably just reactive, but they could have been a lead point. If, after really looking closely at this area, I felt like this could be the cause of the intussusception, then I would resect and create a primary anastomosis.

Anything else you want to do?

I don't think so, no.

Sure?

Yes.

You are ready to close the abdomen then?

Yes sir, I would close the abdomen now.

(Remember, the examiners will test you confidence as well. Just because they are pushing you to do something does not mean they want you to do it. Hold your ground and be strong. If you are confident then let it show. If you are unsure, then say so and let them move on).

(0) NEC

H&P

Patients will often be in the NICU and they will have fever, acidosis, thrombocytopenia, and pneumatosis intestinalis.

Physical exam may reveal a distended abdomen which may or may not have cellulitis. They are usually on ventilators.

Diagnosis

Electrolytes, WBC and platelet count, blood and urine cultures, and coags need to be done. The pediogram is done to rule out free air, fixed dilated loop, pneumatosis intestinalis, portal vein gas, and ascitis.

Ultrasound can be used to show portal vein gas, pneumatosis, and ascitis as well.

Treatment

Initial management is non-operative therapy. Place an NGT, make them NPO, and start TPN. Begin broad spectrum antibiotics. Maintain good urine output with IV fluids, check serial KUBs, and follow their CBC and ABG. Send blood, urine, and paracentesis cultures.

If there is free air, they have clinical deterioration with non-operative management, have persistent acidosis or worsening thrombocytopenia, portal venous gas, abdominal wall erythema, or positive paracentesis cultures, then you have to operate.

Try to preserve the illeo-cecal valve and small bowel length, remove the necrotic bowel, and keep a low threshold for a second look.

Single area of isolated NEC calls for a resection, proximal stoma, and mucus fistula.

(3) Pediatrics

Multiple areas of NEC may call for multiple resections and anastomosis, stomas, and mucus fistulas.

If there is pan-necrosis then you will need to do a high proximal stoma with healthy jejunum. Irrigate and suction out the distal small bowel. Create a mucus fistula of the distal small bowel.

Additional Therapy

Contrast study should be done on these patients about 2 months after they recover to evaluate for stricture. If this is ok then you can close the stomas.

(0) Hirschsprung's Disease

H&P

This presents as a new born with a distal obstruction. They may have enterocolitis and diarrhea, sepsis, or present as older children with chronic constipation.

Physical exam is consistent with abdominal distension and maybe sepsis.

Diagnosis

Pediogram should be done to rule out free air, small bowel dilation pattern or double bubble syndrome. If there is no free air, then you can get a barium enema. Look for a saw tooth pattern of the recto sigmoid. There may be a failure to pass the contrast after 24 hours.

Rectal biopsy is done for definitive diagnosis. Full thickness biopsy is done 2 cm above the dentate line. There will be no ganglion cells in the myoenteric plexus. Histological stains are positive. If they are less than 6 months old, then do a suction biopsy to make the diagnosis. If you are doing a diagnostic laparotomy, you can make a diagnosis with resection and frozen sections of the proximal margins.

Treatment

Immediate decompression is done with a large, soft rectal tube. Serial saline enemas are given to wash out the stool. If they are unstable, they should be taken to the operating room.

A leveling colostomy is placed through a LLQ incision, the descending colon transition zone is found and serial seromuscular biopsies are done with frozen section until you there is normal colon. This is brought out as an end colostomy.

Reconstruction is done in 3 to 6 months.

(0) Imperforate Anus

H&P

This is a neonate who has not passed a meconium stool, has a bowel obstruction, and may be septic.

Physical exam shows no anal opening and abdominal distension.

Diagnosis

Pediogram is done to see if there is dilated small bowel and rule out free air. US can show if there is air in the bladder (high) or not (low).

Check a UA for meconium. If there is, then there is a high fistula to the bladder, and they need a colostomy.

24 hour inverted pediogram is where you place a coin on the anal wink and shoot an inverted x-ray. You should see an air fluid level at the level of the rectum.

Treatment

If they are septic, they need a double barrel colostomy. If there is no sepsis, then you proceed with the work up for high or low fistula.

If there is a low rectal stump, then you can puncture the covering membrane if present and enlarge the tract with dilators. Cut back anoplasty is a Y-incision in the skin; the external sphincters are retracted posteriorly, open the rectal stump and sew the rectal edge to the external sphincter and sew the skin edges to the external sphincter. Anal transposition involves a tennis racket incision, fistula is dissected out and closed, rectal stump is brought posteriorly in another levator ani incision, and the neo anus is created.

If there is a high stump, then get a contrast study to show fistula. Bowel preparation is ordered for the patient. Place them in the prone position and make a Y-incision with the midline incision into the external sphincter muscles. The rectal stump is found, dissected out, and closed. It is then mobilized and the external sphincter is closed anteriorly and posteriorly to the stump. The skin is closed and the neo-anus is created.

(0) Surgical Jaundice in Infancy

H&P

If the infant has been jaundice for more than 2 weeks, it is not normal. The differential includes biliary atresia, choledochocyst, hematological disorder, hepatitis, sepsis, or spontaneous perforation of the bile duct.

They may give a history of acholic stools.

Physical exam may reveal splenomegaly, hepatic mass, abdominal mass, ascitis, jaundice, or fever.

Diagnosis

Check the conjugated bilirubin that is increased in diseases of the liver or biliary tract. Unconjugated bilirubin is elevated in hemolysis. Check the other liver functions.

Ultrasound will show you the gallbladder size (small with atresia), CBD size, or fluid collections.

HIDA scan differentiates biliary vs. hepatocellular dysfunction.

Percutaneous needle biopsy of the liver will determine the type of liver disease.

Treatment

Hypoplasia has a patent biliary system (diminutive ductal system). There is no hepatic obstruction. Work them up for hepatocellular causes.

Biliary atresia is an entire extrahepatic biliary tree is a fibrous cord. The gallbladder is tiny with small lumen filled with white bile. The treatment is a Kasai portoenterostomy. The jejunal limb from a roux-Y is sutured to the transected porta hepatitis. Post-operatively you want to see green stools. If there are no green stools, give them steroids. All patients are given actigall and fat soluble vitamins.

Choledochocyst is treated by excision. See that section.

Spontaneous bile duct perforation is treated with a cholecytostomy tube and external drainage. Post-operative cholangiogram is done to ensure healing.

Transplant is considered if the patient is more than 60 days old, has failed a Kasai, has portal hypertension, or has decreased liver function.

(0) Abdominal Mass in a Child

H&P

They are generally more than 2 years old and present with a painless mass in the abdomen that rapidly increases in size.

Physical exam is of the abdominal mass.

Diagnosis

Check the LFTs and AFP, LDH, and ferritin levels, VMA (neuroblastoma), and neuron specific enolases.

Ultrasound can tell you if the mass is cystic or solid.

CT scan is the best test to diagnose the mass.

MRI is done if you suspect a neuroblastoma.

Treatment

A retroperitoneal mass can be renal or extra renal. Renal masses that are solid are Wilm's tumors and sarcomas. Wilm's tumors are resected and given chemotherapy. Sarcomas are resected and given radiation. Cystic masses can be polycystic or multicystic, which are excised and reconstructed.

Extra renal masses include neuroblastoma. These are resected and given chemotherapy.

Intra-abdominal masses can be hepatic or extra hepatic. Hepatic tumors include hepatoblastoma and hepatocarcinoma (resect and chemotherapy), FNH or adenoma (complete excision), and vascular lesions (which usually regress by age 14). The chemotherapy regiment for hepatoblastoma is doxorubicin, vincristine, 5-FU, Cisplatin, and ifosfamidie.

Extra hepatic tumors include solid lesions like Adenexal torsion or tumors and lymphoma. Cystic extra hepatic lesions may be intestinal duplication which is resected and reconstructed.

(2) Inguinal/Scrotal Conditions in Children*

H&P

Patient will present with a groin mass. Get a history of trauma, increase in size over time, increase in size with valsava (or crying), or obstructive symptoms.

Physical exam is concentrated on inguinal hernia, hydrocele, bilateral testes descended, and reducibility of the mass.

Diagnosis

Ultrasound is used to differentiate hernia vs. hydrocele and document blood flow to the testicle.

Treatment

Cryptorchism is a failure of the testis to descend properly and may be found in the suprapubic area, groin, or thigh. If the patient is less than a year old, then just observe because a high percentage will descend eventually. If the patient is more than a year then do an orchipexy through a groin incision to evert the scrotum and suture the teste to the dartos fascia in four quadrants. Do not do the other side. The testicle is pexied to increase fertility, prevent easy trauma, decrease chances of torsion, and make it easy to examine for tumors.

Incarcerated hernia is reduced and then the patient is admitted and the hernia repaired within the next 24 hours. If you can not reduce, you need to do an urgent operation through a groin incision and look at the bowel and fix the hernia by simply closing the sac at the internal ring. You should explore the other side if the child is less than 3 years old.

Testicular torsion pain is relieved with elevation of the testicle and is treated with an urgent orchipexy through a midline

319

scrotal incision. The torsed testicle is detorsed, and both testes are pexied.

Epididymitis is tender with elevation of the testicle and is treated with antibiotics.

Hydroceles are repaired at age 2. Most hydroceles involute by age 2.

Suspicious masses for testicular tumors with elevate HCG and AFP should have an excisional biopsy.

Varicocele is a swollen cord. On the right could be from a retroperitoneal tumor, but on the left side it could be due to the direct drainage into the renal vein. Ligate and divide the spermatic veins and tributaries.

Example Case

You are seeing an 8 year old boy in the emergency room for a tender bulge in the right groin. He is otherwise healthy and takes no medications. He has no allergies and has never had surgery before.

The boy may have a hernia. I would ask the boy and his parent or guardian that he is with if he had ever noticed this bulge before and if it had swollen off an on depending on his activity. A good physical examination will really tell me what I need to know. If the mass seems to be coming from the internal ring, and I can not get it reduced, then this is concerning for an incarcerated hernia.

He has a bulge extending to the top of the scrotum which is very tender and firm. There is mild erythema.

I am going to assume that the testes are descended bilaterally and they are not tender. So I think this is an incarcerated hernia and I would take this child to the operating room for exploration through an inguinal incision and dissect out the sac, open it, and examine the bowel.

If the bowel was necrotic how would you deal with it?

If I could pull it into the field easily through the defect, then I could attempt a small bowel resection with primary anastomosis there and then reduce this. But if there was any concern about doing this, or if it was at all difficult, then I would make a transverse incision in the RLQ and reduce the hernia from the abdominal cavity and do the resection.

How would you close the hernia?

I would ligate the hernia sack high on the abdominal wall and if the internal ring was excessively dilated or I had cut it then I would place interrupted sutures there.

You wouldn't place mesh nor do traditional tissues repair for this 8 year old boy?

Not in a child, no sir.

Wouldn't you explore the other side in a child?

I would only explore the other side if they are less than 3 years old or symptomatic.

(0) Congenital Diaphragmatic Hernias

H&P

Most are diagnosed before birth by ultrasound that shows no gastric bubble, bowel in the chest and polyhydraminos. Patients usually present in respiratory distress after 24 hours of birth.

Physical exam may show a scaphoid abdomen and decreased breath sounds in the chest.

Diagnosis

A pediogram is taken after placement of a 10 Fr. NGT will show the tube in the chest. Echocardiogram is done to rule in any cardiac abnormalities (because of the hypoplastic lung, these children general have a patent foramen ovale and ductus arteriosum).

Treatment

Once the baby is delivered, place an OGT for stomach decompression and give surfactant to help the lungs. Stabilize the patient in the NICU.

If there is no respiratory distress, the go to the operating room in the next 24 hours for repair of the CHD.

If the child is in distress, then intubate and put them on the ventilator. You want to see spontaneous respirations, allow hypercapnia, and keep low tidal volumes. If they have worsening hypoxemia, then place them on ECMO. Once their hypoxia improves or they are off ECMO, and then go to the operating room for repair.

Two types of CHD are Bochdalex (posterior-lateral) and Morgagni (anteriomedial, posterior to the sternum).

To repair a Bochdalex type, you make a left subcostal incision, reduce the contents, excise the sac, and place 2-0 prolene sutures in a horizontal fashion anteriorly. Explore the abdomen for other anomalies and close (using a silo if you must).

Morgagni is done the same as above, but with diaphragm is also sutured to the posterior sternum and posterior rectus sheath.

(0) Thoracic

(0) Mediastinal Mass

H&P

Consider the differential diagnosis of thymoma, teratoma, germ cell tumor, substernal thyroid, lymphoma, sarcoidosis, or neurogenic tumors.

Patients may present with chest pain, fever or night sweats, cough, dyspnea, dysphagia, weakness, fatigue, or hyperthyroidism.

Physical exam is of the head and neck, lymph node basins, and look for testicular masses.

Diagnosis

Initial test should be a CXR and CT scan of the chest so that it can tell you where in the mediastinum it is (anterior are the terrible T's; middle lymphoma, sarcoid, TB, bronchogenic, or pericardial; and posterior are neurogenic tumors, esophageal duplication and mesotheliomas).

You want to check labs like AFP, HCG, VMA, and metanephrines.

CT guided biopsies can be done for diagnosis. Mediastinoscopy and thorcoscopy are also used as needed to take biopsies. All mediastinal masses are excised or biopsied unless it is a substernal thyroid, diffuse thymic enlargement, or small pericardial cyst

Treatment

Lymphoma is treated with CHOP or MOAP

Sarcoid is treated with steroids.

Antibiotics are used to treat infectious causes (e.g. TB).

Seminomas are treated with chemotherapy and XRT, but non-seminomas are treated with chemotherapy alone.

Neurogenic tumors are excised with WLE, radiation, and chemotherapy.

Thymomas need preoperative plasmaphoresis to remove the acetylcholine receptor antibodies. They are given steroids and a median sternotomy is used to remove the tumor. Radiation therapy is given afterwards.

(0) Lung Nodule/Cancer

H&P

You have to get the old CXR and look at it to make sure that this is not an old scar from infection. You want to know about the history of cancer in the past (could this be a met?). You certainly want to ask about smoking and family history to lead you more toward a diagnosis of cancer.

Physical exam involves examination of the lymph node basins.

Diagnosis

CXR is a good place to start and compare it to the old one. This may also show a pleural effusion that may be malignant (T4).

CT scan will help define the mass, its location, and surrounding structures. In addition, percutaneous biopsy may be an option. The scan should go low enough to include the adrenal glands and the liver (common sites of mets). Consider scanning the brain if you suspect brain mets.

You will need a diagnosis one way or another. Bronchoscopy may show invasion into the bronchus or carina. It can also provide brushings and cytology to get diagnosis.

PET scan is very sensitive but not specific (false positive with sarcoidosis). It is useful in detecting positive nodes, revealing bone mets, and ruling out cancer in larger nodes. When trying to determine if a patient has contralaterl paratracheal nodal involvement (N3, thus unresectable), the PET scan is very useful and may aid in this diagnosis.

Mediastinoscopy plays a role in staging of possible lung cancer as well, especially for left sided nodules. It is used for upper and lower para-tracheal nodes, subcarinal nodes, and anterior mediastinum for LUL tumors.

Thorcoscopy can be used to biopsy peripheral lesions that cannot be accessed percutaneously.

Treatment

Before any resection, the patient's pulmonary function must be assessed. This includes ABG, PFTs, and V/Q scans to determine the post-operative FEV1. In order to do a pneumonectomy you need an FEV of 2 L, lobectomy 1 L, and wedge resection 0.6 L.

The stage of the tumor should be sought to determine resectablility.

T0: No evidence of primary tumor - this would be the case if the sputum cytology found cancer cells, but no tumor can be found. This is very rare.

Tis: Carcinoma in situ. The tumor has not grown completely through the thickness of the airway lining where it is located. This is rare.

T1: Tumor is less than 3 cm in size and is completely surrounded by lung tissue.

T2: Tumor is larger than 3 cm but is still surrounded by lung tissue and is not invading the chest wall or any of the structures in the mediastinum.

T3: Tumor of any size that invades the chest wall, diaphragm, or the pericardium.

T4: A tumor of any size that invades the structures of the mediastinum or other structures.

N0: No evidence of cancer in the regional lymph nodes

N1: Cancer in lymph nodes close to the tumor and on same side of the chest

N2: Cancer in the lymph nodes in the mediastinum

N3: Cancer in lymph nodes on the opposite side of the chest as the tumor, or at the base of the neck

Any distant spread of the lung cancer automatically moves a person to stage IV. If distant metastasis is present and a person's stage has been established as IV, no further staging procedures are needed

Stage I disease (T1 or T2) and Stage II (T1-2N1, or T3N0) are treated with lobectomy with mediastinal lymphadenectomy +/- XRT for nodes. Stage IIIA (T3N1, N2) and pancoast tumors are treated with XRT then resection. Stage IIIB (T4 with any N, N3) get chemotherapy and XRT, then re-stage in 2 months. Stage IV gets palliative chemotherapy.

In general T4, N3, and malignant effusion contraindicate a curative resection. Extra-thoracic mets are generally a contraindication to resection except isolated brain met. SVC syndrome, recurrent laryngeal nerve involvement, and great vessel involvement are contraindications

Once resectability is determined, and the patient is a reasonable candidate for resection, it is usually a lobectomy or pneumonectomy with lymph node dissection.

Additional Therapy

Chemotherapy and XRT are both used in the post operative setting.

(0) Tracheal Stenosis

H&P

Previous intubation, malignant tumors, and tracheomalacia in infants are usually the presenting scenario.

Physical exam is on the patient's airway, as they will present with complaints of strider and difficulty breathing.

Diagnosis

The diagnosis is clinical mostly. An x-ray of the neck may reveal stenosis.

Treatment

Place the patient on oxygen and calm everyone down. If the patient is saturating ok, then you have time to get everything ready for intubation. If the patient has lost their airway, you have to get a surgical airway.

Go to the operating room and get the rigid bronchoscope ready. Have the tracheostomy tray ready. You may even have ECMO on standby in case you cannot establish an airway. You then start trying to dilate or core out the stenotic tissue.

Once you have established a good airway, you will eventually have to do a tracheal resection with primary anastomosis (if you have to do a tracheostomy, be careful not to damage too much trachea, keeping in mind the need for future tracheal reconstruction).

(0) Massive Hemoptysis

H&P

Lung abscess, brochiectesis, tumors, AV fistulas, post-operative complications, and trauma may all result with a patient that is coughing up more than 500 ml of blood in a 24 hour period of time (massive hemeoptysis).

Physical exam is on the stability of the patient. Listen to the breath sounds (one side may be filled with blood and not have sounds).

Diagnosis

It's obvious.

Treatment

Get an x-ray of the chest immediate to try and figure out which lung is bleeding. This is the most important question to answer so that you can save the other lung from drowning. Give them oxygen by mask, put the good lung up (if you know which lung that is), and get to the operating room for a rigid or flexible bronchoscope (flexible bronchoscope may not be ideal if there is a lot of bleeding and you cannot suction very well, but it may be better to tell you which lobe is bleeding because you can get down in the smaller bronchials).

Since the left bronchus is smaller, you can put a Fogarty catheter down this side and occlude the lumen, then intubate. If it is coming from the right side, you will have to selectively intubate the left main bronchus.

Arteriogram may be life saving in this situation if the bronchial artery is suspected to be the cause of bleeding. This is the first course of action; however, if the patient deteriorates or continues to bleed, then you will have to go to the operating room, do a throacotomy and resect the part of the lung that is bleeding.

(0) Empyema

H&P

Recent history of pneumonia, sepsis, hemothorax, pneumothorax, upper abdominal infection, esophageal perforation, or lung abscess can all lead to empyema.

Diagnosis

Chest x-ray and CT scan are used to make the diagnosis.

Treatment

If the empyema has not been there very long then tube thoracostomy may be all that is needed. Follow serial x-rays and place addition chest tubes if needed to drain all the areas. If the lung does not fully expand, or all the fluid collections cannot be drained by the chest tubes, then a limited throacotomy or VATS is used to break up all the loculations, clean the thorax out, and leave chest tubes.

If the lung is plastered to chest wall and you cannot see anything, then convert to a throacotomy and decorticate the lung. If the patient will not tolerate this well, then do an Eloesser flap and get out.

(0) Lung Abscess

H&P

Patient may have a history of aspiration and present with fevers, abnormal CXR or CT scan.

Diagnosis

CT scans and x-rays are used to make the diagnosis.

Bronchoscopy should be done to rule out obstruction by tumor or foreign body.

Treatment

The patient is placed on antibiotics and CT guided drainage is done. Use aggressive pulmonary toilet for these patients.

If they have hemeoptysis, persistent fever for 2 weeks despite antibiotics, the cavity doesn't change in size (shrink), the drain doesn't fully remove the abscess, or they develop a bronchopleural fistula, then you have to operate.

Cut into the abscess by following the drain down and leave a large chest tube in the cavity. Lobectomy may be needed if the patient is having massive hemeoptysis, empyema, or large pneumothorax.

(31) Vascular

(9) AAA*

H&P

Patient may present emergently with back pain, abdominal pain, groin pain, syncope, or hypotension. They could present with an enlarging AAA. Ask about family history, and risk factors for rupture (COPD, HTN, shape and size of AAA, etc).

On physical exam, assess how stable the patient is, feel the abdominal mass, femoral and popliteal.

Diagnosis

Check their labs (send a T&C), and put them on a monitor. Get an EKG. If they are symptomatic but stable, then you can get a CT scan and ultrasound to determine if the aneurysm is intact or ruptured. If they are unstable, then quickly get an US on the way to the operating room.

Get an US every 6 month if the aneurysm is asymptomatic and < 5.5 cm in males and < 4.5 cm in females. Take this time to assess their cardiac risk factors and co-morbidities.

Below 5 cm, there is about a 20% risk of rupture at five years. Between 5 and 7 cm, there is a 33% risk of rupture over 5 years, but once the AAA gets larger than 7 cm, then there is a 95% risk of rupture within the next 5 years.

Greatest Diameter (cm)	Annual Rupture Risk (%)
3.0–5.5	0.6
5.6–5.9	5–10
6.0–6.9	10–20
7.0–7.9	20–30
>8.0	30–50

If the AAA is > 5cm and the patient is asymptomatic, then do a cardiac work up, place on peri-operative B-blockers, plan operation.

Treatment

Asymptomatic aneurysms that are being following with q 6 month US need elective repair if they grow larger than 5.5 cm for men and 4.5 cm for women or if they grow more than 0.5 cm in a 6 month period.

If the aneurysm is intact, and the patient is symptomatic, then you need to do a semi-urgent repair after doing a cardiac work up.

Consider endovascular aortic repair (EVAR) if they are candidates. Contraindications to EVAR include a short and wide proximal neck, neck angulations > 60°, horseshoe kidney (the collecting system and the ureters are medial, so don't divide it down the middle), accessory renal arteries, tortuous iliac arteries, calcified iliac arteries, and poor compliance for surveillance.

If the aneurysm has ruptured, then keep the SBP around 100 and get to the operating room. Heat up the room, have blood and blood warmers available, place an NGT and Foley, prep the patient prior to induction from the chin to the knees, make a midline incision (if the patient crashes on induction, then do a left throacotomy and clamp the thoracic aorta. Clamp the supra-celiac aorta through he gastro-hepatic ligament and get distal control of the illiacs. Open the retroperitoneum once anesthesia has caught up, and find the AAA. Move the supra-celiac clamp below the renals now so the kidneys can have a drink. Open the AAA, remove the thrombus, and over-sew the lumbars as needed. Place a straight Dacron tube graft and check the bowel viability.

You may have to re-implant the IMA if the back bleeding is slow or pressure is less than 40 mmHg, but don't reimplant when there is no flow. Also, you should reimplant the IMA when the patient has had a colon operation that may compromise the collateral flow.

Check the pedal pulses before you leave the room.

Example Case

A 77 year old man is asymptomatic from a 6 cm AAA found by ultrasound. He is S/P transverse colectomy 10 years ago for colon cancer. He has a remote history of an MI, but has good functional status.

Well, considering he is in good functional status, we may consider repairing this. His risk of rupture in five years is about 33%, and he should be alive in 5 years. So I think this is a reasonable option. So I would begin his work up with cardiac stress testing and coronary angiogram if this is positive, and I would want to see a recent colonoscopy in the last 3 years, or else I would do one myself to make sure there is no recurrence of the colon cancer. Also, I would duplex the carotid arteries to make sure there is no significant disease here before I go doing an elective procedure. If all this clears out, then I would evaluate the AAA with a CTA to give me a good idea of the disease pattern and if the iliacs are involved. In addition, CTA can tell you if he is a candidate for endovascular stenting.

I am not a vascular surgeon, but had a good experience with this procedure. The real question is what is the benefit of stenting this man. He will get out of the hospital faster, but the complication rate and survival rate at five years is the same. Endovascular stenting is very costly and may not be a great option for this man. Therefore, I would reserve that for the relatively younger patient who is still working and would benefit from the shorter hospital stay.

Ok, you find a 50% stenosis of the right iliac on your CT angiogram. Other than that, it seems like a straight forward 6 cm, fusiform AAA just below the renal vessels.

(31) Vascular

I would approach this through the abdomen and fix this with a bifurcated limb to the right iliac.

Just the right or bilateral?

Just the right, unless there was aneurismal involvement of the left or he had significant disease on that side.

What about the IMA, would you re-implant it?

Yes, I would. I would do that because he had a transverse colectomy and the middle colic is gone. Therefore, he has very little collateral flow through the left colon.

Good.

(5) Acute Lower Extremity Ischemia*

H&P

Patient may have a history of acute onset of leg pain, a-fib, CAD, DM, PVD, or hypercoaguable state.

Physical exam is done for bilateral pulses, neurosensory, neuromotor, ulceration, and assess the viability of the leg: viable (no deficits, audible doppler), marginally threatened (slight decrease sensory and inaudible doppler), immediately threatened (no sensation, decreased motor, rest pain), or irreversible (profound sensory and motor deficit).

Diagnosis

Check their labs, coagulatation studies, CPK, and hypercoaguable state (antithrombin III deficiency, protein C&S deficiency, factor V Leiden, lupus anti-coagulant, and hyperhomocysteinemia).

Doppler signals of the extremity should be sought, and check ABIs.

Treatment

Start a heparin drip as soon as you see an ischemic limb. Give a 100 unit/kg bolus and then give 15 units/kg/hour.

Then get an angiogram to find out where the thrombus or occlusion is.

If there is an isolated femoral or popliteal embolus, then do a thrombectomy, postoperative heparin and Coumadin, echocardiogram (to rule out mural thrombus), and get a hypercoaguable states work up).

If there is a femoral embolus and distal propagation, start thrombolytic therapy, put them in the ICU and monitor their fibrinogen levels (keep > 100), repeat the angiogram the next day. If there is no improvement then do a bypass.

If the limb is immediately threatened, then start a heparin drip and go to the operating room. Do a thrombectomy proximally and distally and repeat until there is no more thrombus. Send the thrombus for pathology (rule out myxoma). Get a completion angiogram and if you find a focal lesion then stent it, if there is diffuse disease then bypass it, and if there is no other finding then you are done. Consider doing 4 compartment fasciotomies if the onset of ischemia is more than 2 hours. Keep the patient hydrated well to keep the urine output more than 100 ml/hour, pH >7, follow the CPKs, and put HCO3 in the fluids if needed.

Example Case

You are called in to see a 78 year old woman with an 8 hour history of a cold, painful leg. She had an MI 3 weeks ago.

So I am concerned that this lady now has some ischemic myocardium that's not moving very well, developed a mural thrombus and some of that thrombus has embolized to her leg. Assuming she is otherwise stable and I do not need to be resuscitating her, I would start evaluate her with a history focused on risk factors for atherosclerosis, because these vessels may be very narrow as demonstrated by the fact that she had a heart attack. Hopefully she does not smoke, and she is on ASA and Lipitor (and a beta blocker) since her MI.

To examine the foot, I would start at the groin fist and feel for a femoral pulse that will tell me if the illiacs are open; I suspect they are unless this is a large saddle embolism. The popliteal and the distal pulses may be absent if this clot has lodged in the popliteal artery.

Her left leg is pulseless from the femoral arteries down.

Assuming that the other side is normal to give me some access for angiogram, and then I would heparinize her and draw standard lab work including coagulation labs. I would get an EKG to make sure is not in any dysrrythmia.

She is in a-fib and her glucose is a little high, but otherwise everything is normal.

Then I would take her to the operating room. I would put her to sleep, prep and drape her from the chest down to the toes on both sides and perform an angiogram, access the right side and starting with an aortogram with runoff. This should tell me where the blockage is.

Anesthesia refuses to give her general anesthetic because of her recent MI?

I agree with them, she should not be put to sleep; I would do the arteriogram and embolectomy under local.

How do you do this?

I would have her prepped and draped out from the nipples all the way to the toes. I would keep her covered with sterile drapes to keep her warm, I want access incase I need to put her to sleep and fix an aortic or iliac problem emergently. I would inject local anesthetic over the femoral pulse, just as I would to insert a femoral a-line. Once access the artery with a needle, I would place a flexible J-shaped glide wire into the aorta under fluoroscopy, remove the needle, and then place a sheath.

What size sheath?

I'm not a vascular surgeon and I don't do this everyday. If memory serves me correctly this is like a #6 or #8 Fr sheath. I would place a pig tail catheter over the wire and into the distal aorta, just above the bifurcation and try to get in the left iliac. Inject the contrast under live fluoroscopy and visualize the blockage in the left side.

At this time, I would plan the embolectomy, leave the sheath in for post operative angiogram and under local, make an incision over the superficial femoral artery and dissect this out. I would get control of the common femoral, deep femoral and distal superficial femoral arteries, open the superficial femoral and pass a Fogarty catheter proximally and distally until I get good blood return.

You do this and good blood flow back, but the foot remains pulseless. No more clot is coming back though.

I would repeat the angiogram.

It shows clot in the popliteal system.

Then I would make a medial incision on the leg just below the knee and get proximal and distal control of the popliteal, open it and perform the thrombectomy here as well.

The foot pinks up and has good pulses.

I would close all the arterotomies, the tissue layers, and then shoot another angiogram before leaving the room.

All looks good.

Check the pulse one more time as we are leaving the room and take her to the ICU, continue the heparin and consult her cardiologist for the new onset a-fib that is probably the reason she threw this clot.

Is there anything else you would have done while in the operating room.

If the ischemic time had been more than 2 hours I would consider fasciotomies.

It has been about 4 and half.

Then I would do compartment fasciotomies.

How?

Medially, I would make the incision about a centimeter below the tibia and open the deep posterior and posterior compartments, and laterally I would open the anterior and lateral compartment with an incision between the fibula and tibia.

(1) Vascular Bypasses*

Femoral to Popliteal Bypass

Make a groin incision to expose the CFA, SFA, and DFA. Harvest the GSV and ligate the tributaries, obtaining as much length as you can. The proximal anastomosis is done from the SFA to the reversed GSV. The popliteal is exposed through a longitudinal medial incision (knee flexed and externally rotated), the adductor canal is exposed by dividing the adductor magnus tendon and retracting the Sartorius posteriorly and vastus medius anteriorly. The popliteal artery is posterior and medial to the femur. The distal anastomosis is created from the GSV to the popliteal.

Femoral to Anterior Tibial

Make a longitudinal incision 1 cm medial to the tibia and 2cm distal. Incise the deep fascia and retract the soleus anteriorly and the gastrocnemius posteriorly. Expose the anterior tibial artery and the tibioperoneal trunk here.

Femoral to Peroneal

Same as the anterior tibial and tibioperoneal trunk exposure, but you detach the soleus muscle anteriorly. The peroneal artery is found 2 to 3 cm distal to the tibioperoneal trunk.

Distal Anterior Tibial

Make a longitudinal incision anterior to the tibia.

Distal Posterior Tibial

Make a longitudinal incision medial to the tibia.

Example Case

You are asked to see a 72 years old nursing home patient for a left heal ulcer. He lives in a nursing home and is a diabetic. He has normal mentation.

So I will assume that this patient is up and walking around and would like to keep his foot. So there is no reason not to really try and get this to heal. If the wound is not infected and it is a consult to try and get this to heal, then the question here is does the foot have adequate circulation? If the patient has a palpable pulse, no further testing is needed, and we should be able to get this foot to heal. If he does not have a palpable pulse, then I would feel the rest of his pulses to determine where the disease may be, and I would use a Doppler to listen for pedal pulses.

He has diminished pulses pulses in the groins bilaterally. The ulcer is open with surrounding erythema, but it is not infected. The Doppler reveals monophasic pedal pulses.

OK, so I have some proximal disease and there is some flow to the foot. So is there enough flow to the foot to heal this? The next test to do is a toe pressure. You can do this with a pulse ox diode and measure the pressure. It should be about two-thirds the pressure of the ankle pressure. If it is greater than 40 mmHg, it is likely to heal. If it is lower than this, it probably will not heal. Since this is not healing, I will assume that this is lower than 40.

So the next step is angiography of the vessels to find where there is any obstruction. I would perform an aortogram with bilateral lower extremity run off. CTA and MRA are options, but I am not very familiar with these modalities and the reliability of them because of the calcification of vessels below the knee makes it hard to tell if the disease is recontructable. Above the knee, CTA is probably a good test; nonetheless, contrast angiography is probably the best because you may be able to do endovascular therapy at the time of diagnosis.

He has bilateral iliac disease with left greater than the right.

If this is the case, then balloon angioplasty and stenting would be a good option for this patient. By increasing the in-flow, we may be able to get the toe pressure up high enough to get the ulcer to heal.

What if he has distal disease as well?

I am sure he does. I am not a vascular surgeon, but I understand that they really have advanced their endovascular technologies far enough to even hollow out distal vessels enough to increase the inflow. So this may be an option. If this fails, then he would need a distal bypass.

Well, let's say that he can not lay flat long enough to anything. He gets very short of breath.

Well, he has diabetes, he is old, and he has peripheral vascular disease, so it is no surprise that he has so coronary atherosclerotic disease. He should have and EKG, echocardiogram, and stress test. If the nuclear medicine stress shows any reversible ischemia, then he should undergo a left heart catheterization and stenting of any coronary lesions.

He does that, and the LHC shows un-stentable and non-recontructable CAD.

Well, then that is going to limit us to what we can do. Endovascular techniques would be the best option in this patient and we may have to do it in several trips and short episodes with the help of the medicine team to optimize his cardiac status with beta blockers and nitrates to decrease his after load and myocardial oxygen demands.

Let's say he gets his heart stents and you stent his iliacs, but the distal disease is still sever enough on the left that he still can't heal the ulcer.

So then I will have to do a distal bypass. Assuming that on the runoff, I can find a good distal vessel with adequate outflow and the superficial femoral has adequate inflow, and then I would construct a femoral to distal bypass with GSV graft.

(2) Intermittent Claudication*

H&P

Patient will have pain in the calf, reproducible with exercise, relieved with rest, worse going up hill, better with standing or sitting, and may have a history of risk factors like smoking, CAD, DM, high cholesterol, HTN, or sedentary lifestyle.

Physical examination is a full cardiovascular exam, check the ABIs, check the pedal pulses, check for pallor with elevation of the foot, rubor with dependency, decreased temperature, do a neuro and spine exam.

Diagnosis

Initially, you want to get an arterial duplex with ABIs. Claudication occurs with ABI 0.5 to 0.6. Less than 0.3 is consistent with rest pain.

An exercise treadmill test may show that their ABIs decreases to less than 0.3 with exercise. MRA can evaluate stenosis and the level of the lesion.

Treatment

Claudication is not an emergent surgical problem, but the atherosclerotic disease is. They should stop smoking, get tight control of their DM and HTN, start them on Lipitor and ASA, may benefit from pletal, start them on an exercise program where they walk until they claudicate and then return (3 times a week for 30 minutes), and have them lose weight.

If they improve with conservative management then evaluate with annual arterial duplex studies.

Surgery is indicated for rest pain, gangrene, non-healing ulcers, and failed conservative therapy. When considering surgery, get a full cardiac work up work up with EKG and stress test. An arteriogram must be done to evaluate the level of the lesion and to decide if bypass or endovascular interventions are possible.

If the patient is found to have aorto-illiac disease, consider the following: Severe aortic disease can be treated with an aorto-bifemoral bypass, diffuse bilateral iliac disease is best treated with an ABF as well, focal iliac disease is amendable to PCTA and stenting, and diffuse unilateral iliac disease may best be treated with a femoral-femoral bypass.

All of these procedures are concluded with a completion angiogram. A good run-off a-gram shows 2 of the 3 three vessels seen with at least one vessel going to the foot and a patent distal popliteal.

If the patient has infra-inguinal occlusive diseases then consider the fem-pop, fem-ant tibial or fem-peroneal bypasses. Non-candidates for a bypass include extensive necrosis, sepsis, and non-ambulatory patients.

Example Case

72 year old male with 2 block claudication comes to see you in your office.

I would try to get a good idea about the type of pain he is having. I am assuming that this is the typical calf pain that hurts with exercise and then is relieved by resting. I would get a history it pertains to his risk factors. Assuming he is probably a smoker, may have a history of coronary artery disease or PVD, does he have high cholesterol, and is he a diabetic. The next thing I would do is get a good idea of how this claudication is affecting his lifestyle.

I would ask him about rest pain and examine his feet. I would feel the pulses in both lower extremities from the femoral vessels to the feet and look for evidence of chronic ischemia like hair loss, and hypertrophied nail beds.

He is a smoker and has no rest pain. This man is a rancher. His left leg is normal. His right leg has a weak femoral pulse with a bruit and nothing below it.

His right iliac has disease in it. I would encourage him to stop smoking right now. At this time, it would be formal to get some ABI's, but I know that the right side has high disease on it and if I cannot feel a pedal pulse, then we have problems. I would check his creatinine because I will plan an angiogram and that will involve contrast. I would check an EKG as a baseline and make sure there is no obvious heart disease, and I would send him for a nuclear medicine stress test.

Are you planning on an angiogram? So, why are you working up his heart?

I am planning on an angiogram and probably a balloon angioplasty and stenting of the iliac on that side. If the vessel ruptures during the balloon dilation and I have to put him to sleep and fix it, the last thing I will need to worry about is his heart.

Ok, the angiogram shows a tight stenosis of the SFA distal to the profunda.

Oh, I was fooled there; thought the iliacs would be stenosed. Assuming there is no other disease and he otherwise has good run off, then I would consider a femoral to above the knee popliteal bypass using a PTFE graft. Another consideration would be to just do a superficial femoral endarterectomy with patch angioplasty.

OK, let's say he had a popliteal occlusion and an anterior tibial that was patent and fills the arch, but he has had the saphenous vein harvested on both sides for his CABG.

Ha…upper extremity vein mapping may reveal a good conduit, but if that did not work then you could use gortex below the knee with a vein patch and start him on Coumadin which should give you patency rates of 70-80% at 2 years.

(1) Thoracic Outlet Syndrome

H&P

These patients typically present with numbness and pain in the upper extremity that is worsened by stress positions. They may have upper extremity claudication and emboli to the fingers.

Physical exam is focused on discoloration or swelling of the upper extremity. Do a complete CVS exam and neurological exam.

Diagnosis

Check a CXR and C-spine series looking for a cervical rib or elongated transverse processes.

EAST test is the "elevated arm stress test". The patient is to keep the arm elevated and clench and unclench the fist with the arms abducted to reproduce the pain.

MRI, CT and NCV can reveal neurogenic causes (95%). Venous duplex will reveal venous thrombosis (4%), and an arterial duplex is used to diagnose aneurismal or thrombosis or the artery (1%).

Treatment

For neurogenic causes, treat them with 6 weeks of physical therapy. If the symptoms persist, then anterior scalenectomy and 1st rib resection is the treatment.

Venous thrombosis is treated acutely with heparin drip and arm elevation. Thrombolytic therapy is started and the patient is started on Coumadin for at least three months to allow intimal healing. 1st rib resection is the treatment of choice (especially in younger patients).

Once you have lysed the clot with thrombolytics, you should shoot a venogram to find the obstruction. This is where the rib resection comes in. Once you have removed the physical obstruction, if there is still a bend in the vein, then a stent may be needed.

Arterial aneurysm is treated by resection and reconstruction. Thrombosis is treated by bypass from the subclavian to the axillary artery.

(2) Carotid Stenosis

H&P

Patients can have emboli from the different territories of carotid (localized in one hemisphere), vertebrobasilar (ataxia, dizziness, and drop attacks), and global (syncope, dizziness, and weakness). Risk factors sought are tobacco, CAD, high cholesterol, DM, and HTN. Ask about history of A-fib or prior CVA.

Physical exam looks for bruits, neurological deficits, CVSA exam, carotid exam, and cardiac exam.

Diagnosis

Start with a duplex scan of the carotids if there is concern for disease. Get an MRI if there is any question if the vertebrobasilar disease exists and rule out proximal common carotid artery or arch disease. EKG can rule out cardiac disease.

Treatment

If the patient had non-hemorrhagic strokes then start TPA within 3 hours. Once there is resolution, get a duplex. Do carotid endarterectmy (CEA) 4 weeks out.

If there is a hemorrhagic stroke, then treat medically.

If the patient is symptomatic and > 70% stenosis (peak systolic velocities > 135 cm/s), symptomatic and > 50% (PSV > 125 cm/s) with ulceration, and asymptomatic patients with > 80% stenosis (end diastolic velocities > 140 cm/s) all get a CEA

Additional Therapy

NASCET (North American symptomatic CEA trial) found that CEA had a 9% vs. medical treatment's 26% stroke rate within 2 years in symptomatic patients with > 70% stenosis, but 50% stenosis no difference.

ACAS (asymptomatic carotid atherosclerosis study) found that asymptomatic patient with > 60% stenosis had a stroke rate within 5 years of 5% with CEA and 11% with medical treatment.

(1) Varicose Veins*

H&P

History of pregnancy, phlebitis, DVT, ulceration, the veins are worse with standing.

Physical examination should be done on the lower extremities to look for edema, pain, ulceration, and cellulitis.

Diagnosis

Brodie-T-Berg test (lay supine with the leg elevated, tourniquet below the knee, stand for 30 seconds, remove the tourniquet and see if there is more blood coming in from above to suggest vein incompetence).

Treatment

Varicose veins without deep venous disease are treated with therapeutic stockings or variceal ablation.

Deep venous obstruction cannot be ablated. The duplex and ascending contrast venography will locate the level. Femoral to femoral bypass for iliac thrombosis or saphenopopliteal bypass for SFV or DFV thrombosis.

Deep venous reflux requires valvuloplasty, vein transposition, or venous valve transplant.

Combined deep obstruction and reflux is not reconstructable and is treated with compression stockings and/or ablation (ligate at the saphenofemoral junction, strip out the saphenous vein, stab avulsion of perforators or radiofrequency ablation of them).

Additional Therapy

Venous stasis ulcers

Example Case

A moderately obese 38 year old woman comes to your office with her six children, complaining of an ulcer over the medial malleolus of her left foot, as well as ankle swelling and calf swelling, on the same side.

The swelling and edema in that one leg is concerning that she has a deep venous clot or insufficiency that is giving her venous stasis, and that is what has resulted in the ulcer on the medial malleolus. Therefore, assuming that she has no history of varicose veins, deep venous clots, hypercoaguable state, or cancer, then I would start by examining the leg to make sure it is unilateral and examine the pulses with duplex if I have to because of the edema. Assuming that there is good arterial flow, and this appears to be a venous stasis ulcer, then I would order a lower extremity duplex ultrasound.

She has good arterial flow and the duplex is positive clot in the femoropopliteal system.

Then I would admit her and start her on IV heparin, then start Coumadin.

But she has no one to watch her kids. Why can't she just start some Coumadin at home?

If she has a protein C & S deficiency, and she starts Coumadin without heparin first, she can actually become hypercoaguable and clot tiny vessels in her skin, causing necrosis. So, for her safety, we really should start heparin. Another choice would be for her to purchase injectable LMWH and learn to give it to herself at home while she started the coumadin.

She agrees to be admitted and start the heparin and Coumadin. What is your plan for discharge and follow up.

I would get her INR between 2 and 3 on coumadin and keep her on this for at least 6 months while the clot is dissolving, but there is the question as to why she got the DVT and if she has any other venous insufficiency. I would test her for protein C&S, anti-lupus antibodies, Factor V Leiden and anticariolipin antibodies. If this is all negative, and her superficial venous system is open and competent, then una boot wraps to the lower extremity for the ulcer and anticoagulation is the only recommended treatment at this time. I would like to see her back every month to monitor the healing of the ulcer.

Yes, her work up is negative just as you say; however, she returns to the emergency room, two months later, with chest pain, SOB, and hemeoptysis.

Sound like she has a PE, but it could be other things like PUD, pneumonia, MI, and bleeding in the lung from over anticoagulation. I would make sure she is stable, on oxygen, assess her vitals, start an IV and check her coagulation studies. If these appear normal, I would start heparin. I would get a stat chest x-ray and a WBC to rule out pneumonia, and an ABG to see how hypoxic she is. I expect low CO_2 and O_2 if there is a PE. To make the definitive diagnosis, I would start with a CTA of the chest.

It is positive.

Then I would admit her to the ICU, continue supportive care and heparin, and place a filter.

Why place a filter?

Throwing a PE while on anticoagulation is an indication.

(10) Mesenteric Ischemia*

H&P

Patient may have non-specific abdominal pain out of proportion to examination.

They may have risk factors such as CAD, PVD, DM, HTN, recent AAA repair and high cholesterol. Acute thrombosis may be caused by a recent MI, a-fib, mitral valve disease and present with pain after meals with subsequent weight loss secondary to fear of eating. Non-occlusive mesenteric ischemia (NOMI) is usually diagnosed in severely ill patients with low flow state.

Physical examination may be of little value. The abdomen is distended and they will have decreased bowel sounds.

Diagnosis

Check the labs, including WBC, amylase, lipase, and lactic acid. KUB may show free air, air in the bowel wall, or "thumbprinting" pattern.

CT scan can help rule out other etiologies. MRA is better than CT scan.

Arteriogram is the gold standard. It allows excellent visualization of the celiac, SMA, and IMA. The trunks can be separately given papaverine. Angioplasty and stents are used for chronic lesions.

Treatment

Exploratory laparotomy is done for abdominal pain, acidosis and high suspicion. You will usually find necrotic bowel.

See if you can appreciate any palpable pulse in the mesentery and use a Doppler as needed. Look for the pattern of ischemia to get an idea if it is embolic (small bowel and proximal colon affected but proximal jejunum and transverse colon are spared because it usually lodges just past the middle colic artery and jejunal branches of the SMA), thrombotic at origin (entire midgut is ischemic, including the descending colon), and NOMI (entire small bowel affected, find weak pulsation at the SMA origin).

Assess the bowel viability. Doppler on the antimesenteric border, uses florescein and woods lamp, and considers a second look laparotomy. Resect any necrotic bowel and leave all marginally profused bowel.

NOMI is diagnosed with an angiogram and the treatment is non-operative. Optimize their fluid status with a SG catheter and improve the cardiac output, eliminate vasopressors, and selectively catheterize the SMA to give papaverine (30mg/hr). The a-gram is repeated within 24 hours. If the patient develops peritonitis, then operate.

Embolus is treated with laparotomy, find the SMA and palpate it as it crosses over the 3rd part of the duodenum. Get proximal and distal control after giving heparin. Create an arteriotomy and pass a 4 Fr. Balloon proximally and distally. If there is no success here, then bypass.

Thrombotic disease is treated with an SMA bypass. In an emergent situation use an infra-renal aortic to SMA bypass or iliac to SMA bypass. Use GSV graft if you can.

Chronic disease is diagnosed by duplex study and is treated with a supra-celiac graft to SMA bypass.

Example Case

You are asked to consult on a 64-year old man S/P mitral valve replacement 2 days ago who has been complaining of diffuse abdominal pain for 12 hours.

Assuming that this patient is still in the ICU is hemodynamically stable, not having fever or tachycardic…

He seems ok, but he is in a-fib, and noted to be pre-operatively, but he has never been anticoagulated.

I am concerned that this patient has thrown an embolus to the mesenteric vessels, probably the SMA. On examination I would make sure that the patient is stable and that there is no peritonitis but he probably has pain out of proportion to exam, which would increase my suspicion for small bowel infarction. A bedside echocardiogram could show me any mural thrombus in the heart that may be the source of the emboli. I would send lab work to include a WBC which may be elevated if the bowel is infracting, similarly a lactic acid may be elevated in this case and ABG should be done to determine his pH and base deficit. I would check his LFTs and amylase to rule out gallbladder and pancreatic disease, and I would check his electrolytes to make sure there is nothing to cause him to have this arrhythmia. EKG to rule out MI and CXR to rule out pneumonia should be done routinely here. Abdominal films may show an illeus, bowel wall gas, or thumb printing.

If this is all pointing toward mesenteric ischemia, then I would heparinize the patient immediately, transfer him back to the ICU, place invasive monitor (like a central line or SGC) to optimize his fluid volume, and order an angiogram.

The angiogram shows a thrombus of the proximal SMA.

Assuming that the celiac and IMA are not collateralizing a portion of the small bowel to make his symptoms consistent with bowel ischemia, and the cut off in the SMA is a couple cm from the origin, then this would be consistent with an embolus. I would give the patient pre-operative antibiotics; take him to the operating room for exploration via a midline abdominal incision. I will assess the bowel for viability and determine the distribution of ischemia; hopefully it is consistent with what I saw on the angiogram. I would lift the transverse colon, find the middle colic and follow it to the SMA. Palpating the SMA, I will most likely not feel a pulse, and since I expect that this is a thrombosis, I will make a transverse arteriotomy in the

SMA and pass a #4 Fogarty catheter proximally and distally to remove all the clot and good forward and back bleeding. I would then close my arteriotomy with interrupted 5-0 prolene sutures. I would keep the patient on heparin. Hopefully the bowel will pink up after this, but if there is any necrotic bowel I would resect it and do a primary anastomosis. If there is any question about bowel viability, I would vac the abdomen open and come back in 24 hours to reassess.

What if the SMA is very hard when you palpate it?

Then this suggests that there is significant atherosclerotic disease in this vessel and so I would plan on doing a bypass to it. I would palpate up the vessel until I found an area that was relatively soft. Then I would get proximal and distal control and make a vertical incision in the vessel. I would endarterectomize the vessel, remove all proximal clot with a fogarty catheter, and use a SVG to bypass from the infra-renal aorta or illiacs (depending on the amount of atherosclerosis in these vessels) to the SMA.

(79) Trauma/Critical Care

In place of the H&P for other subjects, trauma has the ABC's of ATLS at the forefront of all the scenarios. No matter what is presented, you want to do this and be systematic. Likewise, just as you should not tell your examine, "I would do a full H&P," don't tell them "I would do the ABC's." They hate that. Tell them what you are doing. For most traumas, the scenarios will have a victim brought in, they may or may not be intubated. Bottom line is to tell them, "I am going to make sure that they have a patent airway and listen to their chest to make sure that they are moving air on both sides. Meanwhile, I want my nurses to be getting two large bore IV's and getting a blood pressure on the patient. Assuming they are doing ok, moving air, and have a stable blood pressure, I will assess the GCS and have them move all their extremities, then fully expose them and look for any other injuries...etc." These are basic principles that you need to be able to spit out on command.

(3) Polytrauma with Pelvic Fracture*

ABC's

Most of these patients are MVC victims or have been crushed by something. They will usually give you a hypotensive patient. You have to think about this logically and out loud so they hear your thought process. The patient is hypotensive, and in trauma the top three causes of hypotension are bleeding, bleeding, and bleeding. The places that can have significant bleeding are the chest, abdomen, pelvis, or long bones.

Diagnosis

When you listen to the chest, you can rule out a massive hemothorax. On the full exposure and exam of the patient, you will likely need to note the blood at the meatus or the high riding prostate on rectal exam and the unstable fracture. After the primary survey, and fluid boluses, your chest x-ray and pelvic x-ray will reveal the pelvic fractures, and FAST exam will rule out or in the hemoperitoneum. Assess how stable the patient is at this point and start triaging your injuries.

Treatment

If the patient is stable, then you can go to the CT scan for further diagnostic work up. Place a pelvic binder ASAP.

If the patient is unstable, you have to control the hemorrhage with external fixation or MAST trousers. If the DPL or FAST scan appears negative and the pelvis appears to be the only place for the blood loss, then go to the angiogram suite for embolization of possible arterial bleeding. If the abdomen appears to be bleeding as well, go to the operating room for exploration. Control the abdominal bleeding and externally fixate the pelvis. If they continue to bleed, then go to the angiogram suit. Pelvic hematomas should only be explored if there is a rapidly expanding or pulsatile hematoma (which is rare).

Blood at the urethral meatus, high riding prostate or scrotal hematoma should raise the suspicion for injury and mandates a RUG prior to placing a Foley catheter. If there is an incomplete injury, you may be able to pass a Foley and let is heal. If you cannot place the Foley, then place a suprapubic catheter.

Gross hematuria or microhematuria requires evaluation of the bladder with a cystogram. Extra-peritoneal rupture is treated with Foley drainage. Intra-peritoneal ruptures need abdominal exploration and repair in three layers.

Example Case

You have a 22 year old male who presents to the ED after being involved in an MVC. He was a restrained driver. No LOC. Nurse reports that he complains of lower abdominal pain and has blood at the urethral meatus.

I am concerned that the patient has a urethral injury, and perhaps a pelvic fracture that caused this injury. First, I want to do my primary survey and make sure that he is protecting his airway, breathing well and moving air bilaterally, and has a normal blood pressure and two large bore IV's (and send his labs off as they do this, including CBC and a T&C)

He is.

OK, I would assess his GCS and ask him to move all his extremities. I would check his pulses in the extremities then remove all his clothing and look him over head to toe to make sure he has no other injuries. At this time, I would examine his abdomen and do a rectal exam to check for blood or a high riding prostate. Then ask for my c-spine, chest and pelvic x-rays.

C-spine is negative, chest is clear, but the pelvic x-ray shows a superior and inferior ramus fracture of the left pelvis. You notice a seat belt sign of the lower abdomen. His pelvis is tender when you rock it. You notice blood at the meatus, and when you do the rectal exam you notice fullness and cannot palpate the prostate.

The seat-belt sign concerns me that there could be some intra-abdominal injury. The tender pelvis and pelvic x-ray reveal a pelvic injury, but the patient is hemodynamically stable at this time, so it is probably not bleeding, and the blood at the urethral meatus and high riding prostate are pretty good signs of urethral injury. So I would have urology come down and do a RUG to see if there where the urethral injury is, and if there is a bladder injury, do a bedside FAST scan to look for free

363

fluid in the abdomen, and plan on taking the patient to the CT scanner to look at the abdomen and pelvis.

The CT only shows the pelvic fractures, the FAST is negative, and the RUG shows a cut off at the bladder neck.

So, he has a urethral transection. I would place a supra-pubic catheter then.

You do this yourself?

No, I would ask urology to do it.

There are no urologists around.

Well, I have two choices, I could try to do it myself, and I have seen this done using seldinger techniques, or I could go to the operating room and cut down onto the bladder, place a purse-string in it and insert the Foley, then tack the bladder up to the abdominal wall. In this case, I would try it percutaneously first.

Then what?

Then I would transfer the patient to a place where there are urologists so that they could deal with his urethral injury because I cannot take care of that myself. In addition, he will need his pelvic fractures addressed.

What if there was blood on your rectal examination?

That would suggest a rectal injury and I would perform a proctoscopy right there in the emergency room. If there is anything concerning on the proctoscopy to make me believe there is a rectal injury, then I would have to take him to the operating room at some point and perform a loop colostomy and wash out the distal end of the colon. I would start the patient on Zosyn and flagyl post-operatively.

(11) Blunt Trauma with Hypotension*

ABCs

The same principle applies here. There can be bleeding from the chest, abdomen, pelvis or long bones and you need to find the bleeding PDQ.

Diagnosis

Find the source of bleeding. Listen to the chest. If there are bilateral breath sounds and the CXR is clear, then there is no hemothorax. If there is a hemothorax, then place a chest tube and follow that algorithm.

During the primary exam, if the pelvis is unstable, then extrernally fixate and finish the work up. Follow the pelvic fracture algorithm.

If the abdomen is tender and distended, work quickly through the primary survey and put the FAST on the abdomen or do a DPL. If there is fluid in the abdomen and the patient in unstable, they need to go to the operating room for immediate intervention (whatever that may be, follow that algorithm).

Treatment

Go through the ABC's and give them a bolus of fluids (2L for adults and 20cc/kg for children). If they respond to the bolus and remain stable, they can be treated systematically. If they only respond transiently or remain unstable, they have on going bleeding and should be dealt with accordingly to *stop* the *hemorrhage*.

If the patient is stable, then they can go to the CT scanner for further work up and perhaps non-operative treatment.

Blunt trauma to the kidney is less likely to be successful than penetrating trauma, even if the injury is addressed within six hours. Bilateral intimal injury may be addressed with endovascular stenting. Unilateral intimal injuries may be treated with anticoagulation.

Seat belt sign on the lower abdominal wall with abdominal tenderness should be explored. Sometimes, you may find a significantly disrupted abdominal wall, requiring repair at this time or at a later time.

Example Case

You are seeing a 40 year old man who was an unrestrained passenger in a high speed MVA and was ejected for a distance of 30 feet. Go.

Being ejected from a vehicle suggests that this patient may have significant injury. I want to assess his airway and start talking to him to make sure he is responsive. Meantime, I want my nurses to be placing large bore IV's in the upper extremities, drawing labs, and getting a blood pressure. I would continue by listening to his chest and making sure that he is moving air bilaterally and rule out pneumothorax or hemothorax. Assuming that he looks ok and he is hemodynamically stable…

He has a blood pressure of 90/60 and HR of 110.

So this makes me think that he is probably bleeding from somewhere, and it is probably not the chest. I would order the nurses to give him 2 liters of normal saline wide open. I would continue to complete the primary survey by assessing his GCS and checking the peripheral pulses in all his extremities. I would ask him to move all his extremities, and then I would take all his clothes off and look for any obvious external injuries, palpate the pelvis for stability, do a rectal exam and insert a Foley if there is no high riding prostate or blood at the urethral meatus. By this time, I expect that the fluid bolus has gone in; and, hopefully, he has responded to this with a normal blood pressure now.

Well, his blood pressure has come up to 130/60 with the fluid boluses. You notice a significant amount of bruising over the left chest wall. Otherwise there are no other injuries.

Good, he has responded to my fluid bolus and that means that he may not be actively bleeding. I would start the secondary survey by asking for my C-spine, chest, and pelvic x-ray; and, I want to do a FAST scan at this time to rule out free fluid in the abdomen that could be the cause of hypotension. Assuming the c-spine, chest and pelvic x-rays are normal...

There are several broken ribs on the left side, a left first rib fracture, and a medial clavicle fracture; but there is no effusion. The FAST scan is negative. The rest of the x-rays are negative. The nurse notes that the blood pressure on the left arm is lower than the right.

Those injuries are concerning that he can have an aortic injury, and the decreased pressure on the left side makes me concerned about the left subclavian being injured. Since the patient is stable now, and the secondary survey is negative for any other injury to the pelvis or abdomen, then I would proceed to work up this problem. I am between getting a CT scan or angiogram, and I think that I would get a CT. This is because the CT will allow me to look at the lungs, chest wall, heart, and great vessels; furthermore, CTA is pretty good these days and can give you some pretty good information.

Fine, you get the CT and it shows the broken ribs, no peri-aortic hematoma, but there is a hematoma around the medial left clavicle. So, now what do you want to do?

Now, I want to get an angiogram to focus on the left subclavian artery because of the decreased blood pressure on that side. I really suspect an injury and I didn't see it on CT, so I have to go with the gold standard test.

The arteriogram shows a very small intimal flap in the proximal portion distal to the vertebral artery, but there is good distal runoff.

I am not a vascular surgeon or a trauma surgeon. This is a difficult area to get distal and proximal control, but this patient has unequal blood pressures and a defect on angiogram. It has to be addressed surgically. I would immediately begin heparin to prevent any acute thrombosis of this artery while I plan an approach. Ideally, I would get a chest or vascular surgeon available to assist me in doing this because in order to get the control I need, I will have to open the left chest. A posterior-lateral thoracotomy should be adequate enough to get me proximal control, and distal control can be obtained through a supraclavicular incision. Once getting control of this vessel, I would examine the damaged portion of the vessel. If the vessel looked healthy, I may be able to open it and tack the intimal flap down with 6-0 silk. If the arterial wall looks injured, then it should be resected and repaired with a Dacron graft.

Can you think of any other options?

Yes, radiology or vascular surgery may be able to place a covered stent across this injury. My only problem with this, though, is that this patient is only 40 years old. I don't know what is going to happen to this stent in the next 40 years of his life. He will require frequent surveillance for the rest of his life to make sure he does not have any problems from the stent. Endoleaks are also possible with these stents, just as they are with aortic stents.

(5) Liver Laceration

ABC's

The patient may or may not be stable. Do a systematic work up.

Diagnosis

If the patient is unstable and has a positive FAST scan for intra-abdominal fluid or positive DPL (10 ml gross blood or 100,000 RBC) and they do not respond to fluid boluses, then they are taken to the operating room for exploration.

If the patient is stable, they may go to the CT scan to diagnoses their injury and perhaps have conservative management.

Treatment

Stable patients who will be placed in the ICU with liver laceration with intent to manage conservatively should be monitored closely. 50% will need a blood transfusion but should not receive more than 2-4 units over 24 hours without an operation. Angiography and embolization may be useful in this situation (and pediatric, not adult, splenic injury).

Unstable patients in the operating room are placed in the supine position and prepped widely. Midline incision is made and all 4 quadrants are packed off to give anesthesia time to catch up with the blood loss. Each quadrant is systematically examined for ongoing hemorrhage. The liver is palpated over bilateral lobes for any defects.

If liver injury is seen or suspected, the liver is mobilized by dividing the coronary and triangular ligaments. Control the bleeding in the left lobe by hand. The right lobe of the liver can be packed off with lap pads between the liver and diaphragm and anterior costal margin. Pringle maneuver may be done to control bleeding as well. This is done by placing a clamp from the left side by opening the lesser omentum while guiding the posterior blade through the foramen of Winslow. This can be left on for up to an hour and will differentiate bleeding from the hepatic artery or portal vein from the hepatic veins or retro hepatic cava.

If bleeding continues and you think there is injury to the retro hepatic cava or hepatic veins, then there are four options. Hepatic isolation with clamping of the suprarenal and suprahepatic cava is not well tolerated in trauma patients because of the decreased venous return to the heart. Atriocaval shunt requires a median sternotomy, access to the right atrium, guiding a 36 Fr chest tube down the cava and tightening an umbilical tape around this to bypass the injured cava and veins. Moore-Pilcher tube is a balloon placed through the illiacs and guided up to the defect to tamponade the bleeding. Venoveno bypass avoids having to open the chest.

For grade I and II injuries, topical measures may be used to stop the bleeding. Fibrin glue, fibrillar, and neu-net are all used in this case.

Suturing the parenchyma should be used for relatively short lacerations, using 0 chromic on a large blunt tipped needle.

Hepatotomy with selective ligation should be used if the parenchyma suture does not work. This involves finger fracturing the liver and ligating individual bleeders. Major vascular structures should be repaired if you can.

Hepatic artery ligation is used in the case of deep hepatic arterial hemorrhage. Selectively clamp the right and left. If the bleeding stops or slows, then ligate it.

Grade IV and V and coagulopathic patients, you just need to get out of the operating room, so pack them off and go. Beware of compartment syndrome after this.

Hepatic resection is rare these days because of the above options. This is only done in the case of extensive injury to the left lateral segment of the liver with extensive tissue necrosis.

Remember to place closed suction drains to prevent bilomas and infection. Pack large holes in the liver with well vascularized omentum.

(1) RUQ Retroperitoneal Hematoma

ABC's

Diagnosis

Penetrating trauma is explored.

Blunt trauma is more difficult, and you must consider the possibility of pancreatic injury. Amylase is not a great indicator of injury. CT scan and ERCP are the best modalities to evaluate injury to the biliary and pancreatic system. Transected pancreatic duct on ERCP warrants surgery. Midline hematomas, edema around the pancreatic gland and lesser sac, and retroperitoneal bile staining are reasons for evaluation of the duct. Intraoperative exploration can be done and if there is a question of injury of the pancreatic by duodenotomy with ampullary cannulation or by transecting the distal tail and cannulating the duct. For penetrating trauma, only study the duct if there is injury to the pancreatic tissue.

Treatment

Contusion and laceration without duct injury are treated conservatively with hemostasis and wide drainage with closed suction drainage. Start enteral feeds as soon as you can. If the injury is really severe, you may consider placing a feeding J-tube. Check the amylase in the drain in 2 to 3 days.

If the distal pancreases is injured or duct disrupted then do a distal pancreatectomy and shoot a pancreaticogram through the distal duct while you are there to rule out other injury. If the duct is normal proximally, then staple across the pancreas, put a prolene stitch in the duct, and buttress with omentum. Leave several drains and get out. Save the spleen if you can, but if the patient is at all unstable, and then put it in the bucket. If the proximal duct is injured or stenotic, then resect the distal pancreas and drain it internally with a roux-en-Y drainage procedure. Place a feeding J-tube at the time of this operation for future nutritional concerns.

If the duodenum and the pancreas are injured, you have to evaluate the bile ducts and the pancreatic duct. This can be done via the cystic duct, through the duodenal injury via the ampulla of Vader, or via the distal pancreatic duct. If you cannot evaluate or see the ducts, do not do a pancreatectomy. Place a lot of drains and leave it alone.

For severe combined injuries, you may have to divert the gastric contents. Duodenal diverticularization is when the duodenal injury is closed, a distal antrectomy and vagotomy is done, and T-tube drainage of the CBD with lateral drainage of the duodenum is performed. Gastro-jejunostomy is used for drainage. Pyloric exclusion is easier. The pylorus is sewn shut of stapled closed with a TA and a loop gastro-J is created. This will open back up in 2 weeks to 2 months. 3 tubes are left: gastrostomy, duodenostomy, and jejunostomy. Trauma Whipple should only be done if the trauma has pretty much done it for you.

Duodenal hematomas can usually be managed conservatively, but you have to rule out perforation. This is best done with an UGI. Associated injuries occur 20% of the time. Start NGT and TPN. You should be prepared to wait up to two weeks if you have to. After this, go to the operating room and explore the hematoma. Look for a pancreatic injury. Kocherize the duodenum. Release the hematoma, do a leak test, leave a drain, and get out.

Additional Therapy

Complications from pancreatic injuries include fistula, abscess, secondary hemorrhage, and pseudocyst (see their respective sections).

(4) Shotgun/GSW to the Flank/Abdomen*

ABC's

Diagnosis

There are holes in him. In the process of the initial evaluation, you will get an idea of what is wrong. In these situations, think of the tract of the projectile and what could be injured. This is not rocket science. If the bullet enters the RLQ and exits the left flank, then it probably hit, in order, the right colon, small bowel, cava or aorta, renal vessels or illiacs, sigmoid colon, kidney, ureter, and/or spine. So look for blood on the rectal exam, blood in the urine, and paralysis. If he is unstable and out of it, you are going to OR. If they are stable, you have time to get blood and shoot a one shot IVP and then go to the operating room.

Treatment

As a general rule, when you open the abdomen, get vascular control of hemorrhage first, then stop the enteric contamination, and then start exploration and repair. Reperfuse organs and limbs, and then fix the bowel and other organs.

Zone I retroperitoneal hematomas involve injury to the aorta, cava, illiacs and pancreaticoduodenal structures. These should always be explored.

Always have proximal and distal control if you can. Reflexing the spleen and left colon medially will give you exposure to the SMA, IMA, left iliac, and left renal origin. Performing a Kocher maneuver combined with mobilization of the right colon will give you access to the cava, right renal hilum, and right iliac artery. Exposure of the IVC is done by mobilizing the right colon and Kocherizing the duodenum. Statinsky clamps and sponge sticks can be used to control the cava proximally and distally. Posterior holes may need to be closed through anterior incisions.

Zone II hematomas are from the diaphragm to the illiacs lateral to the psoas muscle and implies injury to the kidney, ureters, renal vasculature and/or colon. These hematomas can be observed in blunt trauma if they are not expanding, but they should always be explored in penetrating trauma to rule out collecting system and/or vascular injuries to the kidneys.

Remember to get a one shot IVP when you seen this (if you had not already done it in the ER). You should have control of the proximal and distal renal vessels before opening the hematoma by mobilizing the right or left colon as needed. Assuming the contralateral kidney is functional, do a nephrectomy if the injury is more than 6 hours old, the patient is unstable, has associated life threatening injuries, or has a severely injured kidney. Do not revascularize the bluntly injured kidney (it doesn't work).

Zone III hematomas includes the bladder anteriorly, sacral promontory posteriorly, and iliac crest laterally. Injured structures in this zone may include pelvis, bones, illiac vessels, bladder, and rectum. Following blunt trauma, these should be observed, but following penetrating injury, they must be explored.

Ureteral injuries are sometimes diagnosed with the IVP. If you didn't have time in the ER, then get one in the operating room when things settle down. Use methylene blue to locate the injury if it is not obvious. If you can (you never can on the board) then do a primary ureteroureterostomy with stenting and reimplantation into the bladder. If a long segment of ureter is lost, the low injuries are treated with psoas hitch, middle with a transureteroureterectomy, and upper with either an auto transplantation of the kidney or bowel interposition.

Colon and rectal trauma should be expected if there is gross blood in the rectal exam. If you have time, and they are stable you can think about procto. Give antibiotics to the patient on the way to the operating room. Resect injured colon if there is preoperative shock, severe hemorrhage, more than 2 other organs injured, significant fecal contamination, delayed operative intervention (more than 8 hours), severely destructive wounds, and loss of abdominal wounds requiring mesh. Rectal injuries need proximal diversion with colostomy. Presacral drainage with closed suction drains exiting the perineum is the key to treating injuries here. Irrigate out the rectum to decrease the infection rate.

Example Case

You are called to the ER to see a young man just brought in after sustaining a gunshot wound to the abdomen. He is alert, hemodynamically stable, and his only apparent injury is a single gunshot entry wound in the right lower quadrant, with an exit wound in the left paravertebral space

The fact that he is alert and stable is reassuring, so I assume he is protecting his airway, moving air in bilateral chest by auscultation, and my nurses have established two large bore IV lines and taken a blood pressure with a SBP in the 120's, and there is no tachycardia. His GCS is 15, he moves all extremities, and I can not find any other injuries than the one you just described to me. Then, if this is the case, my heart rate will decrease a little and I would ask him an AMPLE history while I got a CXR and pelvis x-ray. I would do a rectal exam to see if there is blood to suggest a low colon injury, and I would place a Foley catheter if the is no high riding prostate or blood at the meatus. If there is any blood in the urine or urinanalysis, then that may suggest renal or ureteral injury just given the track of the projectile. I would get a one shot IVP.

He will need exploration of the abdomen; there is no doubt, so I start to ask myself just what can be injured. I can see the colon (right and left), small bowel, IVC, aorta, renal vessels, kidney, rectum, illiacs, and spine. With that in mind, and having finished the secondary survey, I would type and cross him, review my films, and take him to the operating room for exploration.

IVP shows two normal kidneys. You find an expanding hematoma in the right inferior retroperitoneum just above the pelvic brim, several small and large bowel injuries, and another hematoma in the right retroperitoneum.

The expanding part gets my attention, and that suggest that there is active and brisk bleeding there. I need to get proximal and distal controlling, fearing an IVC injury, I would medially rotate the right colon and duodenum and get this controlled, then open the hematoma. Once I have the bleeding under control, then I would place clamps on the bowel injury to stop the contamination.

You have a through and through injury to the vena cava. How do you deal with that?

I would attempt to repair this with a 4-0-prolene suture if possible. Posterior injuries may need to be repaired anteriorly even.

How do you deal with the bowel injuries?

If there is just simple through and through injuries, the patient is stable and there is not a lot of contamination, then I would do a primary repair. If the injury is to the left colon, and there is soilage, then I may opt for end ostomy. Several small injuries to the small bowel in a relatively short segment may prompt me to do a segmental resection and primary anastomosis.

(3) Penetrating Trauma to the Chest*

ABC's

Here, things may get crazy at "C". If cardiopulmonary arrest secondary to penetrating thoracic trauma occurs within 5 minutes of arrival to the ER or is witnessed in the ER, or if they have a SBP < 60/palp due to hemorrhage or pericardial tamponade, then open the chest. Do not open the chest in blunt trauma.

If the chest is opened, retract the lung medially and clamp the aorta. Open the pericardium after taking care to identify and preserve the phrenic nerve. Examine the heart to determine rhythm, site of injury, and blood volume remaining in the cardiac chamber.

Diagnosis

The hole in the chest gives away the diagnosis. CXR and decreased breath sounds indicates a hemothorax and may prompt a chest tube. More than 1500 ml is an indication to go to the operating room.

Consider the structures that may be injured, and think in a structured fashion. For the transmediastinal GSW, from one side to the other (left to right), that bullet may have damaged the left chest wall, left lung, heart, great vessels, esophagus, trachea, spine and cord, right lung and the right chest. So, with that order in mind (and try to do this for everything you do, not just for the boards), you have to check that the patient is alive and protecting his airway, doesn't have a sucking chest wound, has bilateral breath sound to rule out a pneumothorax or hemothorax, does not have a pericardial tamponade (no JVD or muffled heart tones) by echo/FAST, doesn't have crepitance in the chest wall to suggest airway disruption, has a negative angiogram to rule out great vessel injury (you get the aortogram or CTA before the contrast study of the esophagus because if the contrast leaks into the chest, then it will obscure the great vessels on imaging), negative UGI to rule out esophageal injury, and a negative bronchoscopy to rule out tracheal/bronchial injury. You covered it all, and you can end this scenario in less then 3 minutes.

Unstable patients with transmediastinal GSW get bilateral chest tubes immediately.

Treatment

Ventricular injuries are found when the chest is opened and pericardium opened. Place a finger in the hole and over sew with interrupted 2-0 prolene. Teflon plegets may be needed if the tissue will not hold the suture. Atrial injuries are controlled with partially occluding Statinsky clamps, then repair with 2-0 prolene in a vertical mattress fashion. If the injury to the heart is very large, you may have to occlude it with a Fogarty or Foley catheter. If the heart is in fibrillation after repair, then you may have to shock it with 20-50 joules directly. If the coronary artery is injured proximally, then cardiopulmonary bypass will be needed to repair it. If the injury is distal, then you can just ligate it with a "U" stitch. In the worst scenario, you may ligate the proximal artery, but the heart will infarct and you may need to do bypass later and place them on balloon pump.

Cardiac tamponade, vascular injury at the thoracic outlet, loss of the chest wall, massive air leak in the chest, tracheal injury, great vessel injury, mediastinal injury, bullet emboli to the heart or PA, and massive (>1500ml) or continuing (>250ml/hr for 4 hours) hemorrhage are all indications for a throacotomy. The choice of incisions is the key.

Left anteriolateral incisions are for resuscitation in the ED. Right side is never done.

Trans-sternal anterior thoracotomy is done (clamshell) to better expose the heart.

Posterior lateral incisions allow better access to the lung, esophagus and descending aorta. Also used for injury to the left subclavian on the left and the tracheal, proximal esophagus, SVC, and IVC on the right.

Additional Therapy

Retained hemothorax should be avoided by early, aggressive drainage to prevent a fibrothorax. If a first thoracostomy tube placed does not adequately drain the thorax, another posterior tube should be placed. If this does not work, then go to the OR. Streptokinase takes several days to work, and a VATS can be done immediately.

Example Case

You are called to see a 25 year old man who has been shot in the chest. He has an entrance wound in the fifth intercostals space in the left axillary line and an exit in the right fifth intercostals space in the right posterior axillary line. He arrives with a HR of 90, and his BP is 110/60.

I am surprised that this person with a transmediastinal gunshot wound is so stable, but I am happy for it. I am assuming that with vitals like that, he is probably alert and talking to me and his airway is therefore intact. I would listen to his breath sounds bilaterally to make sure he is moving air. He could certainly have injury to his lung causing a pneumothorax or hemothorax. If I hear decreased breath sounds on either side, or both, I would not hesititate to place chest tubes in him.

He has decreased breath sounds bilaterally, and you place chest tubes to get out 200 cc in the left chest and nothing in the right.

Ok, so there is not much bleeding in the chest, but I would continue to monitor the output from those tubes and make sure there is not a persistent air leak to suggest a large lung or tracheal/bronchial injury. I would continue on. All this time, I would have directed the nurses to be establishing two large bore IVs and getting another blood pressure to make sure he is stable. I would assume he is going to lose blood from this type of injury and would give him a liter of fluid despite having an adequate blood pressure. I would continue to think about what could be injured, and I would listen to the heart to make sure there are no muffled heart tones and JVD to suggest cardiac tamponade. If this is all good, then I would assess his GCS, have him move all extremities, check his pulses in all four extremities, and remove all his clothing to check for any other injury. I would do a rectal exam and place a Foley, and draw some labs...

Yeah, yeah... what now?

I would get a chest x-ray, and put the FAST scanner on his chest to rule out tamponade.

It is all negative.

Then, if he is still stable, I would take him to the CT scanner to get an idea of the track of the projectile. I would make this a CT angiogram to look at the great vessels. If there is any question about whether the radiologist could call any injury to the great vessels with this scanner, then I would just get a standard catheter based angiogram.

Did you give him any po contrast?

I think that is a reasonable thing to do, because you are going to look for an esophageal injury too. So I would. If it is positive, then you have a diagnosis, but just because it is negative does not rule it out and I would still get a formal UGI.

Well the great vessels look fine, but the projectile does look as if it has penetrated the esophagus and there is extravasation of oral contrast in the left chest.

Then I will need to take him to the operating room to repair this. First I want to think about his injury. So there is minimal injury to the lung and I have chest tubes in, there is no injury to the heart or great vessels, and there is no large air leak to suggest tracheal injury. I would go to the OR now, but right after intubating him, I would bronch him to make sure there is no tracheal injury.

The trachea is ok...what do you do in the operating room?

I would perform a left thoracotomy through the 6th intercostals space. I would check the heart and the diaphragm to make sure these are not injured, and then I would divide the pulmonary ligament and look at the pleura over the esophagus. I would find the hole, and open the pleura to expose the esophagus. I would work proximal to distal and mobilize the esophagus to look at the injury. As long as the injury involves less than 50% of the esophagus, I would debride the edges and repair it in two layers.

Ok, let's say he arrives in the ER with a normal blood pressure but then it suddenly dropped to the 50's with a HR of 50.

That would raise the concern of cardiac tamponade, and I would make an incision in the upper abdomen just below the xiphoid and open the pericardium.

He codes as soon as you open the pericardium.

I would do a left ER thoracotomy through the 4th intercostals space and incise the pericardium. I would clamp the aorta, and look for the injury to the heart.

(1) Penetrating Trauma to the Base of the Neck

ABC's

Think about the airway here because you could have a tracheal injury.

Diagnosis

You have to rule out injury to the trachea, esophagus, great vessels, heart, and lung, nerves in the neck and extremity, and extremity vessels. Arteriogram is the best test in this situation, if you have the time. It is a critical test if there is injury to the subcalvian, inominate, or carotid.

Treatment

Active bleeding or an expanding hematoma in the neck requires immediate exploration in the operating room.

The patient should be prepped from the chin to the knees. If they are in extremis with a thoracic outlet injury, a left anterior thoracotomy is done with extension to the right as needed in order to get proximal control. Once proximal control is achieved, then a median sternotomy can be done.

If the patient is not in extremis, then a high left anterior thoracotomy in the third interspace will help get control of the proximal subclavian. Distal control is achieved through a supraclavicular incision. Try not to remove the clavicle if you don't have to. If you can not primarily repair the artery, then use a Dacron graft.

The right subclavian and inominate artery is approached through a median sternotomy with a right cervical extension for proximal control. Injury to the inominate is not good. If the injury is partial and a Statinsky can be placed on it to close the hole with a running 4-0 prolene, great! Otherwise, you will need to bypass from the ascending aorta to the distal inominate with a 10mm Dacron graft. The inominate vein can be ligated (ALL veins can be ligated, even the IVC).

For the unstable patient with a unilateral injury to zone 2 or 3, make the incision along the SCM. For bilateral neck injuries, make the incision as a transverse collar or bilateral SCM. Thoracic outlet injuries (zone 1) require a supraclavicular incision to get control and you may have to perform a median sternotomy.

The carotid artery can be ligated in the comatose patient who has no forward flow in the vessels. Otherwise, every attempt should be made to repair the carotid. (Blunt trauma to the carotid can cause endothelial flaps in the carotid and cause neurological defects. They are usually managed non-operatively with anticoagulation).

(4) Pediatric Duodenal Hematomas*

ABC's

Usually presents as a stable child that fell off his bike and hit the handle bars. Immediately be thinking about duodenal, pancreas and liver injury.

Diagnosis

Serum amylase is not specific for duodenal injury, but is elevated in most cases. If the amylase level rises, this makes you suspicious for pancreatic injury as well.

CT with IV & PO contrast or an UGI with gastrograffin (or thin barium) is used to confirm that the duodenum has not been perforated.

If you are in the operating room already, bile staining of the retroperitoneum is generally a good sign that the duodenum is injured.

Treatment

Most of the time, duodenal injury can be repaired with primary repair. The severity of the injury (considering size, site of duodenum, mechanism of injury, time from initial injury, and concomitant injury to other structures) mandates the treatment. Pyloric exclusion, duodenal diverticularization, and 3 tube drainage have all been previously discussed and should be used when appropriate.

Duodenal hematomas usually cause obstruction 24 to 48 hour out from the injury when the edema and the fluid in the duodenal wall organize enough to obstruct the lumen. Most of the time, these will resolve on their own and should be managed conservatively. This topic has already been discussed in an earlier section

Example Case

A 10 year old boy comes into the ER after falling off his bike and hitting the handle bars with his abdomen. He complains of epigastric pain where there is some bruising. What do you do?

I am concerned that he could have injury the duodenum, pancreas, liver, small bowel or colon. First thing I would do is see the patient and make sure that he is not in any kind of extremis. If he is talking and breathing well, I would check his blood pressure and make sure he is stable. I would then look him over and make sure nothing else is injured and get a chest and pelvic x-ray. I would examine his abdomen and make sure he does not have peritonitis.

No, but he is very tender.

I would get a FAST scan and make sure there is no free fluid.

What if there was?

It wouldn't change anything as long as he is stable, I would still get a CT.

Then why are you doing it?

Just habit for me when it comes to trauma. I would draw labs on him, checking his CBC to make sure his Hgb is normal, check his electrolytes, and get an amylase. This may be high with bowel or pancreas injury, but if there is an increasing trend over time, it would suggest pancreatic injury. Assuming the labs are normal, I would take him to the CT scanner.

CT shows a duodenal hematoma.

Assuming that the pancreas looks ok and there is no other solid organ injury, then I would place an NGT, keep him NPO, and start him on TPN. I would give this a week to open up. After a week, I would put some contrast down the NGT and watch to see if it goes past the duodenum. If it does not, then I would wait another week. If it has not opened up after 2 weeks, then I would take him to the operating room for exploration, kocherize the duodenum, evacuate the hematoma, and rule out a duodenal injury with air or methylene blue via the NGT.

Good. Now say there is a pancreatic injury on CT.

Most likely place for injury is at the neck, where the pancreas is crushed between the handle bars and the spine. The big question I have to know is if the pancreatic duct is injured. So I have a couple of different modalities at my disposal. ERCP or MRCP are the choices, and I would choose MRCP in a young child, because it is least invasive. I may have to sedate or even intubate him to keep him still in the MR, but that way we could get really good images and anatomy of the pancreas.

You see the injury at the neck, and there is a duct injury.

I would take him to the operating room and go through the midline. My choices are to try and repair the duct over a stent, drain the distal pancreas into the bowel with a pancreaticoenterostomy, or to do a distal pancreatectomy. The first choice would be ideal, but if there is a large hematoma, or the diagnosis is delayed enough to make this difficult, I would not try it. For the same reasons, a distal pancreaticoenterostomy may be difficult if I cannot see the duct very well, or the tissue is friable. That would leave the distal pancreatectomy, sparing the spleen, as the only option.

(2) Pediatric Splenic Trauma/Head Injury

ABC's

As splenic trauma relates to pediatrics, try to preserve as much spleen as possible for immune competence.

Unconscious children are intubated. ETT size is determined by sizing the child's nares or fifth digit. Use an uncuffed tube.

Estimated blood volume of a child is 80 ml/kg. Hypotension is a bad sign in a child because they have so much reserve. Get IV access. IO's can be placed in children under 6 years old. Give 20 ml/kg bolus once, if no response, and then repeat the bolus. If there is no response to the second bolus, then give 10 ml/kg of blood, and if this is not successful, you need to go to the OR.

Diagnosis

As for splenic injury, assess the hemoglobin, do a DPL, FAST scan, and CT is all used to come to the diagnosis of injury. The injury may be graded by CT scanner. Grade I and II are contained hematomas and considered minor injuries. Grade II is a deep fracture extending into the hilum. Grade IV is a shattered spleen.

With respect to head injuries, asses the child's GCS. An unconscious child should be thought to have a space occupying lesion in the head until proven otherwise.

CT scan of the head is the preferred method of diagnosis of head injury.

Treatment

If the splenic injury is isolated, the patient is hemodynamically stable, and they are alert enough to allow serial examination, then you may attempt conservative therapy by placing them in the ICU setting. Repeat CT scan is done in 3 to 7 days. Conservative management has failed when you have to transfuse

50% of the child's blood volume (40ml/kg) in the first 24 hours. Must set a limit for transfusion in the beginning and stick to this. If the child becomes unstable or requires too much blood, then take the child to the operating room.

At exploration, try to mobilize the spleen and assess the injury. Try to salvage the spleen if you can. This may be accomplished by application of omentum or topical hemostatic agents, direct splenic sutures, ligation of individual splenic vessels, partial splenectomy, vicryl mesh application, and large through and through mattress sutures.

If the spleen is shattered, you will likely have to remove this. If there is a lot of ongoing bleeding, compress the splenic artery against the spine to slow the bleeding while you remove it. The spleen is removed by elevating it with sponges and excising the lienorenal and phrenicolienal ligaments and dissecting out the hilum.

If you suspect a head injury, start lowering the ICP by hyperventilation, elevation of the head, and osmotic (0.25-2.0 gm/kg mannitol).

If there is no time to go to the CT scanner, take to the operating room and consider craniotomy or burr hole at that time.

ICP monitors are placed in those who are unconscious and going to surgery and those that are in a coma but do not have a mass lesion. What to keep the ICP less than 25. If there are any neurologic changes as a result of any ICP, it should be lowered.

There may be an epidural (evacuation needed) or subdural (may be just observe)

Additional Therapy

After a splenectomy, you must watch for thrombocytosis. The child should receive triple vaccination. Finally, they are to be placed on penicillin until age 14.

(1) Airway Management in Head and Neck Trauma*

ABC's

Absolute indications for invasive airway management include acute airway obstruction (direct laryngeal injury, expanding neck hematomas, and transected airways), apnea (related to cerebral or spinal injury), hypoxia, expanding hematoma of the neck.

Diagnosis

The patient is dying, bleeding from the neck, has saturations in the dirt, is blue or cyanotic, or is just not breathing.

Laryngeal injuries present with hoarseness, hemoptysis, and crepitance in the neck.

Treatment

Cricothyroidotomy is done by palpating the cricothyroid membrane and stabilize the larynx. Make a transverse incision over the membrane and open it. Bluntly expand the hole and put your tube in it.

Tracheostomy may be indicated in patient with direct injury to the larynx below the cricoids (placing a tube in the cricothyroid membrane may make it worse), and in those patients under the age of 12.

Additional Therapy

Tracheo-innominate fistula may occur after tracheostomy and is heralded by a sentinel bleed. One the diagnosis is made by bronchoscopy or angiogram, then you should overinflate the cuff or use your finger to compress the artery against the sternum until you get to the operating room. Repair is done through a median sternotomy. It should be repaired primarily, do not resect the trachea, and buttress with mediastinal fat.

Example Case

You get called to the ER where there is a 35 year old man involved in a snowmobile accident win which he plowed into a wire which caught his neck. In the ER he has a BP of 130/60, HR 90, and has obvious crepitus and a hematoma of his neck. He is stridorous.

This will require a deliberate and calm manner. He likely has a tracheal injury and his airway is tenuous at best. I would make sure that we have good IV access while I assess how comfortable I am with his current airway. I would place him on oxygen by mask and reassure him that everything is ok, and keep him calm. I would call the OR and tell them we are on the way, and I will need rigid bronchoscopes, flexible scopes, and a tracheostomy tray set up and ready to go. In addition to this, I would have cardiopulmonary bypass standing by in case we lose the airway and need to go on bypass emergently.

Don't you want to assess the rest of patient before you go to the operating room?

No sir, I am stuck on A here.

Ok, go on.

Once I am in the operating room, I would have the patient's neck prepped and draped in a sterile fashion. I would then use local anesthetic and make an incision on the neck that I would use for a surgical airway, and I would dissect all the way down to the trache...

You are going to dissect through the hematoma while the patient is awake?

I'm sorry; I did forget that you said he had a hematoma. There may be some vascular injury there and I don't want to rush in there unless I have to. So I would just have the neck prepped and draped in the OR, and then I would keep the patient awake and take a look down the nose with the bronchoscope.

Nothing but blood and the patient becomes very anxious.

I am going to have to open the neck and perform the tracheosotomy. I will have to deal with any other injuries in the neck as I find them.

There are no other injuries, but he can't move his arms or legs.

He likely has a cervical spine fracture with spinal cord injury. Hopefully, some of this is due to swelling. I would start steroids by giving him a bolus of 30 mg/kg, and then giving him a drip of 5.4 mg/kg/hr.

(7) ACLS*

PEA

You have got to find the reason for PEA. This could be from hypokalemia, hypovolemia hyperkalemia, pneumothorax, hypothermia, PE, acidosis, hypoxia, MI, or drugs. Start by giving epinephrine, 1 mg IV every 3-5 minutes. You may give vasopressin, 40 U as a one time dose. Give atropine, 1 mg IV ever 3-5 minutes.

Bradycardia

Set up for transcutaneous pacing immediately, especially if they are hypotensive. While getting this ready, you may give the patient atropine as a first choice and epinephrine or dopamine as a 2nd choice if atropine is ineffective.

Synchronized Cardioversion

This may be needed in cases of unstable atrial fibrillation. Put the patient on oxygen and get suction equipment ready. Make sure you have good IV lines and be prepared to intubate if needed. Sedate the patient and give them narcotics if possible. The initial shock is 100J monophasic, increase to 200J, then 300J, then 360J as needed if unsuccessful.

Tachycardia

Think about the rhythm and ask yourself is the patient stable, is the complex narrow, and is it regular. IF the answer is yes to all three, then this is probably SVT and you should try vagal maneuvers, followed by adenosine (6mg IVP, then repeat x2 with 12 mg) and Cardizem. Unsynchronized cardioversion is used if the patient becomes unstable. Irregular tachycardias that are narrow include a-fib, MAT, or a-flutter and are controlled with diltiazem or beta blockers. Stable, narrow, regular tachycardias include SVT, a-flutter, and ectopic atrial beats are treated with beta blockers. Stable, wide, and irregular could be Torsades and you should give magnesium. Stable wide and regular should receive amiodarone and/or cardioversion.

Basic Shock and CPR

You should shock at 360 joules every 2 minutes as needed. Between the shocks, you should immediately begin CPR without checking a pulse at a rate of 30:2. At the end of 2 minutes, check the rhythm and feel for a pulse only if there is an organized or unshockable rhythm. Meanwhile, you should be giving epinephrine and consider giving amiodarone 300 mg IV and another 150 mg IV every 2 minutes as need or lidocaine if amiodarone is available. Magnesium is given if the complex is wide and regular.

Example Case

The medical service consults you on a 74 year old female with a near-obstructing left sided colon cancer. She is transferred to your service in preparation for a colectomy. The next day, she develops sudden onset of tachycardia and feels palpitations.

I am concerned that she has an arrhythmia. I would go see her immediately and assess her stability. Assuming she is alert, protecting her airway and has a normal saturation, I would get a blood pressure, and order stat labs for electrolytes and get an EKG right away to diagnosis the tachycardia.

The EKG shows an irregular tachycardia, looks like a-fib.

In that case, since she has no history of a-fib as far as I know, I would attempt to cardiovert her. As long as she is stable, I would attempt to do this medically. Personally, I start with IV lopressor, 5mg IV every 5 to 10 minutes times three to see if the heart rate will slow and become normal again. Of course, I would be look at her electrolytes to make sure there is no underlying disorder that needs to be corrected. If the lopressor fails, I usually don't try calcium channel blocker because I am not used to it, I start amiodarone, loading her with 150 mg in the first 10 minutes, then given her 1mg mg/minute for 8 hours and 0.5mg/minute for the next 16 hours.

None of this works and her blood pressure drop into the 80's, and she becomes more symptomatic.

This is unstable now, and I am going to have to cardiovert her. First, she needs sedation with versed and fentenyl as tolerated by her blood pressure. When I feel that she is sedate enough from the medication or her hypotension, then I would provide synchronized cardioversion with 50 joules. Increasing to 100 joules if that does not work, and repeating as needed.

Ok, that works, now what about her colon?

This is a near obstructing lesion, so it needs to be addressed. Since she is in the hospital, I would get a cardiologist to help me find the cause of her a-fib, and strongly suggest/order an echo and stress test.

(3) Management of ARDS*

H&P

This is usually a sick patient in the ICU and the saturations or blood gasses are getting worse. You have to consider the differential diagnosis here and it can include emboli, pneumonia, MI, pneumothorax, sepsis, atelectasis, and pleural effusion. You want to know about fever, leukocytosis, infiltrates on x-rays, etc.

On physical exam, assess their airway and listen to their breath sounds. Listen to the heart, look for jugular venous distension. Check their ventilator setting and make sure they are appropriate.

Diagnosis

The PaO2/FiO2 ratio of less than 150, alkalosis, hypocapnia (<35), and a chest x-ray that looks fluffed out are all diagnostic for ARDS

Plain x-rays may rule out or in other diagnosis.

If you suspect a pulmonary embolism, you should heparinize the patient and get a CTA or V/Q scan to rule this out.

Treatment

Hypoxemia is treated by increasing the FiO2. In ARDS there is dead space in the lung and this will not help a whole lot. Oxygen is toxic and should only be increased acutely. Every attempt should be made to decrease the oxygen concentration. PEEP improves oxygenation by recruiting collapsed lung, increasing compliance, and reducing the V/Q shunt. High peep can decrease the venous return to the heart and decrease cardiac output, and it can cause direct baro-trauma to the alveoli.

Because the compliance of the lung decreases as ARDS develops, ventilation with lower tidal volumes will be needed to decrease the peak airway pressure and minimize lung injury. Generating a tidal volume to respiratory pressure curve is helpful to find the highest tidal volume that is safe. Pressure control ventilation is the best mode for this disease process because it will decrease the mean airway pressure. To recruit collapsed alveoli and prevent further development of the disease, inversed ratio ventilation is used at times.

Example Case

A multitrauma patient is in the ICU and has a chest x-ray that is read out by the radiologist as ARDS. He is POD#2 from repair of long bone fractures and his saturations are dropping into the 80's and he is getting hard to ventilate. What do you do?

I would confirm the radiologist's suspicion with a PaO2 to FiO2 ratio which should be below 150 in ARDS. Then, I would initially raise the FiO2 to get his saturations up, but that is only a temporary fix because the O2 is toxic and I want that below 40%. So I would put him on a pressure regulated volume control mode so that I could decrease the airway pressures, and I would decrease the tidal volumes as much as possible to decrease the peak pressures so that I do not cause barotrauma as I increase the PEEP. I would slowly increase the PEEP to a level that is tolerable with peak airway pressure around 30 mmHg or so. I want to give him PEEP because this will recruit alveoli, decrease dead space, improve ventilation and gas exchange, and increase lung compliance.

You try to increase the PEEP, but his blood pressure falls.

I am compressing the venous return to the heart with the PEEP, and this would indicate that he needs more volume. I would check his urine output, expecting it to maybe be a little low, and then I would insert a PA catheter to guide fluid resuscitation until I get a wedge of 18.

Well you have him on the highest amount of PEEP you can go, and the tidal volumes are very low, now what?

I would recheck the ABG and see if there is any improvement in the PaO2, tolerating hypercapnia to a certain degree.

There is no improvement.

The next thing to do would be to paralyze and sedate the patient and inverse the inspiration to expiration ration, giving him a longer time to exchange gas and hold the alveoli open. I would start with a one to one ratio.

Thank you.

(11) Surgery after MI*

H&P

Patient will have an obstructing colon cancer, acute cholecystitis, or some other surgical emergency while they are in the hospital recovering from a major MI.

You have to assess the cardiac risk based on their age, time out from MI (>6 months ideal), JVD, aortic stenosis, EKG rhythm (PVCs?), general medical condition (Cr, BUN, lytes, activity level), and the kind of operation you need to do.

Patients who have had a MI in the last 6 months have a 25-40 % change of having another MI if you operate on them, with a 70% mortality rate. So you only want to do lifesaving operations on these patients.

Diagnosis

Nuclear stress test may show the distribution of the disease.

Treatment

Try to do everything you can not to operate on the patient for 6 months (place a colonic stent, cholecytostomy tube under local, etc). If you have to operate, then lower the myocardial oxygen demand with beta blockers and Ca channel blockers. Nitrates can decrease the afterload on the heart.

Place a SGC and a-line in the operating room to avoid episodes of hypotension and hypoxia during the operation.

Example Case

A 56 year old man was admitted to the FP service yesterday with abdominal pain. He has had nausea and vomiting. His WBC is 16K. His only significant history is that he had an MI 4 months ago.

So this gentleman, I am assuming, has only the past medical history you gave me. I take that to mean he has not had any surgeries before, and that is concerning because it sounds like he has a bowel obstruction and adhesions would be the number one cause. I would examine him closely for hernia, and if I find none, I would be concerned for malignancy. Now because he is vomiting, I would make sure his electrolytes are corrected, and NGT is placed for comfort and decompression, and start him on IV fluids for resuscitation. I would examine his abdomen to make sure that he does not have peritonitis.

He does have peritonitis with pain mostly in the RLQ.

Then, I would get a chest x-ray and abdominal films to evaluate the lung fields and bowel gas pattern.

This shows a SBO with a questionable sentinel loop.

I am very worried about the physical exam finding, elevated white count, and this x-ray. It is starting to look like this man will need an operation, but he is only 4 months out from his MI. This puts him at high risk for general anesthesia.

What do you mean?

Well, he has a 25% chance of having another MI during anesthesia, and that may have a very high mortality. So, I would make sure that he is on a beta blocker and calcium channel blockers to decrease the oxygen demand of the heart, I would place a SG catheter and optimize his CO with fluid boluses (creating a starling curve), and place an arterial line. I would also get an EKG. I would explain to the patient that I think he has an acute surgical problem, and we have to operate on him. If we do nothing, his bowel could strangulate, die, and make him much sicker, putting him at a higher mortality risk.

He wants to know if you are exactly sure he needs this.

To be honest, I am not completely sure. I am pretty sure, and now that the patient mentions it, I was considering doing a CT scan to evaluate the degree of obstruction. I think it would be reasonable to do this if it could be done in a reasonable time fashion (an hour or so to get down the po contrast) and his creatinine is normal. CT scan is fairly specific when it comes to complete bowel obstruction.

It shows a complete obstruction.

Then we are going to the operating room for exploratory laparotomy.

Now, you are asked to see a 72 year old woman on the medical service for RUQ pain and E. coli *bacteremia. She had an MI one month ago and had a cardiac catheterization which demonstrated non reconstructable disease. What do you do?*

I think this patient probably has cholecystitis or ascending cholangitis. I would go see her and I will assume she is relatively stable. I would get a history from her that is focused on gallbladder disease, history of stones, and I will assume she still has a gallbladder. I would examine her abdomen. She is tender in the RUQ, positive Murphy's sign, and this would be consistent with gallbladder (but I would not exclude the hepatic flexure of the colon). I would make sure she is NPO, start her on fluids, and place a Foley to monitor her urine output and measure her resuscitation. She should be started on broad spectrum antibiotics. I would start her on Zosyn and flagyl.

I would send off some laboratory for a WBC, I expect this to be high if she is infected, and I would send of LFTs, expecting then to be slightly elevated or normal. If this is cholangitis, then the alk phos and bilirubin would be elevated. Finally, I would get an US of the RUQ.

She is febrile to 101, but she is stable. She has had RUQ before this but was never treated for it. Her WBC is 13,000 and her alk phos is at the upper end of normal. The US shows thickening and fluid around the gallbladder. No obvious stones.

So, this is likely to be the gallbladder. Since she had a recent MI, then general anesthesia and cholecystectomy is not a good option. I would ask the radiologist to place an ultrasound guided percutaneous cholecystostomy tube.

What if the radiologist refuses to place the tube?

We would have an argument. However, if I could not get them to the bedside, then I would do a cut down through a right upper quadrant incision with local anesthetic and place a small Foley in the gallbladder with a purse string suture under direct visualization.

Have you ever done that?

No.

Ok, radiology places that tube for you, and she does well until two days later when she drops her pressure into the 60's out on the floor.

I would immediately go see her and asses her mental status. If she is protecting her airway and is alert, I would make sure she has two good IV's and start some fluid boluses. I would put some oxygen on her and get a stat EKG to make sure it is not her heart. I would immediately transfer her to the ICU.

She is anxious but awake. The EKG looks normal compared to her baseline. What do you do now?

She may be septic, I don't know. I would examine her abdomen. Tenderness around the drain would be concerning. Assuming the drain has been working normally, it probably has not fallen out. I would place a Swan-Ganz catheter and get some numbers.

Her wedge is 8 and her CO is 5.5. Her abdomen is tender in the RUQ.

Her heart is good, but she could use some more volume. I would give her a couple of liters to get her wedge up to 15.

I would put some contrast through that cholecystostomy tube and get a flat plate of the abdomen to see if it is still in the gallbladder.

There is extravasation.

Then I have to take her to the operating room, wash out the abdomen and remove the gallbladder.

The anesthesiologist is giving you a hard time.

She will die if we don't take her to the operating room. This is an emergency. We have to go.

(7) Management of Septic Patient/Patient in Shock*

H&P

Sepsis is fever, tachypnea, tachycardia, and end-organ dysfunction. Shock is hemodynamic instability. H&P are guided by the diagnosis and cause of septic shock.

Diagnosis

Determine the cause of shock: septic, hypovolemic, neurogenic, and cardiogenic.

Vitals, cultures, EKG, CXR, ABG and cardiac enzymes are all used to assist in the diagnosis of the type of shock.

Treatment

Septic shock can be high cardiac output or low cardiac output. In the high cardiac output state, the SVR is very low and the high CO is not enough. Fluid boluses should be given to try and increase the CO. Low output results in oliguria and renal failure. Invasive monitors (a-line and SGC), respiratory support, fluid boluses to get the PCWP to 15 mmHg and Hgb to 12, antibiotics, and inotropic support are used.

Cardiogenic shock is pump failure. Swan-Ganz catheter (SGC) shows a low CO (index < 2.2) and a normal SVR with elevated filling pressures (> 18). Give them oxygen therapy (ventilate as needed), and optimize their cardiac support to keep the wedge pressure around 15 or optimizing contractility with dobutamine. Nitrates and morphine can be used to lower the filling pressures when there is no hypotension. Find the ideal place on the Starling curve. If you absolutely cannot get their pressure up despite aggressive medical therapy, then place an IABP (especially in the case of massive MI, consider LHC).

Example Case

A 72 year old man is on the operating room table for a ventral hernia repair. When the Foley is placed, with some difficulty, there is only a small amount of cloudy urine obtained and then the patient promptly spikes a temperature to 39C.

I think the patient probably has a urinary tract infection. I would stop the case right there because I am not going to operate on an infected patient. I would wake him up and bring him to the PACU. I would then send an urinanalysis to confirm the diagnosis, and send a sample for gram stain, culture and sensitivity so I could tailor my antibiotic regimen. Until I have that data, I would cover some broad spectrum UTI bugs by starting Cipro and flagyl. Since he is having fever, he could use some fluid boluses. I need to draw some blood cultures as well, and I would check basic labs to see if he has a leukocytosis (which I would expect) and to make sure his electrolytes and creatinine is ok. I assume that now he is awake and his vitals are stable.

He has a WBC of 15, BUN 32 and Cr 1.8. The rest of the labs are normal. The urine output has only been 10cc/hr for the last 2 hours.

That is concerning. He has a bad urine infection his creatinine is rising, and he is not making adequate urine.

What is adequate urine?

0.5 ml/kg/hour

Go on.

So, I am worried that he can go into renal failure. I would transfer the patient to the ICU and place a SG catheter to determine his fluid status and make sure he is not in shock. Furthermore, I can optimize his cardiac function by creating a Starling curve and then I know I have his fluid volume where I want it.

CI is 2.2, PCWP is 6, and SVR is in the 600's.

Well his wedge is low; I would continue to give him volume until his wedge comes up to around 12-16, watching his CI the entire time, because this should go up as well until I get him too full.

Ok, his wedge is 12 now, and the CI goes up, just as you said, to 4.4; however, his BP is in the 90's and the SVR is still very low.

Well, he is in shock. He has urosepsis. I have him "tanked up" on fluids, his cardiac function is good, so I need to get him to vasoconstrict a little, but I don't want his heart rate to get too high because of his age (and he probably has some CAD). So I would start him on norepinephrine. Dopamine is another option, but it will increase the heart rate more than norepinephrine.

The urine output is still only 15 ml/hour.

So I have his preload as good as I can get it, I have his pressure head up with pressors to keep his MAP around 80, and he still not making urine. I would flush his Foley to make sure there is no post renal obstruction. If this is fine, then this must be a renal cause. I would send urine electrolytes, expecting the sodium to be high if this is ATN.

It is high, what do you want to do now?

I have to support him, try to keep his urine flowing. ATN is probably from hypotension, so that is corrected. I would try some diuretics to keep him urinating; and, since I have a swan, I can add fluid as he responded so he did not drop his pressure. I would review his medications and stop any nephrotoxic drugs.

(10) Oliguric Renal Failure*

H&P

Oliguria should immediately be addressed by assessing the only three causes of renal failure: pre-renal, renal, and post-renal. Go through a thoughtful history and physical with ruling in or out these causes. Did the patient have surgery around the ureters? Is he on nephrotoxic drugs? Is there a Foley in and is it working right? Is he in shock?

Diagnosis

Check the BUN and creatinine, measure the urine output, check the urine electrolytes, and calculate the FeNa. If there is concern for ureteral injury, get an IVP or RUG, place a Foley, place invasive monitors for a CVP or PCWP, get an H&H to rule out bleeding, send a UA to look for cast or cells, and an ultrasound may show hydronephrosis.

Treatment

Find the cause and treat it.

Place invasive monitors and improve the patient's volume status. You may need to start low dose dopamine and give diuretics to prevent anuria if the patient is volume repleted.

Nephrotoxic drugs must be stopped. Monitor K levels and treat as needed.

Indications for dialysis include acidosis, hyperkalemia, fluid overload, and symptomatic uremia (bleeding, nausea).

Example Case

You get called to the PACU to see a patient who had an APR performed by your partner who had 30 minutes of hypotension during the case. His urine output over the last hour is 15 cc.

Anytime, I am presented with oliguria, I think about pre-renal, renal, and post-renal causes. In this patient, my immediate concerns are on going bleeding, hypovolemia, injury to the ureter, and blood transfusion reaction. I would go to the bedside and see the patient. Assuming that he is awake, extubated and alert, I would make sure that he is saturating ok, and that he has a normal blood pressure. I would then examine his abdomen and make sure that it is not overly distended to suggest bleeding, and I would make sure that he is not tender. I would then flush his catheter and make sure that it is working properly. Assuming all this checks out good so far, then I would send off labs to include a CBC to check his hemoglobin and hematocrit and rule out bleeding, chemistries to check his potassium and creatinine, and urinanalysis and urine lytes to calculate the fractional excretion of sodium.

He has a HR 90 and BP 130/60 and he came to the hospital with Hct 42 and now it is 30. His creatinine is 1.2.

The Hct is a little low, but this may just be dilutional. I am not sure what is going on at this time, so I would move him to the ICU and get the urologist to do a cystogram and look at the ureter.

Urologists are not around.

Then I would get an ultrasound of the kidneys to look for hydroureter and shoot an IVP.

There is no hydroureter and the IVP looks normal bilaterally. His urine output for the next hour is only 12 ml.

I would place a SG catheter to get a better idea. Although his blood pressure has been normal, I would check an EKG to rule out the chance of myocardial ischemia.

EKG is normal. His wedge is 18 and his Co is 5.0 with an index of 2.1.

So he has a good volume and no pre-renal cause, good CO and heart function, there is no post renal cause, so it has to be the kidney itself. I never did get that fractional excretion of sodium, but now I am assuming that it is greater than 1.

Let's say the urine sodium is low and the IVP shows a ureteral injury.

Then I would have to take him to the operating room, find the injury and fix it.

You do that and find that the left ureter is transected. How do you find the ureter and repair it.

I would look where the ureter crosses the iliac vessels and trim the edges. If I would spatulate the two ends and bring them together without tension over a stent. If I could not get them to reach, then I would re-implant the ureter into the bladder using a psoas hitch technique.

Ok, let's say the wedge was 18 and his CO was 1.9 with an index of 1.1.

That is concerning that he is have a cardiac issue. So I would start him on dobutamine, and give him nitrates and beta blocker if his blood pressure would tolerate it. I would give him an aspirin and put him on oxygen, then consult a cardiologist.

(6) Pulmonary Emboli in the Postoperative Patient*

H&P

Patient could have pneumonia, pulmonary contusion, fat emboli, ARDS, pneumothorax, sepsis, and MI

Diagnosis

Check a WBC to rule out pneumonia, ABG will usually show PaO2 < 60mmHg and the PCO2 will be very low as well. If *hypoxia* and *hypocapnia* are not present together, then it is not a PE. Get an EKG to rule out MI and a CXR to rule out pneumonia, pneumothorax, esophageal perforation, or CHF. VQ scan can be done to tell you the probability of PE. Venous duplex can tell you if there is a DVT. Arteriogram is the gold standard for diagnosis and can be therapeutic.

Treatment

If you are suspicious for an embolus, then start heparinization now and ask questions after. A filter should be used in situations in which anticoagulation cannot be used or if coagulation has failed.

Thrombolytic therapy is used for a major PE with hemodynamic instability. Contraindications include active bleeding, intracranial disease, and recent eye operation. Relative contraindications include recent operation, recent serious trauma, postpartum, recent external cardiac massage, uncontrolled HTN, and history of GI bleed.

Pulmonary embolectomy is done by placing the patient on bypass, median sternotomy, cannulize the SVC, open the PA and remove the clot. Mortality is 40% and should only be done in those that thrombolytic and catheter embolectomy could not be done.

Example Case

A 70 year old man that you did a colectomy on 7 days ago is getting ready to go home when the nursing staff calls you because the patient has become short of breath.

I am immediately concerned that he is having and MI or a pulmonary embolism, and I would rush to his bedside. I would immediately decide if the patient needs to be intubated. If he is awake and moving air, then I would just place him on 100% face mask and listen to his chest to rule out pneumothorax and make sure he is moving air bilaterally. I would check his blood pressure and make sure he is stable.

His respiratory rate is in the 20's and he is saturating in the 90's now that you put him on oxygen. He is a little hypotensive with SBP in the 80-90's, and his heart rate is 110.

I still do not have a cause for this, but he needs to be moved to the ICU. I would get a chest x-ray to make sure his lung fields are up and clear, an ABG to look at the PaO_2 and PCO_2 to determine if there is a shunt, an EKG to rule out acute myocardial ischemia, and send off cardiac enzymes to make sure he is not having a heart attack. Because I am suspicious that he is having a pulmonary embolism, I would go ahead and heparinize him.

His PaO_2 is in the 60's and the PCO_2 is in the 20's, chest is clear, and EKG shows sinus tachycardia.

This is looking more like a pulmonary embolism because of that ABG. Since he is a little hypotensive, I would give him a couple of liters of IV fluids to help his pressure. If his pressure comes up and he remains stable, then I would send him for a CT of the chest PE protocol.

CT shows the PE, now what do you want to do?

As long as he remains stable, I would continue the heparinization and supportive care. Eventually I would need to Doppler the lower extremities and see if there is clot in the deep venous system and switch him to oral Coumadin to keep the INR between 2-3.

While on heparin, he begins to bleed, requiring transfusions.

If I could not continue to anti-coagulate him, then I would ask radiology to place an IVC filter.

What if he remains hypotensive?

If the blood pressure does not get any better, then I want to send him to the angiogram suite to diagnose the PE and then start a thrombolytic.

Aren't you concerned about starting thrombolytic therapy in a patient that is only 7 days out from surgery?

Absolutely, but I would rather transfuse the patient several units of blood and have him alive. So there is definitely a risk there, but he is dying without it.

Aren't there other options?

Catheter based suction embolectomy and surgical embolectomy are options that I am not familiar with. If my hospital had the staff and ability to do this, then that would be an option to consider before thrombolytics.

(14) Miscellaneous Example Cases

(1) Hyperkalemia*

A 72 year old man has just undergone an embolectomy of a saddle aorto-iliac embolus through bilateral femoral incisions, and then his surgeon left town. As he was leaving, he told you that there was some significant ischemic time of both lower extremities. The ICU calls you because the patient has a serum potassium of 5.8 on post-operative labs.

That is a high value for potassium and could be causing some arrhythmia problems. I am assuming that this patient is probably still on the ventilator and is sedated. So I would get a stat EKG as I evaluate him to make sure that he is ventilating and oxygenating well, his chest is clear and his vitals are stable.

Yes, he is stable, on the vent, saturating 100% on 40% FiO2.

Ok, assuming that the EKG does not reveal any peaked T-waves, then I would first focus on starting to get the potassium down, and then I would focus on finding the cause. So, I would give this patient insulin and glucose to immediately move the potassium intracellular, and I would give him kayexalate enemas to bind the potassium. To focus on the source, I expect that the ischemic muscle is necrotic and releasing the potassium. I would check his pulses and examine his legs to make sure they are still warm and have blood flow. Assuming that they are good pulses, I would check the compartment pressure and make sure this is not contributing to the problem.

His pulses are fine, and his calves are soft. The nurse does report to you that his urine output is only 20 ml for the last hour, and it is very dark.

He probably has a significant myonecrosis and serum and urine myoglobin levels would be high. I would send off these labs to confirm that. Meanwhile, I have to keep the kidneys functioning well or the hyperkalemia will get worse. I would give him a fluid bolus and insert a SG catheter to make sure that he is well hydrated. I would look at his creatinine.

Are you worried about arrhythmias when you insert the SG catheter, specifically because of his hyperkalemia?

Yes, I can stabilize the myocardium with calcium gluconate before I do this. Even in the normal patient, there is a risk of arrhythmia when you are putting a SG in.

Ok, you do all this and his repeat potassium is 6.8 now.

I would give him more insulin and glucose, calcium gluconate to stabilize the myocardium, and more kayexalate. The only other way I can get the potassium down faster is with CVVHD or hemodialysis. I would consult a nephrologist now.

(1) Paradoxical Aciduria*

A 54 year old man presents to you with a known history of PUD. Recently he has not been able to hold any of his food down. He complains of bloating, early satiety, and vomiting after eating. This has been going on for the last several days.

I am concerned that he is obstructed, and with his history, I think this is probably gastric outlet obstruction. If this has been going on for several days then he is probably pretty dehydrated. I would admit him to the hospital and start IV fluids on him. I would get some labs on him, expecting to find a hypochloremic, hypokalemic metabolic alkalosis. Assuming he does not have any peritonitis on physical examination or any hernias that may be obstructed, then I would proceed with an UGI contrast study to diagnose the obstruction.

Yes, you find a gastric outlet obstruction. Why do you expect this hypochloremic, hypokalemic metabolic alkalosis?

He is vomiting hydrochloric acid and losing his potassium from the kidneys.

Can you explain paradoxical aciduria?

Sure. The body is volume contracted, and it wants to try to hold onto the volume by concentrating the urine. As a result, it tries to hold on to the sodium so that water will follow. Unfortunately, it trades potassium instead. This results in hypokalemia. When the potassium gets so low that the kidney cannot exchange this for Na any more, it starts to use hydrogen ions. The loss of these protons results in aciduria and a worsening of the alkalosis.

What do you think his ABG would look like?

I expect that he would have an alkalosis with a respiratory acidosis to try and compensate for it.

His creatinine is 3.4. What will you do about that?

He is probably just dehydrated. I would place a Foley catheter and start normal saline infusion (couple of liter boluses first), and when he started to make urine, I would start correcting the potassium. His creatinine should come down with time and hydration. I would start TPN when the fluids were corrected and wait seven days, using nasogastric decompression to let the duodenal scaring resolve. Hopefully he will open in this time.

If he has not…

That's ok; we're done with this question.

(3) Post-Splenectomy Abscess*

A 50 year old lady underwent a splenectomy last week for ITP. She now has fever and LUQ abdominal discomfort.

I am most concerned that she has an abscess in the LUQ. It could also be an injury to the splenic flexure of the colon, injury to the stomach, or injury to the pancreas. Assuming that she is otherwise stable, maybe a little tachycardiac but normotensive, then I would make sure she is NPO in case this is a stomach injury or she needs surgery, give her IV fluids in case she becomes septic and because I am making her NPO, start broad spectrum antibiotics because she is running fever, draw blood cultures to rule out bacteremia, and draw labs. If her creatinine is normal, then I would get a CT scan of the abdomen and pelvis with PO/IV/and rectal contrast.

So the CT shows a fluid collection in the LUQ.

I would ask the radiologist to place a percutaneous drain and send the fluid for gram stain, culture, sensitivity, and amylase. If the gram stain is positive and the amylase is negative, then I would tailor my antibiotics to the specific organism. The organism may also tell me the source of the injury. If this is polymicrobial, growing gram negatives and anaerobes, I would worry more about colon injury. Hopefully, the drain will drain the fluid collection, the antibiotics will control the infection, and she will get better. I would treat her with antibiotics until the drain comes out. The drain should stay in until the fluid collection is completely gone on serial CT scans done every week.

Well, let's say the amylase comes back 20,000.

Then that is a pancreatic fistula. Most of these should heal spontaneously. I would make her NPO and start her on TPN. I would also give her somatostatin to decrease the pancreatic secretions. I would follow the drain output and expect it to decrease over the next week to ten days. I would continue antibiotics for ten days, and then hopefully she is afebrile and her WBC is normal. If the drain output does not decrease, then I would have an ERCP performed to see where the injury is and ask them to leave a stent, thinking that this may decompress the duct and get it to drain through the stent preferentially.

What if the fluid had budding yeast on the gram stain?

That makes me worry about a stomach injury too. I would get an UGI study to rule out gastric perforation and start anti-fungal medication (diflucan 800mg IV for the first dose and then 400mg IV daily). If there is no obvious gastric perforation, then I would wait it out, thinking she should get better with drainage. If there is an obvious leak that is not drained adequately with the percutaneous catheter, then I would go back to the operating room to wash her out, repair the perforation and leave drains.

What about the pancreas?

I would drain the heck out of it. If it was an obvious injury at the distal end of the pancreas, then I would just do a distal pancreatectomy.

(1) Perirectal Abscess*

A 32 year old male comes in to your office because he is having rectal pain. When you examine him, you find this 1 cm right peri-rectal abscess. What do you want to do with this?

I am assuming that he has no previous history of rectal problems (including abscesses or fistulas), Chron's or UC, or recent surgery. I would also make sure he has not had any recent trauma to the area. The reason I ask is that if this just "popped up," it is probably due to an infected anal gland or fistula. The treatment for this is incision and drainage, and in my experience, these are best done in the operating room because they are so tender and then you can also get a better look at the anus and rectal canal to see if there is any underlying pathology.

I would try a rectal exam in the clinic to make sure there is no mass, but I wouldn't push it, so to speak, and defer the exam until we are in the operating room.

I would admit him to day surgery immediately, make him NPO, give him fluids and give him IV cipro and flagyl on call to the operating room. I would do a rigid proctoscopy and look for any fistula or bulging abscess in the rectal vault. If this all looks negative, then I open the abscess, cut open it just big enough to get my finger it, drain the pus, take samples for culture, and then do some blunt debridement to get an idea of how big this abscess is.

It is very large and extends posteriorly to the other side.

So this is a horseshoe abscess. These must be adequately drained before they can get better. If you just open the entire abscess cavity, the patient will be left with a large rectal wound that will be difficult to deal with, and may eventually need a colostomy to get it to heal. Therefore, my preference is to make another, or even several, counter incisions connected with Penrose drains so that the abscess cavities can drain. These heal a lot faster. My only problem doing this comes when I find really bad necrotic and foul smelling tissue at the base. Then I have this overwhelming erge to open the wound more and debride the necrotic tissue.

He does well, what is your plan for discharge and follow up.

I would keep him in the hospital for a couple of days on antibiotics until his leukocytosis is resolve, he is afebrile, up and walking about and able to void on his own. I want he pain controlled with oral medications, and I would like to see him have a bowel movement. I would put him on a stool softener, have him take sitz baths twice a day and after every BM, and I would see him back every week in the office until the cavities have significantly collapsed and feel comfortable removing the Penrose.

Two months later you see him the ER again with another abscess.

Now I getting concerned that I missed something at the first go around, like a fistula in ano. I would go through the same routine. Try to get a really good look on procto; however, this time, after he heals, I am going to perform a colonoscopy on him. I am looking for inflammatory bowel disease, so if that is negative, I would get an upper GI with SBFT to rule out Chron's (but I should see that in the rectum if there is rectal involvement). If I still don't find anything, then I am at a loss, and this may be a good time to refer this patient to a colorectal surgeon.

(1) Pulmonary Embolism in the Pregnant Patient*

A patient in her third trimester of pregnancy presents with a swollen leg and her primary care sent her to you with an US report that shows a DVT in that leg.

Assuming that the primary care doctor doesn't want to take care of his patient, I would explain to her that she needs to be admitted to the hospital to receive anticoagulation to prevent further propagation of the clot and embolization.

How would you dose the heparin?

I would start with a 5000 unit (100 u/kg) bolus and then start a drip at 1000 units (15 u/kg/hr) and hours. There is a standing heparin scale in my hospital that will check the PTT every 6 hours and adjust the drip as needed. Pregnant woman have a larger blood volume than normal and they may require more heparin than usual.

Fine, you do this, and the patient wants to know if she is going to have to stay in the hospital for the rest of her pregnancy and how long will she need to be on anticoagulation.

She will be able to go home on LMWH, not Coumadin because that is toxic to the baby at any gestational age. So once she is therapeutic, I would start the change over and educate her on how to give herself the shots and then I would discharge her with frequent follow up (every 2 weeks) to make sure her levels are adequate (have to test factor X levels). I would also tell her really focus on staying on her left lateral decubitus when she lays down and to keep that swollen leg elevated as much as she can for symptomatic relief.

She present back in the ER with spontaneous bleeding.

I am worried that she has heparin induced thrombocytopenia or is heparin toxic. I would send a type and cross match, send off the coagulation studies, factor X levels, a HIT panel, and platelet count.

Her platelet count is low and the HIT panel returns positive.

I would transfuse her platelet until they are above 100 k and that should stop the bleeding. Since I have to stop all heparin products and I cannot give her Coumadin, then I have an indication to place an IVC filter. I do not do this myself, so I would consult vascular surgery or radiology to do this.

What if she develops a contralateral DVT?

I don't think this would change the treatment plan at this time. This is a bad problem, she is obviously hypercoagulable and cannot tolerate heparin, I would send of a hypercoagulation panel. I would discuss her case with the obstetrician and decide if the baby should be delivered any earlier so we can get her anticoagulated and prevent thrombotic syndrome.

(4) Necrotizing Fasciitis*

An elderly man has undergone a right hemicolectomy 3 days ago and begins to have some clear looking fluid coming out of his wound.

I am concerned that he has a dehiscence or a wound infection. So I would go to the bedside and get a better idea of this drainage. If it is infected, I would expect to see some indurations and cellulitis, the wound may be tender and the fluid may be cloudy or foul smelling. Dehiscence would be clear or serosanguinous. Assuming it looks like an infection, then I would open the wound, culture it, and examine the tissue.

The drainage is brown and has bacteria on the gram stain. The patient does not appear toxic. What might the gram stain show?

I expect that most surgical wounds are caused by gram positive cocci from the skin. However, after colon surgery the gram negative rods and anaerobes can be found.

What would you do now?

Well if the patient is doing well and the wound is clean looking, I would pack it open with wet to dry dressings.

The wound is nasty, and the preliminary report on the culture is clostridium. What now?

Now I am concerned for necrotizing fasciitis. I would start PCN and clindamycin if the gram stain showed GPR (clostridium), and I would take him to the operating room for debridement of any necrotic tissue. I would not stop until there is healthy bleeding tissue.

Would hyperbaric oxygen be helpful here?

I suppose it could be because these are anaerobic organisms and oxygen therapy may help; however, I have very little experience with this treatment modality.

(3) Burns

A 60 year old female is brought into the ER with 70% burns to her upper body, sustained in her trailer home while smoking in bed. She just came in a short while ago. How would you manage her?

I am immediately concerned that this was a closed space fire and probably has significant inhalational injury. Furthermore she has sustained significant burns and will require massive fluid resuscitation. Therefore, I would intubate her immediately and secure a good airway. I would make sure that we are able to ventilate her well and she is saturating well. I would obtain good IV access even if meant I had to place a central line though eschar, but usually the groin is spared because of the underwear. I would begin fluids based on the parkland formula, but would gauge her response to the fluids by placing a Foley catheter and targeting her urine output to about 30-50 cc per hour.

I would draw labs on her including an ABG and check CO level. She is on the ventilator, and I would give her 100% oxygen until the CO levels normalized. Now at this point, I would clean all her burns and dress them with silverdine for the time being and continue this resuscitation for the next 12 hours. As long as she remains stable, I would plan on taking her to the operating room within 24 hours to perform early tangential excision of the burned area and lay down xenograft for most of the area.

I am interested in your ventilator settings?

I generally start with SIMV (spontaneous intermittent mechanical ventilation) and target tidal volumes of 10-15 cc per kg for peak pressures below 30. I would give her 5 PEEP and 5 PS.

Would you be interested in doing a bronchosocpy?

I don't think it is mandatory, but in a patient that has suffered major burns and pulled out of a closed space fire, I think that it is reasonable to put a scope in and look for injury to the lower airway that may alert you to significant ventilator problems in the future.

Would you use hyperbaric oxygen chamber?

If the CO is very high, it would be helpful.

Explain that.

Well the half life of CO is 5 hours on room air, 1 hour on 100% oxygen, 45 minutes on forced ventilation with 100% oxygen (like in our case here), but only 25 minutes with 100% oxygen at 2.5 atmospheres.

Her peak pressures go up over the next several hours and are very high now.

She could have a mucus plug so I would suction her, get a chest x-ray to rule out pneumothorax, check my ventilator settings, and examine her chest. She may have compartment syndrome from the burns to the chest. If I cannot find any other cause of her high pressures then I would do bedside fasciotomies in the anterior axillary lines bilaterally and connect them with subcostal incisions.

Her urinary output is very low and dark.

She may be under resuscitated; I would check the CVP and place a PA catheter if I have to. I would give her fluids and send the urine out for electrolytes and myoglobin.

Thank you.

Procedures

This section is not intended to be an atlas of surgical procedures, nor is this given in any great detail. The point of this section is to hit the highlights of the procedure that you should be aware of as a general surgeon, and this is what they will be testing for on the board exam. During the exam, however, I would not go into details of any operation unless they ask you to. They may not be interested in your description of the procedure, just that you would do a particular procedure. So hold back and don't just shoot right off into the operative report for a ruptured AAA. If they ask you to describe the procedure, give them the bulleted procedure (like the one below), and if they want to know about your knowledge you can go into that with them. Be conservative and safe.

Whipple

- Prep the patient from the chest to the thighs and make an upper midline or bilateral subcostal incisions (go with the later if the patient is large).

- Assessment of the abdomen for metastatic disease.

    o You can start off with a laparoscope and do a quick assessment of the liver and peritoneal surface. If this is negative, make your open incision, feel the liver look at the transverse mesocolon and small bowel mesentery, feel the peritoneum, and biopsy anything suspicious

- Mobilization of the duodenum and the head of the pancreas, with identification of the superior mesenteric vein.

    o Kocherize the duodenum to the LOT and

look at the renal vein and cava. Rule out unresectable disease with a biopsy of any mass involving either of these structures

- Mobilization of the stomach and proximal duodenum, with transection of the proximal stomach at the level of the gastric antrum. The proximal stomach is retracted to expose the porta.

- Skeletonize the structures of the porta.

  o The gallbladder is removed and the CBD is divided just proximal to the cystic duct.

- Mobilization and divide the proximal jejunum.

- Transection of the neck of the pancreas and division of the remaining attachments of the specimen.

  o Hemostatic Prolene sutures (3–0) are placed through the pancreatic parenchyma at both the inferior and superior margin of the pancreas, on either side of the proposed line of transection (i.e., four sutures total), which usually overlies the vein.

- Reconstruction of gastrointestinal continuity.

  o Pancreatic anastomosis results in invagination of the cut end of the pancreas into the lumen of the bowel

  o end-to-end pancreaticojejunostomy

  o a 5- or 8-F pediatric feeding tube is inserted well into the duct so that it can be easily seen during the anastomosis

  o Biliary anastomosis is done with a single-layer anastomosis using interrupted sutures of 4–0 or 5–0 PDS.

o If the duct is smaller that 1 cm it is wise to leave a T-tube in the CBD (going into the jejunum).

o Gastrojejunostomy is created 30 cm distal to the choledochojejunostomy

- Two closed-suction drains (e.g., no.10 Jackson Pratt) are placed close to the pancreatic and hepatic duct anastomosis.

Graham Patch

- Open the abdomen through a midline incision.

- Culture the abdomen and wash it out.

- Find the duodenal perforation and debride the edges.

- If it is amendable to graham patch, then place the interrupted 2-0 silk sutures through the duodenum and mobilize a part of the omentum to reach.

- Place the omentum over the perforation and tie down the sutures to hold it in place.

Thyroidectomy

- Place the patient in a supine position with the arms tucked and the neck extended.

- The incision is placed in a natural skin fold for about 5 cm in length.

- Skin flaps are mobilized superiorly to the thyroid cartilage and inferiorly to the sternal notch.

- Strap muscles are divided.

- The dissection is carried bluntly to the carotid artery medially and superiorly to identify the superior pole vessels. Identify the middle thyroid vein and ligate it to avoid tearing.

- Superior vessels are taken (be to retract the thyroid laterally and caudally, to avoid injury to the external laryngeal nerve).

- The inferior vessels are identified and taken close to the gland as well.

- Repeat on the other side and mobilize the gland off the trachea.

Parathyroidectomy

- Four gland exploration:

    o Place the patient in a supine position with the arms tucked and the neck extended.

    o The incision is placed in a natural skin fold for about 5 cm in length.

    o Skin flaps are mobilized superiorly to the thyroid cartilage and inferiorly to the sternal notch.

    o Strap muscles are divided.

    o The dissection is carried bluntly medial to the carotid artery and superiorly to identify the superior pole vessels. Identify the middle thyroid vein and ligate it to avoid tearing.

    o The lower parathyroid gland is normally found in the thyrothymic tract, inferior to the thyroid lobe and anterior to the recurrent laryngeal nerve.

    o A common location for the superior parathyroid gland is within 1 cm of the recurrent laryngeal nerve as it pierces the cricothyroid membrane, posterior to the superior pole of the thyroid.

    o All glands should be identified and their locations recorded before excision.

- Minimally Invasive Technique:

    o You should inject the patient with radioactive material pre-operatively (about 2 hours before surgery).

    o Use an intra-operative radio-probe to find the

gland.

o Any gland with more than 20% background noise is considered positive.

o If you feel that you found the responsible gland, check a PTH and remove the gland.

o Check a PTH at 5 and 10 minutes, expecting a > 50% decrease in the level.

o If you don't get this (49.9%), then go to the 4 gland exploration.

Laparoscopic Nissen Fundoplication

- You must circumferentially mobilize the distal esophagus.

    o The gastrohepatic ligament is widely opened to expose the right crus of the diaphragm, and it is fully dissected.

    o The posterior esophagus is mobilized away from the left crus to open the posterior space and an adequate window is created behind the esophagus so a medium Penrose drain can be used to encircle the distal esophagus and both vagal trunks.

- The short gastric vessels are divided and the stomach is mobilized.

- The esophageal hiatus is closed.

    o After the crural closure is complete, the fundus is again passed behind the esophagus. A 56-F Maloney dilatator is then carefully passed into the stomach.

- A short, floppy, 360-degree fundoplication is created.

    o Two sutures of 2-0 silk are placed 3 to 4 cm apart. Each suture incorporates the left gastric wrap, esophagus, and right gastric wrap.

Sentinel Node Biopsy

- 99mtechnetium-labeled (99mTc) sulfur colloid is usually given in a single dose of 0.5 to 1.0 mCi on the morning of surgery.

- Blue dye is injected under the skin around the lesion. Methylene blue of lymphazurin can be used. The later is associated with allergic reactions. The former can cause skin necrosis and may not be as good of a tracer.

- All SLNs that are blue or "hot" should be surgically excised for analysis.

- If the remaining axilla shows more than 10% of the radioactivity count of the "hottest" SLN the surgeon should continue exploration to identify additional SLNs.

- The specimen is sent to surgical pathology for analysis.

Laparoscopic Cholecystectomy

- The surgeon uses the left hand to grasp the infundibulum and provide traction inferolaterally to expose the critical view.

- Dissection begins high on the gallbladder, and the loose areolar tissue is gently teased away to expose both the cystic duct at its point of entry into the gallbladder and the liver bed behind it, creating the critical view.

- Identifying the gallbladder-cystic duct junction provides essential anatomic confirmation, which allows attention to be safely turned to the careful placement of metallic clips.

- Gallbladder is removed from the abdomen

Distal Splenorenal Shunt

- The gastrocolic ligament is taken down to the first short gastric vein, and the inferior border of the body and tail of the pancreas is mobilized.

- The splenic vein is identified and meticulously dissected from the pancreas by ligating and dividing multiple small pancreatic branches.

- After mobilizing 4 to 6 cm of the splenic vein, it is brought down in a gentle arc and anastomosed end-to-side to the left renal vein, which can be found in the retroperitoneum posterior to the splenic vein.

- Ligation of the coronary vein, gastroepiploic vein, and any other collateral vessels connecting the decompressed gastrosplenic and hypertensive superior mesenteric venous networks is an essential component of the operation if hepatic portal perfusion is to be preserved.

Femoral Hernia Repair

- Make an infra-umbilical incision, incise the fascia, and the preperitoneal balloon dilator is placed.

- Dissection begins at the pubis and is carried laterally along Cooper's ligament to the iliac vein

- Expose the spermatic cord

- The hernia sac is identified and freed from any attachments

- In the event of a chronically or acutely incarcerated hernia, it is sometimes helpful to place trocar into the peritoneal cavity to inspect for possible injury to the peritoneum during dissection or reduced bowel contents, to check the viability of reduced bowel, or to aid in the reduction of the hernia.

- Half the time they can be can reduced laparoscopically, or you will have to make a small incision to open the femoral ring by incising the inguinal ligament to release the hernia (you may have to open the sac to reduce the contents).

- If all else fails, open anteriorly.

- The Prolene mesh is then inserted and placed in proper orientation for easy positioning.

- It is sutured or tacked in place.

AAA Repair

- A midline incision is made, and the transverse colon and omentum are retracted cephalad, and the small intestine eviscerated to the right.

- Distally the iliac arteries are dissected for clamp placement

- Systemic heparinization is initiated with 60 to 70 U/kg IV bolus, and clamps are positioned distally on the iliac arteries before placing the proximal clamp to reduce the risk of distal embolization.

- After the aorta is clamped and there is no pulsation within the aneurysm, it is opened longitudinally and the thrombus extirpated.

- Back-bleeding from lumbar arteries and the inferior mesenteric artery (IMA) is controlled with silk sutures from inside the aneurysm sac.

- There must be 1 cm of normal aorta below the clamp, and the proximal anastomosis is performed using a 2–0 polypropylene suture in a running fashion, starting along the posterior wall.

- When complete, the graft is clamped and the proximal clamp is gently released to test the anastomosis.

- Before completing the distal anastomosis, the anesthesiologist is prepare for the possibility of declamping hypotension and the anastomoses are flushed proximally and distally to remove any remaining plaque or thrombus.

- The clamps are removed and distal pulses verified.

- The aneurysm sac may be closed over the graft.

CEA

- The patient is placed in the supine position in the modified semi-Fowler position.

- The incision is made along the anterior border of the SCM.

- The common carotid artery (CCA) is dissected first, to identify the vagus nerve, carry the dissection toward the bifurcation, sweep the hypoglossal nerve away from the ICA and reach a point beyond the visible disease.

- The ECA is dissected to its first branch, the superior thyroid artery.

- Modified Rumel tourniquets with umbilical tapes are positioned around the carotid arteries.

- Intravenous heparin (70 U/kg) is given to the patient.

- Patients with back-pressure measurements of less than 25 mm Hg receive shunts.

- A longitudinal arteriotomy is made in the CCA and extended through the lesion into the ICA, the distal end of the shunt is placed in the ICA and allowed to backbleed, and the proximal end of the shunt is placed in the CCA.

- Endarterectomy is carried from the ICA proximally and circumferentially into the CCA and tack down the leading edge with suture.

- The endarterectomize artery is generously flushed with heparinized saline solution, and all residual debris or loosely attached intima is removed using fine forceps and loop magnification.

- Patch angioplasty closure using a continuous 6-0 polypropylene suture starting at the distal apex.

- Flow in all vessels should be confirmed by Doppler examination or arteriography.

Fasciotomies of the Extremities

- All tissue compartments must be decompressed.

- For the lower extremity:

  o Make the medial incision just below the tibia, longitudinally down the leg and open the fascia, then open the deep fascia. This releases the posterior and deep posterior compartments.

  o The lateral incision is made between the tibia and fibula and extended longitudinally to release the anterior and lateral compartments.

- For the upper extremities:

  o Incisions are made anteriorly (volvar surface) to release the anterior compartment, and

  o Incisions are made posteriorly (extensor surface) to release the posterior compartment

- Wounds are left open and may be closed in 3 days or STSG should be placed.

Liver Resection Left and Right Lobes

- Right Hepetectomy

    o The right liver is mobilized.

    o The right hepatic artery is transected close to the liver,

    o The porta is then encircled.

    o the right bile duct is divided within the liver

    o The right hepatic vein trunk is divided with a stapler.

    o The liver is split, and the retrohepatic venules and the right hepatic vein are controlled within the liver

- Extended Right Hepatectomy (right trisegmentectomy)

    o This is a right hepatectomy plus removal of segment 4.

    o The segment 4 feedback vessels can be divided within the liver.

- Left Hepatectomy

    o After the left liver is mobilized, the left hepatic artery is located at the left edge of the porta hepatis.

    o The left portal vein is then dissected and ligated.

    o The liver demarcates along the principal plane. Outflow control can be obtained within the liver.

- Extended Left Hepatectomy

- o Remove the anterior section of the right liver (segments 5 and 8).

- Left Lateral Sectionectomy

  - o The left lateral section (segments 2 and 3) is mobilized by dividing the left triangular ligament.

Highly Selective Vagotomy

- Denervation of the parietal cell mass via a true highly selective is most often performed by combining a posterior truncal vagotomy with an anterior seromyotomy.

    o Following the truncal vagotomy, the seromyotomy is started at the level of the first branch of the crow's foot, which is usually found approximately 6 cm from the pylorus.

    o The superficial gastric incision proceeds along the lesser curve, crosses over the anterior aspect of the cardia to the angle of His and as far posteriorly as the lateral aspect of the left crus.

    o The seromyotomy is closed with a running stitch of 2–0 silk or Vicryl.

Modified Radical Neck Dissection

- **Central neck dissections**

    o You are to remove all lymph tissue from the carotid arteries laterally, the cricoid cartilage superiorly, the clavicles caudally, and the trachea and esophagus medially.

- **Modified Radical Neck Dissection**

    o The incision is made like an "H" and flaps are raised posteriorly to the trapezius and anteriorly to the strap muscles on the thyroid.

    o You are to remove levels 2 through level 4 jugular lymph nodes.

    o Identify and preserve the phrenic nerve, the thyrocervical trunk, the brachial plexus, the thoracic duct, and the spinal accessory nerve.

    o The posterior triangle of the neck is cleared of the tissue; the spinal accessory nerve is preserved.

    o Carry the dissection along the clavicle and the omohyoid muscle is visualized. The phrenic nerve is visualized lying on the scalene. The thoracic duct is seen here as well.

    o Identify the carotid artery and remove all tissue as you dissect superiorly.

    o Once you reach the bifurcation of the ICA and ECA, look for the hypoglossal nerve and preserve it.

    o The submental area of the neck is exposed

with the anterior belly of the digastrics and all loose tissue is removed in this area.

o The submaxillary gland is removed and the linguinal nerve is seen and preserved.

o Working posteriorly, you find the posterior belly of the digastrics and the internal juglar.

o The lymphatic tissue is removed as high up as you can, even including the tail of the parotid if tumor extends that high.

o The skin is closed in layers over closed suction drains

Peustow

- A bilateral subcostal (chevron) incision is made and a thorough exploration is performed to rule out malignancy.

- Expose the entire anterior surface of the pancreas.

- Locate the pancreatic duct by aspirating it with a 22-gauge needle.

- The main pancreatic duct is entered, and a right-angle clamp is then used to guide the process of opening the rest of the pancreatic duct.

- A Roux-en-Y jejunal limb is created and anastomosed to the pancreatic capsule alongside the opened pancreatic duct with an interrupted or continuous 3–0 nonabsorbable suture

Zenker's Diverticulectomy

- Endoscopic

    o Under direct vision, the bivalved diverticuloscope is introduced into the hypopharynx

    o Endoscopic gastrointestinal anastomois (GIA) stapler (3.5 cm in length), introduced under endoscopic visual control, and opened; its jaws are then advanced over the parting wall and fired.

- Open

    o The incision is made along the left anterior border of the SCM and the carotid sheath is pulled laterally while the trachea is pulled medially to expose the posterior-lateral diverticulum.

    o A myotomy is performed of all transverse muscle fibers for about 3 cm up and down until all the muscle of the cricopharyngeous are divided.

    o For diverticulum less then 2 cm, a pexy can be performed, but if it is >2cm then a diverticulectomy is performed using a TA stapler over a 60 Fr. Bougie.

    o Test for any leaks (using air or methylene blue)

    o Place a closed suction drain.

    o Close the neck in layers.

Thyroglossal Duct Cyst

- Patient is prepped and draped in same way you would for a thyroidectomy.

- Incision is made slightly high than you would make for a thyroidectomy and the strap muscles are divided.

- The cyst is dissected out and its track is identified tracking superiorly to the hyoid bone.

- The track and portion of the hyoid bone it is attached to are excised up to the base of the tongue. If this is not done, there is a high rate or recurrence.

- The cyst and track are removed and the neck irrigated.

- Closed suction drain is left in place and the neck is closed in layers.

Adrenalectomies

- Position the patient in the lateral decubitus position

- Expose the adrenal gland by incising the lateral attachment to allow medial rotation of either the spleen/pancreas or liver and dissect peritoneum free from the interface between the adrenal and either the spleen/pancreas or liver.

- Starting with the most cephalad attachments to the diaphragm and moving toward the renal hilum, carefully dissect one layer at a time between the adrenal gland and either the spleen/pancreas or liver.

- Identify the adrenal vein.

- Be careful not to ligate a superior pole vessel to the kidney because this may cause postoperative hypertension, and be sure to maintain your dissection plane right over the renal capsule.

- Cut through the fat between the kidney and adrenal gland, hugging the kidney, using the LigaSure, harmonic scalpel, or cautery.

- Pushing the clamp on the top of the kidney will define the perfect plane.

- Remove the gland via an incision wide enough to remove it via an endocatch bag.

Open Inguinal Hernia Repair

- Make a curvilinear incision about 1 cm above the line from the pubis symphysis to the anterior superior iliac crest.

- Dissect down to the aponerosis of the external oblique and open it superior to the external ring and in line with it such that the ring is obliterated. Isolate and preserve the ilio-inguinal nerve

- Clean off the preperitoneal tissue from the inguinal ligament and tranversalis shelving edge down to the pubic tubercle.

- Isolate the spermatic cord, find the hernia sac on the anterior medial aspect of the cord, dissect it off the cord structures and obtain hemostasis.

- In a primary tissue repair, approximate the inguinal ligament to the conjoint tendon and internal oblique musculature with interrupted non-absorbable 0-suture (Bassini repair). A releasing incision on the external oblique may be required if there is too much tension (McVay repair).

- Lichtenstein repair involving laying a piece of mesh into place and suturing it onto the pubic tubercle, along the inguinal ligament, and cooper's ligament in a tension free manner. Do not entrap nerves.

- Irrigate the wound and close in layers to create the external ring again.

Heller Myotomy

- Free the upper third of the gastric fundus

- The GE junction is then exposed by dissecting the gastro esophageal fat pad and retracting it laterally.

- Once the esophagus is mobilized and GE junction exposed, the myotomy is performed.

- The myotomy is carried both proximally and distally for a total distance of 4 to 6 cm and for 2.5 to 3 cm onto the surface of the anterior stomach.

- Visualize the distal extent of the myotomy with an intraluminal endoscope.

- The procedure is completed by fashioning an anterior (Dor) or posterior (Toupet) partial fundoplication.

Paraesophageal Hernia Repair

- The surgery is generally performed laparoscopically through the abdomen by most surgeons today.

- Ports are placed like you would for a Nissen Fundoplication, the hernia sac and contents are reduced along the cardia of the stomach (to reduce the chances of recurrence), and the fundus of the stomach is mobilized.

- The esophagus is cleared off circumferentially, taking care not to injure the vagi. You should achieve an adequate length of esophagus in the abdomen (at least 2 cm) or else you should consider a collies' gastroplasty.

- The diaphragmatic crura are closed with non-absorbable suture (e.g. 0-ethibond), and the hernia is patched with an alloderm patch to decrease the recurrence rate.

- Depending on the manometry studies and the surgeon's preference a wrap should be performed at this time.

- A suture should secure the repair below the diaphragm. For toupet closure sutures to bilateral crura is used.

- For Nissen and anterior stitch to the right crura is used.

- There is no benefit to gastrostomy tube placement, but it is still done with the thought that it will prevent the entire stomach from slipping back into the chest.

Splenectomy

- Place the patient in the right lateral position.

- The spleen is first mobilized from its attachments to the colon and retroperitoneum.

- The short gastric vessels can be clipped and divided or taken with a harmonic scalpel.

- The vascular pedicle can then be isolated and divided.

- The specimen is placed in a bag, morcellated, and removed from one of the subcostal port sites.

- Accessory spleens must be removed. The most common location is in the splenic hilum region, the pedicle and tail of the pancreas, and the greater omentum. Ovary and mesentery are much rarer locations.

Surgical Cricothyroidotomy

- Vertical incision is made in the neck over the cricoid membrane.

- Blunt dissection is used down to the membrane, and it is sharply incised with the knife.

- The opening is enlarged with the knife handle or clamp.

- Endotracheal tube is placed in the airway.

Delorme

- A Delorme is done in the prone jack-knife position with epidural or local anesthetic.

- A circular incision is made in the mucosa 1 cm above the dentate and a mucosal sleeve is dissected circumferentially off the muscle until you get resistance.

- The rectal muscle is then pleated longitudinally in 4 quadrants with 2-0 vicryl.

- The mucosal sleeve is transect and removed and the distal and proximal edges are re-approximated with 3-0 chronic.

CBD Exploration

- CBD exploration is done through a right subcostal incision.

- Perform an IOC. If there are just a few small stones, give glucagon and flush.

- If the stones persist, do a Kocher maneuver, trace the cystic duct to the CBD and aspirate it to ensure that it is the CBD.

- Place 5-0 vicryl suture as stay suture and make a 1.5 cm longitudinal incision in the duct.

- Flush it with saline via a 10Fr red rubber catheter.

- Place a flexible choledochoscope and pass a 4 Fr Fogarty or use a basket to retrieve stones.

- Leave a T-tube in after you are done.

- Perform a completion cholangiogram to ensure the stones are gone.

Final Thoughts

We all suffer through hard times, wishing we could simply disappear to make it all go away or maybe just be able to put it behind us and forget it. We have all been there, maybe thinking how nice it would be if we could just jump in a time machine and go back a few days to do it differently. That is exactly how I felt when I received a letter informing me that I was unsuccessful in my attempt to pass the certifying examination for the American Board of Surgery.

The week before the exam had been a very hard week. I was a junior faculty taking emergency general surgery call. I had just finished operating on an elderly woman with a massive retroperitoneal sarcoma. I did not want to operate on her, and I told her family that it would be very difficult, carrying a relatively high mortality. Nonetheless, the patient, her family, her doctor, and her oncologist were all pushing for an upfront surgical resection. I unwisely abided by all their wishes, and found that the tumor was not resectable. I was only able to debulk the high-grade malignancy, knowing the results would not be satisfactory.

I went to see my patient in the ICU the day before I left town to take the exam. She vaguely smiled and in a soft whisper she told me she understood I had done all I could, but in her face, I could see that she did not understand. She was not prepared to die. She was very ill and scared, and it left a hole in my heart. There was nothing I could do. I had never felt so powerless.

As a result, I was not in the correct place of mind when I took my exam on January 28th, 2008. Nonetheless, I believed I was "well prepared", and I felt good about my answers when it was over. There were no major disasters. The trauma room was a little scary, but I thought the other two rooms would save me.

On January 31, 2008, my 33rd birthday, my patient with the sarcoma died, and I found out I was not successful in my attempt to pass the certification exam. Those were two very hard pills to swallow. I went home early that day and felt really sorry for my patient and myself. All I could think about was what a failure I was. "Maybe I was not safe; maybe I should not be doing this."

My wife and two young boys did their very best to console me that evening. We had a little celebration of my birthday for the kid's sake, but it was in no way a joyful time. However, later that night, before going to bed, my wife had one final gift to give me. I opened a box wrapped in light blue wrapping paper and found a baby's blanket. She undecidedly told me that she was pregnant with our third child, concerned how I would take the news after this protracted, miserable day. However, my eyes lit up, and everything fell into perspective. This news was the perfect cure to transport me out of that dark cloud which had sadistically surrounded me the entire day. "It was only a test for crying out loud!" Everything was going to work out.

So, life went on. I swore to myself that I would take this test again with vengeance. I would make sure that I absolutely knew everything there could be to know about this examination.

However, a month into this plan, my wife and I lost the baby, a girl. My fragile world quickly fell apart again. We were devastated and looked for answers. Soul searching vivaciously ensued. What was really important in this life? It was clearly not this test. As a result, it was difficult for me to re-focus on the orals. Nonetheless, over the course of the next nine months, I experienced the highs and lows that life can throw at us; needless to say, they were emotional. In the course of this time I wrote this book, my wife became pregnant again, and I retook the certifying examination.

Sometimes, I wish bad things never happened to me; on the other hand, I wouldn't change a thing because I am happy where I am now and this is how I got here. Aldous Huxley wrote, "Experience is not what happens to a man; it is what a man does with what happens to him." The events in our life are the essential effects which make us into the people who endure to success or succumb to failure. Realizing that they are all we have to deliberately create our own wisdom is reason enough to endure. Failing this exam has fashioned me into a more humbled surgeon who is dedicated to teaching other surgical residents and fellows how to take this test by thinking critically and producing a focused and complete answer. Potential harm to patients by my hands has fortunately amplified my integrity and allowed me to wholeheartedly accept my innate flaws as a human being, thus restoring my faith in God, His will, and His healing powers. Sorrowfully losing an unborn child has facilitated my acceptance that all people will suffer loss, frequently without explanation. There are many clichés that tell us how failures and hard times make us a stronger person: fill your favorite one in here.

These nine months are over, and my third son, Treyson, is a living reminder that we never give up or give in but just do our best and let it work out in the end. There is a destiny for all of us, and it has already started!

Good Luck!

Brad Snyder M.D.

P.S. And yes, now board certified.

Made in the USA
Columbia, SC
14 August 2021